• • • • • • • • • • • • • •

Plato's Vision

The Classical Origins of Social and Political Thought

Irving M. Zeitlin

University of Toronto

PRENTICE HALL
Englewood Cliffs, New Jersey 07632

Library of Congress Cataloging-in-Publication Data
ZEITLIN, IRVING M.
　　Plato's vision: the classical origins of social and political
　　thought / Irving M. Zeitlin　　p. cm.
　　Includes bibliographical references and index.
　　ISBN 0-13-681628-2
　　1. Plato-Contributions in political science. 2. Plato-
Contributions in sociology. I. Title
JC71.P6Z45 1993　　　　　　　　　　　　　　92-24746
320'.01 --dc20　　　　　　　　　　　　　　　CIP

Acquisitions editor: Nancy Roberts
Editorial/production supervision and interior design: Marianne Peters
Prepress buyer: Kelly Behr
Manufacturing buyer: Mary Ann Gloriande
Copy Editor: James Tully
Editorial Assistant: Pat Naturale

© 1993 by Prentice-Hall, Inc.
A Simon & Schuster Company
Englewood Cliffs, New Jersey 07632

Printed in the United States of America
10 9 8 7 6 5 4 3 2 1

ISBN 0-13-681628-2

Prentice-Hall International (UK) Limited, *London*
Prentice-Hall of Australia Pty. Limited, *Sydney*
Prentice-Hall Canada Inc., *Toronto*
Prentice-Hall Hispanoamericana, S.A., *Mexico*
Prentice-Hall of India Private Limited, *New Delhi*
Prentice-Hall of Japan, Inc., *Tokyo*
Simon & Schuster Asia Pte. Ltd., *Singapore*
Editora Prentice-Hall do Brasil, Ltda., *Rio de Janeiro*

For Rose and Albert Zeitlin
in memoriam

Contents

Preface   ix

1   Introduction: History and Social Structure   1

The Emergence of Democracy   4
Tyranny   6
Athenian Democracy   10
Solon (c. 594/3)   13
Cleisthenes (c. 508/7)   15
The Persian-Greek Wars   16
Slavery in the Democracy   19
The Athenian Empire   20

2   From Religion to Philosophy   25

Greek Polytheism   25
Plato's Predecessors 1
The Sophists   5

Protagoras   38
Gorgias   39
Notes   41

3   Socrates   43

The "Spartan" Habits of Socrates' Associates   50
Socrates in Aristophanes' The Clouds 52
The Theory of "Forms" or "Ideas"   54
The Forms as Manifestations of Moira   57
The Trial and Execution of Socrates   69
Notes   63

4   Plato   65

The Apology and the Crito   70
Other Early Dialogues   74
The Meno, Protagoras, and Gorgias   77
The Protagoras   79
The Gorgias   83
Notes   90

5   The Republic   91

The Debate with Thrasymachus   96
Plato's Ideal Society   99
The Classes of the Ideal Society   103
Sparta or Athens   107
Plato's Theory of the Mind   109
Education in The Republic   111
Education of the Philosopher-Rulers   112
Plato's Theory of Communism   116
Communism of Wives   121
The Republic: Utopia or Program for Actual States?   125
Social Systems   127
Rebuttal of Thrasymachus' Argument   132
Plato's National Ideal   133
Notes   134

6   The Statesman: A Transitional Phase in Plato's Thinking   135

   Plato's Weaver Analogy   142

7   The Laws: Plato's Last Thoughts   147

   The Central Principle of the Laws   151
   War and Peace   152
   Property and Wealth   155
   Marriage and the Family   159
   Government in the Laws   161
   The State Apparatus in the Laws   166
   The Return to the Republic   170

   References   173

   Acknowledgments   175

   Index   177

Preface

The safest general characterization of the European philosophical tradition is that it consists of a series of footnotes to Plato.[1] What did Alfred North Whitehead mean when he made this now famous statement? Did he mean that Plato had already solved all the fundamental philosophical problems and that later thinkers merely explained and elaborated his solutions? Was it Whitehead's meaning that Plato had discovered all the eternal verities which, like minted coins, lie stored in his writings, and, therefore, that in order to find those coins all we need to do is to study Plato? No, that is not what Whitehead meant. Instead, he was alluding to "the wealth of general ideas" scattered throughout Plato's writings which, during the past 2,000 years, has constituted "an inexhaustible mine of suggestion." That is why we regard Plato as a great pioneer-philosopher and that is why it is an extraordinarily rewarding experience to read his dialogues and letters with care.

In order to understand Plato as a thinker we need background in at least three areas: (1) the history and social structure of the societies on which he reflected; (2) the rich intellectual tradition to which he was heir; and (3) his personal endowments and associations. In Chapter One of this book I try to provide an adequate background for the first of those areas, describing the various political systems of Greece and outlining the history of the Persian-Greek wars as narrated by Herodotus and the Peloponnesian Wars so brilliantly analyzed by Thucydides. Ostensibly those wars were fought between states for material gain, power and spheres of influence; but those wars also represented an underlying struggle between social and political systems. The Persian Empire was a form of what

Montesquieu first called "oriental despotism." The struggle of Greece against Persian domination was, therefore, a struggle to preserve the integrity of Greek institutions. To appreciate what was at stake, had the Persians won the battle of Marathon and had Xerxes' invasion not been repulsed, the subsequent history of the West would have been quite different. Similarly, the Peloponnesian War between Sparta and Athens and their respective allies, was a life-and-death struggle between oligarchy and democracy. Within each of the Greek city states there was a continuing tension and strife between the pro-Spartan oligarchical and the pro-Athenian democratic parties. It is impossible to understand what animated Socrates and Plato without taking those conditions into account.

In Chapter Two, actually a continuation of the Introduction, I try to provide the background necessary for an understanding of the religio-philosophical tradition which Plato had inherited. Much of the pre-Socratic theorizing about the *physis*, I argue, was little more than a translation of religious concepts into those of Greek philosophy. Moreover, Plato's Theory of the Forms is also an adaptation of a Greek religious idea. Finally, the personal characteristics and associations of Socrates and Plato are considered in Chapters Three and Four, thus setting the stage for a critical exposition of Plato's social and political thought.

The main aim of this work, then, is to make clear what Plato was affirming, and what he was arguing against, and why. Although there are, of course, significant differences between the Greek societies of 2,000 years ago and our own, it is also true that we face some of the same questions and issues. This may be illustrated simply by listing the subjects discussed by Plato and therefore touched upon in this book: abortion, adultery, alienation, anarchy, art, atheism, bad men, beauty, censorship, child-upbringing, citizenship, class struggle, communism, corruption, crime and punishment, demagoguery, democracy, despotism, equality, eugenics, extremes of wealth and poverty, family, gods, goodness, homosexuality, justice, law, monarchy, needs, oligarchy, private property, religion, sex and marriage, slavery, the soul, statesmanship, the state, tyranny, vegetarianism, virtue, war and peace, the status and capacities of women, and more. Clearly, these are subjects which continue to concern us; and it may therefore be worthwhile to ask ourselves, whether this critical discussion of Plato's thoughts yields any trans-historical truths that might serve us as wise guidelines as we prepare to enter the 21st Century.

Notes

[1]Alfred North Whitehead, *Process and Reality* (corrected Edition), edited by David Ray Griffin and Donald W. Sherburne, New York: The Free Press, 1978, p. 39. Originally published in 1929 by Macmillan Publishing Co., Inc.

1

● ● ● ● ● ● ● ● ● ● ● ● ● ● ●

Introduction: History and Social Structure

It was not until the fifth century B.C. that anything like a historical record of events was written down by the Greeks. Herodotus, the first historian, was born about 490 B.C. in Halicarnassus in southwest Asia Minor. A wide and observant traveler, Herodotus surveyed the history and ethnography of many parts of Asia, as well as Egypt, Libya, and southern Russia. In the first part of his history he traced the growth of the Persian Empire and the development of Greece from the middle of the sixth century B.C.—although the latter was accomplished quite unsystematically. In the second part of his work Herodotus provided an account of the Greco-Persian wars from the Ionian revolt of 499 B.C. to the repulsion of Xerxes' invasion of Greece in 479 B.C.

The second pioneer Greek historian was Thucydides, an upper-class Athenian intellectual born about 460 B.C. It is to him that we owe the bulk of our knowledge about the first twenty years (431–411) of the Peloponnesian War between Sparta and Athens. As we read Thucydides, we sense throughout that he tries to be objective by carefully sifting reports from many sides. He is concerned with causes and consequences, and he effectively conveys the temper of the times by means of elaborately composed speeches delivered, presumably, by leading historical individuals. For the remaining years of the Peloponnesian War (411–362) we rely on a rather selective historical account by Xenophon, another Athenian. These histories, together with the surviving comedies of the playwright Aristophanes, various inscriptions which the Athenian State engraved on stone, and a sprinkling of inscriptions from other cities, enable us to be reasonably well informed about Greece during the fifth and fourth centuries B.C.

If, however, we wish to gain insight into the earlier history of Greece and the origins of its institutions, we have to do so without the aid of historical records, strictly speaking. For we learn precious little about the earlier periods from Herodotus and Thucydides, and we must therefore rely on inferences from other sources such as the works of Homer and Hesiod, which, used with care, yield relatively reliable glimpses of early Greek social structure, just as the various writings of Aristotle can help us grasp the quality and concerns of pre-Socratic philosophy.

By the end of the eighth century B.C., the primitive Greek monarchy depicted in the Homeric epics was no more. Although there remained some hereditary kings who held office for life, they were actually little more than magistrates with limited authority. Most often kings reduced to magistrates no longer held their positions for life. The hereditary privilege was removed from the family in which it had originally resided, and magistracy became an annual office open to the families of the ruling nobility. At the same time the king's role was reduced and restricted to sacred functions. In Athens, for instance, the king was only one of nine archons (chief magistrate), and his sole responsibility was to oversee and administer the cultic ceremonies.

The weakening and gradual breakdown of the primitive monarchy turned to the advantage of the powerful noble chiefs who had been working toward that end for some time. It was they who now became the masters of the city-state (*polis*) and remained so for centuries. Tracing their origin to some deity and taking immense pride in their noble blood, these chiefs carefully preserved their genealogical tree and the traditional history of their house (*patria*). They belonged to illustrious families and clans who controlled land and revenues from sizable domains and who enjoyed the riches won at the point of the sword over many generations. Throughout Greece a class emerged designated by such terms as "the good," "the best men," "the great and good," "men of blood," "men of quality," "men of honor." They were also called "well-born men," "lords of the earth," and "knights." Landowners and warriors, they devoted themselves to raising horses. While the foot soldier was armed with the short javelin or sometimes only with a sling, the noble knight approached his adversary clad in heavy brass armor, his head enclosed in a visored helmet, and his body protected with leather or metal sheets. In his left hand he held a shield, in his right a long lance, and by his side hung a sword. The war-horse, whether yoked to a chariot or mounted, became the distinctive mark of the nobility who ruled a large number of city-states.

In the seventh century B.C., however, the expansion of commerce, and with it mining, manufacturing, and shipbuilding, brought about significant social and political changes. Money increasingly replaced the old natural economy. The large, noble landowners, who were used to taking the lion's share of the booty through raids on land and piracy at sea, were advantageously situated to gain from the new commercial developments. They owned and controlled fields, forests, vineyards, olive groves, mines, and quarries. They built ships, made forays into foreign lands, and, through trade or piracy, brought back wealth in many forms. In this way the noble aristocracy changed its character. It was money and not only landed wealth that now gave the nobles their power.

They, however, were not the only ones to benefit from the large volume of trade stretching from one end of the Mediterranean to the other. In most city-states the *demiourgoi*—artisans and traders—were able to take a portion of the profits and thus to form an intermediary class between the nobility and the *thetes* (hired laborers). Although the new commercial class owned neither land nor horses, they had sufficient wealth to arm themselves and thus to form a heavy infantry called *hoplites*. In time they became sufficiently numerous and strong to threaten the position of the knights, and even to defeat them in battle. A new type of aristocracy was formed in which the noble-warrior landowners retained their social prestige, but in which wealth, however gained, also rose in the scale of social values. The old warrior-aristocracy was being transformed into a plutocracy.

In the many city-states affected by such economic and social developments, power was always concentrated in the hands of a few, the *oligoi*; it was for this reason that the Greeks gave this form of government the name of *oligarchy*. The meaning of oligarchy for the Greeks was very different from that of *aristocracy*—a term that earlier had referred to the "best men," the ancient nobility, but which the future philosophers Plato and Aristotle would reserve for those who were morally and intellectually the best. Oligarchy meant the division of the populace into two classes, only one of which had the right to participate in government. Participation varied with the city, depending on the size of the upper class and thus extending either to a large minority or to a small and exclusive one. Extreme oligarchy was a situation in which the supreme magistrate, possessing hereditary authority, controlled such great wealth and ruled so many subjects that sovereignty effectively resided in the hands of one man.

There were, however, less extreme oligarchies in which power was still confined to a minority, but to a comparatively numerous one. Aristotle discusses this form in prescriptive terms: The highest offices "must have expensive duties attached to them, in order that the common people may be willing to be excluded from them, and may feel no resentment against the ruling class, because it pays a high price for office" (*Politics* VI. IV.6). Whether the ruling minority was small or large, however, the system was oligarchical nonetheless. The major defect of the system was that it created more and more inequality, even among the privileged. The monopoly control of the magistracies gave to certain families and circles such power that the majority of the economically privileged, who were excluded from government, refused to submit to this state of affairs. Aristotle informs us that time and again oligarchs were assailed:

> ...the nobles frequently form parties among their friends and the common people and so bring about a suspension of government, and form factions and engage in war with one another. Yet such a condition of things really means that for a time such a state is a state no longer, but the bonds of civil society are loosened. (*Politics* II. VII. 7–8)

The Emergence of Democracy

While the great noble families of the eighth century B.C. were monopolizing power in the *polis*, what was the condition of the people? The less-skilled artisans struggled to make a living, and the unskilled *thetes* were even worse off. And judging from Hesiod's description of the lot of the peasants, their position was steadily worsening. Their small patches of land that barely sufficed for scratching out the necessities of life were increasingly swallowed up by the giant estates. On the other hand, the land of the nobles was expanding, protected as it was from permanent alienation by the kinsmen's right to buy back any portion of the original inheritance that might have been sold. On top of that the nobles had successfully encroached on the traditionally common pasture grounds. Like the Hebrew prophets of social justice who denounced the oppressive landlords of ancient Israel, Hesiod reflects the plight of the oppressed peasants of Greece. He does so, however, in a pessimistic philosophy of life, expressed in his myth of the five ages of the world, in which there has been a continuing moral deterioration of humanity. It has gone so far that Shame, Righteousness, and Justice have fled to Olympus, having found no abode on earth. Hesiod's *Works and Days* contains myths, ethical maxims, and practical advice for the peasant, teaching that divine blessings depend on diligence and industry. Hesiod's pessimism results from the belief that humanity has degenerated from the Golden Age to the Iron Age and that he himself now lives in that era of rapacious landlords and their accomplices, the crooked judges:

> I wish I were not of this race, that I had died before, or had not yet been born. This is the race of iron. Now, by day, men work and grieve unceasingly; by night they waste away and die. The gods will give harsh burdens, but will mingle in some good; Zeus will destroy this race of mortal men, when babies shall be born with greying hair. Father will have no common bond with son, neither will guest with host, nor friend with friend; the brother-love of past days will be gone. Men will dishonour parents, who grow old too quickly, and will blame and criticize with cruel words. Wretched and godless they, refusing to repay their bringing up, will cheat their aged parents of their due. Men will destroy the towns of other men. The just, the good, the man who keeps his word will be despised, but men will praise the bad and insolent. Might will be right, and shame will cease to be....(*Works and Days*, [165–94], p. 64)

Continuing, Hesiod then speaks of the magistrates "who judge dishonestly and swallow bribes":

> The deathless gods are never far away; they mark the crooked judges who grind down their fellow-men and do not fear the gods....
>
> The eye of Zeus sees all, and understands, and when he wishes, marks and does not miss how just a city is, inside. And I would not myself be just, nor have my son be just among bad men: for it is bad to be an honest man where felons rule; I trust wise Zeus to save me from this pass. But you, O Perses [Hesiod's no-good brother to whom *Works and Days* is addressed], think about these things; follow the just, avoiding violence. The son of Kronos made this law for men: that animals and fish and winged birds should eat each other, for they have no law. But mankind has the law of Right from him, which is the better way. And if one knows the law of Justice and proclaims it, Zeus far-seeing gives one great prosperity.
>
> And now, for lords who understand, I'll tell a fable: once a hawk, high in the clouds, clutched in his claws a speckled nightingale. She, pierced by those hooked claws, cried, "Pity me!" But he made a scornful answer: "Silly thing. Why do you cry? Your master holds you fast, you'll go where I decide, although you have a minstrel's lovely voice, and if I choose, I'll have you for a meal, or let you go. Only a fool will match himself against a stronger party, for he'll only lose, and be disgraced as well as beaten." Thus spoke the swift-flying hawk, the long-winged bird. (*Works and Days*, [195–223], p. 65.)

Hesiod remarks that the wisest of the peasants had only one son, thereby preventing the parcellization of their land. There thus prevailed a middle stratum of cultivators, possessing their yoke of oxen for plowing, and capable in times of war of arming themselves at their own expense. The majority of the agricultural population, however, lived in privation. In bad years, when harvests were insufficient for both subsistence and sowing, this population was compelled to borrow grain from the neighboring lord and to return it with substantial interest. Insolvent debtors, together with their families, thus fell into the hands of the creditors. Compounding the misery of the impoverished peasants and making their situation utterly hopeless was the fact that the grasping noble lords were in a position to bribe the magistrates who, like themselves, were members of the powerful and privileged circles. For such magistrates— "eaters of bribes" in Hesiod's words—there was no more lucrative source of revenue than their iniquitous practices. Hesiod, witness and victim of "crooked" verdicts, could only call upon Zeus the protector of Diké (Justice), since the unhappy wretches who had fallen into the clutches of the oppressors were like the nightingale caught in the talons of the hawk.

When democracy was first organized as a political party, it therefore sought to counteract the iniquity of the magistrates by demanding the publication of the laws. Virtually all of the critics and opponents of oligarchy were united on this point. The people had had enough of the crooked judicial sentences that the *eupatridae* (hereditary aristocrats) handed down as the presumed expression of the divine will, but which were all too often a cynical exploitation of their power. Many generations had waited in vain for the judges, delivering sentences under solemn oath, to remember Orcus, the avenger of perjury. They had waited patiently for the lamentations carried by Dike before the throne of Zeus to have their effect on earth. Patience had run out. Now the people demanded to know the laws and to have them written down.

Tyranny

Little wonder, then, that neither Solon nor any of the other legislators were able to do their work free from the raging passions of civil conflict. The mandate of the legislator was precisely to put an end to the bloodshed by bringing about reconciliation. It was his task to intervene and mediate between the warring factions by proposing a compromise. To accomplish this he was invested with extraordinary powers, thus becoming the supreme head of the city. It is not known what title was given to such legislators. In Asia Minor the title *aisymnetes* was often assigned to the chief magistrate since, as the term suggests, he was supposed to be well versed in the wise customs, traditions, and laws. Although Solon—whose reforms will be discussed in some detail later—was called *Thesmothetes*, or archon, he certainly fulfilled the functions of an *aisymnetes* in the widest sense. In any event, the legislator's mission was considered temporary, either for an indeterminate period until the task was accomplished, or for a fixed period of one, five, or even ten years. In all cases it placed supreme authority in the hands of a single man. Aristotle called it an "elective tyranny" (*Politics* III. IX. 5). Once the society had been saved by the elected tyrant, he returned to private life. Not surprisingly, the nobility and the other wealthy elements did not always submit to the legislator and accept compromise. In such cases, the people had recourse to an extreme expedient: They placed themselves in the hands of a tyrant, hoping thereby to gain some material improvement of their lot.

The term "tyrant" probably originated in the East and signified master or king as did its equivalent, *basileus*. On account of its origin, however, and because of its association with the despots of the East, the term was applied by the adversaries of tyranny in a derogatory sense to those who had gained absolute power unlawfully, by insurrection. An aspiring tyrant typically began his career as a demagogue leading the discontented poor against the rich or the common people against the nobles. The multitude followed him blindly as long as he promoted its welfare. Tyranny did not establish itself throughout Greece, but only in those cities where commercial and manufacturing interests had created a markedly oppressive regime and where, therefore, a persuasive demagogue could mobilize the masses for an assault upon the privileged classes. Tyranny, as Thucydides observed, was associated with the growing importance of money:

> The old form of government was hereditary monarchy with established rights and limitations; but as Hellas [Greece] became more powerful and as the importance of acquiring money became more and more evident, tyrannies were established in nearly all the cities, revenues increased, shipbuilding flourished, and ambition turned towards sea-power. (Thucydides I. 13)

Tyrants who made themselves champions of the lower classes were, generally speaking, restless, ambitious, and discontented members of the privileged camp. By virtue of the fact that they already held an office of state or a military command, aspiring tyrants, seizing an opportune moment, could mobilize armed partisans and succeed in ousting the reigning monarch. Once in power, a tyrant usually left the civil laws intact and remained content with adapting the existing governmental administration to his own interests. Tyrants frequently disdained public offices for themselves, preferring to turn them over to their sons, relatives, and friends. In this way, a tyranny that began with the usurpation of power soon tended to become a family affair, a dynastic regime. The general principle guiding tyrannical rule was to humble the nobility and appease the lower classes. Herodotus provides a vivid description of extreme tyranny. When Cypselus seized power in Corinth in the seventh century B.C.,

> many of the Corinthians he drove into exile, many he deprived of their property, and still more, by a long way, of their lives. He ruled in Corinth for thirty years, died in the height of prosperity, and was succeeded by his son Periander. To begin with, Periander was less violent than his father, but soon surpassed him in bloody-mindedness and savagery. This was a result of a correspondence which he entered into with Thrasybulus, the master of Miletus. He sent a representative to the court of this despot, to ask his opinion on how best and most safely to govern his city. Thrasybulus invited the man to walk with him from the city to a field where corn was growing. As he passed through this cornfield, continually asking questions about why the messenger had come to him from Corinth, he kept cutting off all the tallest ears of wheat which he could see, and throwing them away, until the finest and best-grown part of the crop was ruined. In this way he went right through the field, and then sent the messenger away without a word. On his return to Corinth, Periander was eager to hear what advice Thrasybulus had given, and the man replied that he had not given any at all, adding that he was surprised at being sent to such a person, who was evidently mad and a wanton destroyer of his own property—and then he described what he had seen Thrasybulus do. Periander seized the point at once; it was perfectly plain to him that Thrasybulus recommended the murder of all the people in the city who were outstanding in influence or ability. Moreover, he took the advice, and from that time forward there was no crime against the Corinthians that he did not commit; indeed, anything that Cypselus had left undone in the way of killing or banishing, Periander completed for him. (Herodotus V, 92E–G)

In addition to disposing in this manner of their actual and potential enemies, the tyrants constantly preoccupied themselves with the task of appeasing the masses by improving their material condition. The urgent agrarian problem of restoring land to the impoverished and indebted peasants may have been dealt with at least partially by distributing the property of the banished nobles. Solon, as we shall see, rejected the peasants' demand for the redistribution of landed property; but we no longer hear such a demand after the rule of the tyrant Pisistratus. To keep the peasants attached to the soil and away from the *agora* (marketplace), where they might swell the urban plebians, the tyrants employed ingenious devices: Pisistratus sent out to the countryside itinerant justices; Ortyges' regime administered justice at the city gates of Erythrae, allowing no inhabitant of the rural demes (unit of local government) to enter; and Periander created local councils at the outskirts of the Corinthian territory.

The most urgent task of all, however, was to find a means of maintaining the social peace within the *polis*. This the tyrants sought to accomplish by ensuring to the *thetes* a higher remuneration for their labor and a larger measure of public respect. The tyrants also initiated and sponsored large-scale public works: aqueducts, breakwaters, and monuments to the gods. This achieved many things at once. It enormously enhanced the tyrant's prestige; it provided employment and kept the laborers occupied and, hence, less inclined to rebel; and it inspired in the people a civic pride that made them forget their loss of liberty (Herodotus III, 60).

It is a noteworthy historical fact, however, that tyranny nowhere endured for long. After a tyranny had accomplished what the disadvantaged classes had expected of it, it disappeared. The Orthagoridae at Sicyon appear to be the only case we have of a tyrannical dynasty maintaining itself in power for a century. Elsewhere power was retained by the son of the founder but went no further than that. Herodotus relates that when Cypselus, the father of Periander, consulted the oracle, he received an answer "which cut both ways," as it were:

Fortunate is he who steps down into my house, Cypselus, son of Eëtion, lord of famous Corinth: Fortunate he and his sons, but not the sons of his sons. (Herodotus 92E)

Whether this was an actual prophecy or, more likely, prophecy after the fact, the oracle reflects the general pattern. Tyranny was a system directed against oligarchy; it persisted, therefore, as long as it had the support of the people, for whom it was a temporary expedient. The people used it as a weapon with which to demolish the strongholds of the oligarchs; and once this had been achieved, they destroyed the weapon. The founding tyrant, placed on the pinnacle of power by the multitude, was almost always succeeded by a more harsh and less capable ruler. For as tyranny became less useful to the people, it also became more oppressive and thus doomed to death. And yet, it had fulfilled a historic role in activating the people and thereby contributing to the birth of democracy.

Athenian Democracy

By the close of the sixth century B.C., then, the people had stirred in some city-states and moved into history—albeit under the leadership of tyrants. In other states, however, the large noble families succeeded once again in seizing power and restoring their hereditary prerogatives. The future of Greece from the fifth century on was shaped by a struggle between competing and even antagonistic sociopolitical systems. For although the wars between Persia and Greece, as related by Herodotus, were a struggle for territory and spheres of influence, they also represented a struggle between "Oriental despotism," in which the people had no voice, and the Greek city-states in which the people had some voice. Aristotle, recognizing that the Oriental monarchy was significantly different from that of the Greeks, remarked that because the Asiatics were more servile than the Europeans, "they endure despotic rule without any resentment" (*Politics* III. IX. 3). And Herodotus, in his discussions of Egypt, Babylon, and Persia, provides some insight into the political system that scholars, from the time of Montesquieu, have called "Oriental despotism"—a highly centralized agrarian bureaucracy of which pharaonic Egypt was the prototype. Often but not always, the economic corollary of this political system was a vast and complex system of artificial irrigation (Herodotus I, 185; I, 193).

And if the Persian-Greek wars represented a struggle between two opposing sociopolitical systems, so did the Peloponnesian War, which was at one and the same time an ideological struggle between oligarchy and democracy. This is a fact that Thucydides repeatedly stresses:

> Practically the whole of the Hellenic world was convulsed, with rival parties in every state—democratic leaders trying to bring in the Athenians, and oligarchs trying to bring in the Spartans. (Thucydides III, 82)

> Society had become divided into two ideologically hostile camps, and each side viewed the other with suspicion. (III, 83)

> The two parties in Megara were both apprehensive. One party feared that he [Brasidas, the Spartan commander] might restore the exiles and drive them out; the other party that the democrats, just because of this fear of theirs, might attack them and so, with fighting going on inside and the Athenians on the watch so close outside, the city would be lost. They therefore refused to let Brasidas in, both sides preferring to remain quiet and see what the future would bring. (IV, 71)

Directly after the return from the Megarid, the Athenian general Demosthenes arrived at Naupactus with forty ships. There had been some people in the cities of Boeotia who had been intriguing with him and with Hippocrates with a view to overthrowing the regime and introducing a democracy, as at Athens. (IV, 76)

The Mendaeans were now split into two factions, and someone from the democratic party answered Polydamidas back and said that they would not go out and that they did not want a war. For this reply Polydamidas dragged the man forward by the arm and began to knock him about. This infuriated the people, who immediately seized hold of their weapons and set upon the Peloponnesians and those of the opposite party who were collaborating with the Peloponnesians. (IV, 130)

The pro-Spartan party wanted to overthrow the democracy in Argos, and now, after the battle, this party was in a much better position to persuade the people to accept the proposals. They wanted first to make peace with Sparta, to follow this up by making an alliance, and then finally to launch their attack on the democratic party. (V, 76)

Although there are many more examples of the internal political struggles that went on during the war, we will conclude with just one more—a segment of a speech that Thucydides places in the mouth of Athenagoras, a man who represented the democratic standpoint, but who adequately characterizes both ideological positions:

There are people who will say that democracy is neither an intelligent nor a fair system, and that those who have the money are also the best rulers. But I say, first, that what is meant by the *demos*, or people, is the whole State, whereas an oligarchy is only a section of the State; and I say next that though the rich are the best people for looking after money, the best counsellors are the intelligent, and that it is the many who are best at listening to the different arguments and judging between them. And all alike, whether taken all together or as separate classes, have equal rights in a democracy. An oligarchy, on the other hand, certainly gives the many their share of dangers, but when it comes to the good things in life not only claims the largest share, but goes off with the whole lot. And this is what the rich men among you are aiming at; but in a great city these things are beyond your reach. What fools you are! In fact the stupidest of all the Hellenes I know, if you do not realize that your aims are evil, and the biggest criminals if you do realize this and still have the face to proceed with them. (Thucydides VI, 39)

Thucydides thus makes it clear that Athens everywhere encouraged democracies, and Sparta encouraged oligarchies; and though there were exceptions, the rule cannot be denied. The propertied classes, generally fearing and distrusting the people, regarded the imposition of democracy as an act of tyranny; but the lower classes looked forward to Athenian victory as offering at least some protection against their native oligarchs. In due course we shall see how the Greco-Persian wars led to those between Sparta and Athens and their respective allies; and how the issues raised in those wars influenced Plato's theory of the State. But first we need to say more about the Spartan and Athenian systems.

Sparta, as the leader of the Peloponnesian League, commanded enormous forces—so enormous, in fact, that there was no question that she would lead the Greek army and navy in the conflict against the Medes and Persians. The Spartan warrior-aristocracy was, of course, an oligarchy, its economic and social system resting on the subjugation of a large population of peasant cultivators called *helots*. The *helots*, first of Laconia and later also of Messenia, were assigned to individual Spartans for work on the land and other services. The *perioikoi*, in contrast, were free Greeks, living in their own Laconian communities, but subject to Spartan control in foreign-policy matters and obligated to provide military units to the Spartan armies. The aim of the Spartan warriors' education was to train them to fulfill two functions, preparedness for war and internal security— keeping the subject *helots* under control.

Athens, in contrast, prided herself from earliest times on having neither a dominant ethnic group nor a subjugated one in her midst. Athenian society had nothing comparable to the *helots*—although we shall need to qualify this statement in a later discussion of Athenian slavery. In Athens as in other city-states the declining monarchy had been supplanted by the nobility. Nevertheless, a modicum of the ancient political equality had prevailed for a time both among the clans and within them. For beneath the nobles the common people—composed of freeholders, shepherds, artisans, fishermen, and sailors—had been accustomed to deliberating and having a say in matters of common interest. The ancient, communal traditions were undermined, however, as the nobility became more and more oppressive. The rural poor, in particular, were subjected to debt-bondage by the rich landlords. The poor were called dependents and "sixth-parters," because it was for a sixth of the yield that they worked the land of the rich. Much if not all of the best land was concentrated in the hands of a few powerful families; and if the poor failed to pay their rents, both they and their children were liable to seizure as debt-slaves. At this time, before the reforms of Solon, all loans were made on the security of the person. As one would expect, political power was likewise concentrated in the hands of the well-born and the very rich. They ruled through the nine archonships and the council of the Areopagus. The Athenian political structure had become an oligarchy; and strife between the nobles and the people had become the rule.

Solon (c. 594/3)

In these circumstances a mediator and lawgiver emerged. Deeply disturbed by the prevailing social conflict, and inspired by the ethical teachings of Delphi, Solon sought to apply the lessons of limit and moderation to social and political life, and thereby to restore social peace and unity. Solon reintroduced the ideal of social equality and made a real effort to prevent the rich from exerting their power without limit. At the same time he tried to soften the burden on the poor by cancelling the debts accumulated on mortgages by the impoverished peasantry. He imposed a limit on the extent of landed properties, and he restricted, by means of sumptuary laws, the ability of the rich to flaunt their wealth. In addition, he attempted to reestablish the peasants as freeholders on their own farms. Equally important for the future of Athens, Solon provided legislation permitting foreign, skilled craftsmen to settle in Attica, thereby encouraging the rise of manufacturing. In the long run this proved to be a safety valve for the poor, since it rescued them from the misery of exclusive dependence on a strictly agrarian source of livelihood. To protect the weak and needy, Solon stipulated that any Athenian citizen might undertake, on another's behalf, to prosecute a criminal offender, thus enabling the common people to take a large stride forward in ensuring evenhanded justice. But Solon's work went even further. His aim, as we learn from his elegiac poems, was to institute a general rule of balanced equality (*isonomy*) in which no class could claim either social superiority or undue political privilege. In Solon's own words:

> I gave to the people as much esteem as is sufficient for them, not detracting from their honour or reaching out to take it; and to those who had power and were admired for their wealth I declared that they should have nothing unseemly. I stood holding my mighty shield against both, and did not allow either to win an unjust victory. (Aristotle, *The Athenian Constitution* 12)

Since Solon was a great mediator, it turned out that the nobles were disappointed with him because of his cancellation of debts and that, indeed, both the rich and the poor came to regret his appointment because his reforms were contrary to their expectations. The common people had wanted him to carry out a complete redistribution of property, while the notables had assumed that he would make only small changes. But Solon was in principle opposed to the extremes of both parties; and though he was in a position to align himself with either one and become a tyrant, he followed his principles instead and incurred the hostility of both. In the face of such ingratitude and animosity, Solon left his homeland to trade and travel in Egypt, declaring that he would stay away for ten years.

In his lifetime, then, Solon incurred hostility because he conceived of the neutral, mediatory state as a means of moderating the strife raging between the notables and the people. But by the end of the fifth century B.C., some 200 years after his reforms, he was honored by both. On the one hand, the democratic party claimed him as the father of Periclean democracy; on the other hand, the oligarchical party that attempted a political revolution in the year 411 B.C.—or at least the more moderate among them—regarded Solon as the father of an "ancestral constitution" (*patrios politeia*) of a mixed type, neither democratic nor oligarchical, to which, they urged, Athens ought to return. And Aristotle appears to have perceived both the aristocratic and democratic elements in Solon's constitution:

> As for Solon, he is considered by some people to have been a good lawgiver, as having put an end to oligarchy when it was too unqualified and having liberated the people from slavery and established our traditional democracy with a skillful blending of the constitution: the Council on the Areopagus being an oligarchic element, the elective magistracies aristocratic, and the law courts democratic. And although really in regard to certain of these features, the Council and the election of magistrates, Solon seems merely to have abstained from destroying institutions that existed already, he does appear to have founded the democracy by constituting the jury-courts from all the citizens. (*Politics* II. IX. 2)

But Solon's reforms failed to achieve their aim, and it was not for long that Athens remained free of civil discord. Since none of the conflicting parties had achieved full satisfaction, they refused to lay down their arms. There were three factions in conflict, each representing a socioeconomic class and a distinct area of the land, and each having at its head a powerful family: the *eupatridae*, or nobility, of the plains were led by the Philaedae; the merchants and fishermen of the coast by the Alcmaeonidae; the small peasants of the mountains by the Pisistratidae. Pisistratus (c. 560) won the day by seizing the tyranny, which the lower classes had offered to Solon in vain. Pisistratus introduced far-reaching agrarian reforms. He distributed the waste land and the large estates confiscated from the nobles, and thus created again a vigorous class of smallholders who came to play a significant part in the affairs of Athens. He encouraged maritime commerce through a foreign policy that sent merchants to Thrace for gold and to the Hellespont for corn. At the same time he catered to the rural and urban masses by means of festivals in honor of Dionysius, as well as theatrical productions and the construction of magnificent buildings. And since he allowed the Athenian constitution to remain in effect, he fostered among the people valuable political experience in the sessions of the Assembly and in the courts. On the whole, Pisistratus appears to have enjoyed the support of the masses; for in the words of the *Athenian Constitution*, he gave them no trouble and

> ...always maintained peace and saw that all was quiet. For that reason it was often said that the tyranny of Pisistratus was the age of Cronus; for afterwards, when his sons took over, the regime became much more cruel. Most important of all the things mentioned was his democratic and humane manner. In other respects he was willing to administer everything according to the laws, not giving himself any advantage; and on one occasion, when he was summoned before the Areopagus on a homicide charge, he attended to make his defence— but the prosecutor took fright and defaulted. Consequently, he remained in power for a long time, and when he was expelled he easily recovered his position. He had many supporters both among the notables and among the ordinary people: he won over the notables by his friendly dealings with them, and the people by his help for their private concerns, and he behaved honourably to both. (*Athenian Constitution* 16)

Cleisthenes (c. 508/7)

Cleisthenes continued the work of Solon and gave a more decisive form to the democratic structure of Athens. His major aim was to prevent the return of tyranny, and to accomplish this he recognized that he must destroy the strong political organization that the nobles had made for themselves in their clans and in the four powerful Ionian tribes. Under Cleisthenes, the people gained more control over civic affairs. Following the overthrow of Isagoras (c. 508), the last tyrant and his sons, Cleisthenes distributed all the citizens through ten tribes instead of the old four, intending thereby to mix the members of the families so that men of all social backgrounds would have a share in running the State. He created districts in which the citizens were classified according to their domicile, dividing the entire country into *demes*—parishes with their own assemblies, magistrates, and administrations. All citizens were enrolled in these demes, and they bore the deme-name as proof of their citizenship. There were well over a hundred of these demes, which were then grouped in ten sectional tribes (*phylai*). These now became merely topographical units and could no longer be identified as family or kin groups. It was now impossible for the ancient tribes to recognize themselves in the new tribes. Since Cleisthenes made the men in each deme the fellow-demesmen of one another and decreed that they were to bear the deme-name and no longer that of their fathers, it was never obvious who the new citizens were.

The decimal system was applied to the entire political and administrative organization of the city. The *Boulé*, or council, consisted of 500 members, 50 from each tribe, chosen from the demes in proportion to their population. As there had been only nine archons, a secretary was added so that each of the ten tribes would be represented in the college of magistrates. The army was made up of ten regiments called *phylai*, each commanded by a *phylarch*. On all occasions the people were organized in ten groups, and, indeed, the decimal system—a logical criterion and thus contrary to all the traditional principles of social organization—became an integral feature of the democratic regime. Thus the Athenians of the fifth century B.C. lived in accordance with the civil laws of Solon and the political laws of Cleisthenes.

The Persian-Greek Wars

In less than two decades after Cleisthenes' reforms the new Athenian democracy was put to a severe test with the large-scale invasion by the Medes and Persians in c. 480 B.C. Cyrus, the great Persian king, overthrew his Mede overlords and extended his kingdom farther than they had. In a short campaign he defeated Croesus of Lydia and then went on to conquer the Greek coast. Although Cyrus himself made no effort to advance farther west, his successor, Darius I (ruled 521–486) conquered Thrace and Macedon and thus came very close to the Greek homeland. The danger was such that appeals for help against the Persians were frequently dispatched to Sparta, who had brought all of the Peloponnese except Argos under her leadership and formed the powerful organization that historians call the Peloponnesian League. Sparta, however, ignored the appeals and sent no help, although she did make some preparations for resistance within the league. On the whole, our impression of the Persian rulers of Lydia is that although they were not excessively oppressive—in that they tolerated local customs and religions—they nevertheless demanded tribute, general obedience, and, on occasion, military service as well. The one feature of Persian domination that became most offensive, however, was the fact that Persia ruled the Greek cities of Asia Minor through tyrants she herself appointed. But the Greeks had outgrown tyranny, and the Ionian Revolt against Persia (499–494) began with a general uprising that deposed the tyrants. Again, Sparta extended no aid; but Athens and Eritrea did support the Ionians in the first year of their revolt, and it was, therefore, against the Athenians in particular that Darius's seaborne force was directed in 490 B.C. This was the occasion on which Athens made history, for her troops faced Darius's army at Marathon and defeated it without Spartan assistance.

In 480 B.C., however, Darius's son Xerxes I (ruled 486–465) brought by land a much larger army directed to the general conquest of Greece. Sparta now fully recognized the danger, and the Greek city-states came under Spartan leadership, since her league commanded the greatest resources for war on land. Although the Athenian navy, newly created by Themistocles, was much larger than any other contingent, it was not Athens but Sparta that commanded even at sea. The decisive naval action in 480 B.C. at Salamis, which resulted in the Athenian defeat of the Persians, was fought under Spartan leadership, and the important victory by land at Plataea in 479 B.C. was very much the achievement of Sparta and of her general, Pausanias (Herodotus IX). It is reasonable to suggest that had it not been for Sparta's specialization in military technique and the general Greek resoluteness in preventing Persian conquest, much of subsequent Western history would have been different.

Athens not only stood the test of the great invasion but she also came out strengthened. In the course of the war, however, the Areopagus, its members drawn for the most part from the rich and the nobility, had magnified its power in public life. In 462 B.C. the democratic party, under the leadership of Ephialtes, launched an assault upon this stronghold of the aristocracy, depriving it of the function that had made it the guardian of the constitution and that had enabled the notables to exercise control over governmental affairs. Retaining only its religious functions, the Areopagus lost all its other powers, which were transferred to the Assembly of the people and to the Boulé. Described as a "champion of the people" and "uncorrupt and upright in political matters" (*Athenian Constitution* 25), Ephialtes was assassinated, thus paying with his life for his dedication to the people's cause. But he had as his lieutenant a man who was to become the most famous representative of Athenian democracy—Pericles, the son of Xanthippus and the great-nephew of Cleisthenes.

Pericles addressed the question of how to enable the common people, totally engaged in earning their livelihood, to give their time to the service of the republic. The administration of justice throughout the country was so complex and demanding that it required many thousands of judges and other officials. The business of public affairs not only required the occasional presence of all the citizens in the Assembly, but it also made necessary the ongoing participation of more than a third of them. But at least half of the citizens earned scarcely enough for their subsistence. How could they go without their income for even a few days? And if such working people were to be excluded from the council, the courts, and other offices of State, why would this be a democracy rather than a timocracy or oligarchy? It was therefore Pericles's innovation to institute pay for those citizens who, in order to serve as officials of the State, had to abandon their occupations. Salaries were paid to members of the council, to the judges, and to the majority of other officials, especially those elected by lot. And now that the office of archon was also furnished with a salary and filled by lot, there was no longer any reason for limiting it to the proprietary classes.

Thus Athens at the height of her democracy governed herself by the service of a substantial portion of her citizens. They were daily engaged in State duties, either civil or military. But this was not a leisure class, since the citizen was paid for his civic work under the Periclean system. Plato, as we shall see, objected to the system of pay on the ground that it attracted the lower classes into politics. But Pericles believed that the alternative to paying the citizens would have been either corrupt lower-class officials or oligarchy. The Periclean system sought to prevent both of these developments by attracting into politics those who were not independently wealthy and who had to work for a living. In words attributed to Pericles:

> Here each individual is interested not only in his own affairs but in the affairs of the State as well: even those who are mostly occupied with their own business are extremely well informed on general politics—this is a peculiarity of ours: we do not say that a man who takes no interest in politics is a man who minds his own business; we say that he has no business here at all. (Thucydides II, 40)

Work was no stigma in Periclean Athens. The Athenians took pride from membership in their craft. Work was a part of a full and harmonious life. Yet individuals did in fact object to some occupations as "menial," either because these occupations were unduly monotonous or because they precluded a good physique. But people nonetheless worked with self-respect and pride in making good blades in a sword factory or artistic vases in a pottery, or even in the fulling of wool and the tanning of leather.

For Plato, as we shall see, politics is an art or craft that, like all arts, requires specialized knowledge. Furthermore, one individual can attain such specialized knowledge in only one art. It followed that the art of politics can be practiced only by a professional class that has acquired the requisite knowledge and skills. This is the direct opposite of Pericles's conception that an adequate knowledge of politics can be combined with attention to private affairs. Again, in the words attributed to Pericles in his funeral oration:

> [Our] constitution is called a democracy because power is in the hands not of a minority but of the whole people. When it is a question of settling private disputes, everyone is equal before the law; when it is a question of putting one person before another in positions of public responsibility, what counts is not membership of a particular class, but the actual ability which the man possesses. No one, so long as he has it in him to be of service to the State, is kept in political obscurity because of poverty. (Thucydides II, 37)

Nevertheless, we have to remind ourselves that Athenian democracy was a democracy only for Athenian citizens, who were a minority. Side by side with them lived an equal number of slaves and about half their number of *metics*, who were originally foreigners. By the time of Pericles, the metics grasped at every opportunity to gain citizenship through marriage. This was perceived as a direct threat to the material advantages and political privileges of the citizenry, and about the year 450 B.C. a law was passed at Pericles's initiative restricting citizenship to those who were born of Athenian parents.

Slavery in the Democracy

The Greek philosophers were united in postulating for the citizens of their ideal cities abundant leisure for the higher things in life; and there could be no such leisure without slavery. It is estimated that in the period under consideration the total population of Athens numbered between 300,000 and 400,000. These included: (1) citizens and their families, about 160,000; (2) metics, or resident aliens, about 45,000 adults or upwards of 90,000 if we include the children; (3) slaves, between 80,000 and 100,000. A large number of slaves belonged to or worked for the State as clerks and police officers. Apart from these there were about 20,000 slaves employed in the silver mines at Laurium. Many if not all of the latter were the property of private individuals who purchased concessions and used slave labor to work the mines. This was slave labor in its worst form. In addition, wealthy Athenians often had a large number of slaves whom they employed in their own businesses or hired out to contractors and factory owners. In this light it may be said that the Athenian State was enriched by mining royalties and that the wealthy Athenian citizens owed their riches to the labor of slaves. But the important question remains: What was the relevance of slavery for the ordinary Athenian artisan or farmer? It seems to be true that many potters and other craftsmen employed slave-apprentices in their workshops. But when we take account of the vast majority of slaves owned by those of means, there can be no doubt that the bulk of Athenian citizens had no slaves at all but nevertheless had the time to sit in the Assembly, serve on juries, attend the theater, and watch the athletic competitions and games. In a word, an Athenian who possessed no slaves at all could enjoy the benefits of the political and cultural life of Athenian democracy.

Apart from the slaves in the mines, it may be reasonable to surmise that Athenian slaves lived and worked in conditions that were not inhumane. In Athens the majority of slaves appear to have been skilled workers—masons, potters, sword-makers, and the like; and it is generally agreed that where skilled craftsworkers are concerned, they can be made to do their best work only by decent treatment. Furthermore, under Athenian law, slaves could purchase their liberty, or be assured of emancipation after a definite period of service, or gain freedom by their master's will. Inflicting bodily injury on a slave was an indictable offense. Finally, it is worth noting that in the everyday life of Athens, slaves were treated as social equals. There having been no color line between masters and slaves, nor any other badge of servility, slaves were often indistinguishable from freemen. This social equality or near-equality of slave and freeman must have been conspicuous since it evoked the following sardonic comment from Plato: "And the height of popular freedom, my friend,…is attained in such a city when the purchased slaves, male and female, are no less free than the masters who paid for them." (Plato, *Republic* 563B)

With these considerations in mind, we can say that although the State profits derived from the silver mines rested on slave labor, the political democracy of Athens did not rest on slavery. If revenue from various sources is to be the criterion, then we can say that the political life of Athens depended far more on her empire than on the fact that she was a slave-owning State.

The Athenian Empire

The silver mines at Laurium in the southeast corner of Attica did, however, play a significant role in strengthening Athens. At the beginning of the fifth century B.C. a new rich vein was opened there, and Themistocles persuaded the State to use the huge revenues for the construction of a fleet of 200 ships, an unprecedented number. That this was a wise military decision became quite clear soon afterwards, since the same Themistocles was the principal architect of the naval victory at Salamis in 480 B.C. Athens emerged from the Persian wars immensely more powerful than ever before. Although the conflict with Persia continued, it now shifted to Asia Minor and the eastern Mediterranean where Sparta, as a specialist in land warfare, found it increasingly awkward to exercise leadership and therefore withdrew from the struggle. Sparta's prestige among the Greek city-states was damaged still more by the personal disgrace of Pausanias, the victor in the battles of Plataea. In the words of Thucydides:

> The Spartans recalled Pausanias to face a court of inquiry in connection with various reports that they had received. Serious charges had been made against him by Hellenes arriving at Sparta: instead of acting as commander-in-chief, he appeared to be trying to set himself up as a dictator. It happened that he was recalled just at the time when, because of his unpopularity, the allies, apart from the soldiers from the Peloponnese, had gone over to the side of the Athenians.
>
> At Sparta, Pausanias was condemned for various acts of injustice against individuals, but he was acquitted on all the main counts; *one of the most serious charges was that he was collaborating with the Persians, and there seemed to be very good evidence for this....*
>
> So Athens took over the leadership and the allies, because of their dislike of Pausanias, were glad to see her do so. (Thucydides I, 95–96, italics added)

Thucydides then goes on to say that after Pausanias had been tried and acquitted,

> he was not sent out again in an official capacity. However, on his own initiative and without Spartan authority he took a trireme [a galley ship with three banks of oars] from the town of Hermione and sailed to the Hellespont. He pretended that his intention was to join in the national struggle against Persia, but in fact he went in order to intrigue with the King of Persia, as he had already begun to do before, with the aim of becoming the ruler of Hellas. (Thucydides I, 128)

Finally, it was reported that Pausanias was conspiring

> with the helots, and this was in fact the case. He was offering them their freedom and full rights as citizens if they would join him in revolt and help him to carry out all his schemes. (Thucydides I, 132)

In these circumstances, Sparta withdrew entirely inside the Peloponnese, and had to contend with considerable disaffection there; and

Athens took over the leadership of the allies and organized a new maritime confederation, the Delian League, with the aim of continuing the war against Persia and liberating the Greeks of the East. The requirements of wide-ranging naval warfare meant that more ships had to be constructed and rowers paid and fed. Hence, member states of the Delian League had to assume responsibility for building and providing ships for the various expeditions. In time, however, members of the league found this arrangement too burdensome and consented to the making of substantial monetary contributions to finance what became, in effect, an Athenian navy. Athens unhesitatingly employed her newfound power, and by the middle of the fifth century the Delian League had become an empire. Athenian magistrates were installed in a majority of the cities, and the more serious legal cases were referred to Athenian courts. When revolts occurred among the discontented allies, their land was confiscated and allocated to Athenian colonists, and more. Thucydides relates, for example, that when the city-state of Naxos left the Delian League, the Athenians besieged the island and forced the populace back to allegiance. "This was the first case," he wrote, "when the original constitution of the League was broken and an allied city lost its independence, and the process was continued in the cases of the other allies as various circumstances arose" (Thucydides I, 98). The Athenian Assembly often tended to justify this policy, but the allies receiving such treatment regarded it as forcible subjection to servitude.

As we noted earlier, the tension that eventually erupted in the Peloponnesian War was, in a large measure, due to the political-ideological struggle between democrats and oligarchs. As a rule with few exceptions, Athens everywhere fostered democracies, and Sparta oligarchies. Those who feared, despised, or distrusted the common people were the propertied classes who actually paid the tribute money that went to Athens. To such privileged elements the Athenian imposition of democracy was an act of tyranny; but to the lower classes Athenian rule afforded some protection from their native oligarchs. The Greek world as a whole was now increasingly dominated by the conflict between Athens and Sparta, each striving to install in the small cities a regime in its own image, or to destroy the regime favorable to the other side.

And yet for some time after the Persian War the two great cities of Athens and Sparta lived in comparative harmony. Athens was preoccupied with the further prosecution of the war against the Persians in Asia, while Sparta directed her energies toward the threats of insurrection in the Peloponnese. The war against Persia ended in a formal treaty in 449 B.C. But as Athenian power, already great, continued to grow and Sparta effectively stabilized her dominion, she was frequently called upon to help a city against Athenian intervention. A war that had broken out between

Athens and a neighbor ultimately involved Sparta as well. Although a peace treaty concluded this war in 446 B.C., it lasted for only fourteen of the thirty years for which the treaty was made. This was a period of relative calm (446–432) before the outbreak of full-scale warfare between Sparta and Athens—the great Peloponnesian War.

The years of calm were those in which Pericles came to the fore and played so central a role in Athenian politics. This was the period when the Parthenon and the Propylaea were built, when the plays of Sophocles and Euripides were being performed, and when Protagoras and the Sophists frequented Athens as Greece's cultural center. The city had become, in the words Thucydides ascribed to Pericles, "an education to Greece" (II, 41). It was under the leadership of Pericles that the Athenian League was transformed into an empire. The uneasy peace between the two powerful cities of Athens and Sparta came to an end in 431 B.C. as war erupted between Athens and the Peloponnesian League: a war, as Thucydides shows, that was a struggle for the domination of Greece. The cause of the war, as Thucydides saw it, was the Spartan fears "of the further growth of Athenian power, seeing, as they did, that already the greater part of Hellas was under the control of Athens" (Thucydides I, 88).

It cannot be too strongly emphasized, however, that the ideological conflict between democracy and oligarchy was an extremely important component of the war, with practical effects. For the Spartans found partisans among the men of property in the cities subject to Athens, just as the Athenians found supporters among the lower classes in the cities of their opponents. But the support of the common people in those cities was less effective, since they were not the ones who bore arms. The war, a protracted one lasting twenty-seven years, was only briefly interrupted by the compromise Peace of Nicias in 421 B.C. A main reason for the long and drawn-out nature of the conflict was the difficulty the adversaries had in coming directly to grips with one another: The Athenian navy could not strike at the inland strongholds of the Peloponnesian League, and the armies of the latter could not decisively interrupt the seaborne supply routes of the Athenian naval forces. Thucydides relates in detail how the Athenians mistakenly sought to break the stalemate with a large and ambitious expedition to Sicily in 415 B.C. This was a turning point in the war: The Athenian forces were so badly beaten that it took almost a decade to rebuild her fleet. The victory over Athens in 404 B.C. was achieved with Persian assistance to the Peloponnesian fleet.

The defeat of the Athenians brought with it great material damage as the Peloponnesian armies devastated the countryside of Attica. Even before the defeat, the oligarchical party of Athens had made in 411 B.C. a brief revolution. After the Athenian surrender in 404 B.C., Sparta, under Lysander, imposed a second oligarchy, that of the "Thirty," which lasted one year and precipitated a civil war which ended with Sparta's acquiescence in the restoration of democracy. Later, we shall need to take the ideological and political conflicts into account as we consider the social and political theories of Socrates and Plato.

Thucydides describes the secret oligarchic clubs that flourished in Athens during the war and which occasionally came into the open; and the great historian also relates the part played by the clubs in starting an oligarchic reign of terror as a prelude to the revolution of 411 B.C. The second oligarchic coup of 404 B.C. revealed once and for all that the Athenians had no tolerance for oligarchic government.

Democracy was restored after only one year under the leadership of very moderate men who proclaimed an amnesty for the members and sympathizers of the oligarchic party. The people behaved more decently than their opponents. Economically and politically, Athens recovered from the war rather quickly and retained a leading role in Greece right up to the Macedonian conquest. But the tensions between rich and poor remained; and Aristotle, writing after the conquest in the latter half of the fourth century B.C., took it for granted that every *polis* had two opposing parties divided on socioeconomic lines.

2

● ● ● ● ● ● ● ● ● ● ● ● ● ● ●

From Religion to Philosophy

Greek Polytheism

To understand one very important dimension of Plato's philosophy we need the historical and sociological background provided in the Introduction to this book. Socrates and Plato addressed definite problems, questions, and issues in their reflections on society and politics. And there can be little doubt that what gave rise to those reflections was the larger historical context, notably the Greco-Persian wars as a struggle between social systems, and the Peloponnesian War as a political-ideological conflict between oligarchy and democracy. But to understand the other essential elements of Socrates' and Plato's thought, we need to see how their theory of the Forms, the soul, and the nature of the divine emerged out of Greek religion. Indeed, we need to recognize that much of the pre-Socratic theorizing about the *physis* (of which more will be said later) was little more than a translation of religious concepts into those of Greek philosophy and proto-science.

Note: The title of this chapter is the same as that of F. M. Cornford's classic study cited later in this chapter.

Greek religion was a form of polytheism, the belief in a plurality of gods. In the fifth century B.C., in the time of Herodotus, Thucydides, Socrates, and Plato, we have the impression that the highly educated individuals ceased to take literally the theogonic and mythological tales of the gods. Nevertheless, we find in Plato that he continues to refer to "the gods"—although he also employs the singular noun *theos*, which is frequently rendered as "God" in English. Scholars have shown, however, that the Greek word *theos* and the English word *God* are by no means equivalent. To the ancient Greek, god was primarily a predicate as, for example, in "love is god" or "beauty is god." This is the reverse of the Judeo-Christian, monotheistic conception in which the existence of an Almighty God is taken for granted, and in which one makes such statements about God as being "just and merciful," or "God is love." It appears that when the Greeks said that beauty is god, they were telling us something about the reality of beauty. In saying that beauty is a god, the Greeks meant that beauty is more than human—that it is everlasting and not subject to death. That is why they ordinarily referred to their gods as *oi-athanatoi*, the "deathless ones." And more often than not, "god" designated impersonal things: any quality, power, or force that was here before we came into the world and that will surely continue to exist long after we are gone.

Whether it is the noun *theos* or the adjective *theios* (divine), it cannot be translated as *god* or *godly* and still make sense from a monotheistic standpoint. When, for example, the pre-Socratic, Milesian philosophers described the primordial substance constituting the physical world, they called it *theos*. Thus Thales, the first Greek philosopher about whom we have any information, said that the world was full of gods, meaning, apparently, that it was full of water. Thales, Anaximander, and Anaximenes, the first, second, and third of the earliest Milesian philosophers, all concerned themselves with *physis*, which may be translated as "Nature" as long as we bear in mind that Nature, for the Greeks, was no mere object. *Physis* was not "matter" if we intend by that term something lifeless. Nor should we think of it as a "primary substance" in the medieval, scholastic sense. The primary meaning of *physis* is "growth," implying life and motion. Whatever it is that constitutes the "All" or universe, it is alive and self-moving; it has a soul in the same sense that there is a "soul," or life-principle, in the body of organic, animate beings. For Anaximander the *physis* was the "indefinite" or "limitless thing." For Anaximenes, it was "air" or mist.

It is not perfectly clear even from Hesiod's *Theogony* whether the Greeks conceived of the *physis* as having a beginning. Although Hesiod uses the term "chaos," it appears to be nothing other than the space that yawns between Heaven and Earth, a gaping abyss that existed in primordial times (*Theogony* 116–146). Under the influence of the biblical story of Creation, and the Hebrew words *tohu vabohu*, in particular, some readers of Hesiod have been inclined to think of "chaos" as wild, confusing disorder.[1] This is probably an incorrect view, since Aristotle, in his *Physics* (IV.1. 208b31), speaks of chaos simply as empty space. It is possible that for Hesiod even chaos came into being. He does not say, "In the beginning was chaos," but rather, "Chaos was first of all, and next appeared broad-bosomed earth," and so on. The question thus arises whether there was, for the Greeks, a beginning or becoming, a something which, as in the biblical view, had not itself become. In any event, for Anaximander, order comes into being not last but first, when the primordial elements—earth, air, water, and fire—are assigned by eternal motion to their proper and distinct provinces, a conception in which Necessity and Right, Must and Ought, are united.

The most fundamental characteristic of Greek religion is that the gods come into being late, and once they emerge they do not reign supreme. Throughout we find them dominated by a higher order, a *supradivine,impersonal force* to which they always remain subject. In this higher order, Necessity and Right are united; for as we see in Homer, the gods are subordinate to a power that is both inexorable and moral and that the Greeks called *Moira*, Destiny or Fate. The gods of Homer are limited creatures who, although they are exempt from age and death, are not eternal: They were born into a world older than they. Nor are they omnipotent. The power that limits them is *Moira*, which they did not create and against which they cannot stand. The gods are helpless to save a man whom they love when the "dread fate of death" lays hold of him (*Homer Odyssey* III, 236). Zeus, the most powerful of the gods, laments that it is Fate that his son, Sarpedon, dearest to him of all men, must die at the hands of Patroclus (*Homer Iliad* XVI, 433). Zeus cannot undo what Fate has decreed. Herodotus relates that when Lydian messengers "reached Delphi and asked the questions they had been told to ask, the priestess replied that *not God himself could escape Destiny*" (Herodotus I, 90, italics added). And in the same vein: "The god of prophecy was eager that the fall of Sardis might occur in the time of Croesus' sons...but he had been unable to divert the course of Destiny" (Herodotus I, 90). Athena in Euripides says that what is ordained is master of the gods; and Prometheus in Aeschylus states that Zeus himself cannot escape what Fate has decreed. As for the inexorable power of *Moira* over human beings, this is most clearly expressed in Sophocles' *Oedipus Rex*, where Oedipus kills his father and commits incest with his mother in accordance with the oracle, and this despite the father's efforts to foil the prophecy. Fate had its way.

If *Moira* is an inexorable power superordinate to the gods, it is also moral. In F. M. Cornford's words: "Fate is not a mere blind and senseless barrier of impossibility; it is a moral decree—the boundary of right and wrong."[2] The moral dimension of *Moira* is best grasped from the original meaning of the word: "allotted portion." Each of the gods has been allotted a region or domain and may rightly exercise his or her powers solely in that domain. The powers of gods and humans alike are circumscribed by *Moira*; yet gods or human beings may, for a moment, stretch their powers beyond the boundaries of their domain or portion, but only at the cost of provoking an immediate retribution. In the Fifteenth Book of the *Iliad*, Zeus awakes one day to find Poseidon assisting the Trojans who are hard-pressed in battle by the Achaeans. After at first blaming Hera who, however, swears by Styx that Poseidon is acting of his own will, Zeus dispatches Iris with a threatening message, commanding Poseidon to cease from war and battle, and to withdraw into his own domain. Poseidon protests angrily:

> No, no. Great though he is, this that he has said is too much, if he will force me against my will, me, who am his equal in rank. Since we are three brothers born by Rheia to Kronos [Cronus], Zeus, and I, and the third is Hades, lord of the dead men. All was divided among us three ways, each given his domain. I when the lots were shaken drew the grey sea to live in forever; Hades drew the lots of the mists and the darkness, and Zeus was allotted the wide sky, in the cloud and the bright air. But earth and high Olympus are common to all three. Therefore I am no part of the mind of Zeus. Let him in tranquillity and powerful as he is stay satisfied with his third share. And let him absolutely stop frightening me, as if I were mean, with his hands. It were better to keep for the sons and the daughters he got himself these blusterings and these threats of terror. They will listen, because they must, to whatever he tells them. (*Iliad* XV, 185–200)

Iris urges submission, reminding Poseidon that the Erinyes, the spirits of vengeance, are always available to the elder-born. Poseidon then relents but declares that it is "a bitter sorrow to my heart and my spirit, when Zeus tries in words of anger to reprimand one who is his equal in station and endowed with destiny like his" (*Iliad* XV, 207–210). Although Poseidon is resentful, he yields and retires to the sea, his own undisputed domain.

From this passage the original meaning of *Moira* becomes evident. Destiny or Fate represents the ordained apportionment to each god of his or her province. It is clear, then, why *Moira* is superior to any and all of the gods, and why it is *moral* as well as inexorable: *Moira* sets the limits within which a god's powers may be exercised. Poseidon may not rightly or legitimately use his powers outside the province to which he has been assigned. Hesiod states that the *Moirai*, the Fates, track down the trespasses, not only of humans, but also of gods (*Theogony*, 220). So the original conception of *Moira* is not only *spatial* but also *temporal*, in that the division of the universe into domains is older in time than the gods. Cosmogony is older than theogony, and that marks the supremacy of *Moira* over the later-born divinities.

It is clear, then, why *Moira* is supradivine; but it is also *impersonal*. Greek polytheism (and perhaps every polytheistic religion) conceives of the order of the universe as having come into being without the intervention of a conscious, purposeful intelligence. Since all the gods possess only circumscribed powers, limited to their respective domains, no one of them can advance the claim that he or she has created the entire order by an act of will. Such a claim seems to have emerged for the first time in ancient Israel with the monotheistic intuition that a transcendental, Almighty God has created the entire universe, and that he was the first cause. In Greek religion it was literally impossible to attribute such a role to Zeus. For though he was said to reign supreme in the present era, the theogonic literature made it clear that Zeus was not even one of the oldest deities, but rather the head of a later dynasty. Before him lay the age of Cronus and those Titanic deities who reigned in the space of time separating the emergence of the world from the birth of Zeus on the island of Crete.

In the Hebrew intuition, God is not only the beginning of all things, but possesses personal qualities in the sense that one can communicate with God. *Moira*, in contrast, possesses no such personal qualities: It is impersonal, having neither foresight nor purpose, nor the capacity for communication. *Moira* is an inexorable force that allows its subordinate gods and humans to exercise their wills and fulfill their purposes, but only within their own distinctive and legitimate spheres; and *Moira* reacts with certain punishment the moment gods or humans trespass on the allotted portions of others. As a concept, *Moira* states a truth about the disposition of Nature—namely that it acts with necessity or inexorability. But the other integral element of *Moira* concerns itself with what is right and wrong, just and unjust, and that element could not have been derived from observing or contemplating natural forces or processes. The moral element must have a *social* origin, as was first postulated systematically in Émile Durkheim's sociological theory of the origin of religion, a theory that profoundly influenced the work of F. M. Cornford.[3]

The Greek word *Nomos*, which has come to mean "custom," "norm," or "law," has also left traces behind it of an older *spatial* significance: the notion of a province within which definite powers may be legitimately exercised. *Nomos* implies the exercise of power within spatial or "departmental" boundaries. The spatial significance of *Moira* is therefore pertinent to the distinction between the *sacred* and the *profane*. Such a distinction is made in the Greek as in every religion. The sacred is an area "not to be entered," "not to be set foot in" by profane persons—that is, persons who are not themselves ceremonially endowed with a sacred status. If, then, *Moira* stands for the limit or restriction on what one *may* do and what will happen if the limit is exceeded, *Nomos* stands for what one *must* do—the rightful functions one must exercise within one's allotted province. Actually, however, these are simply the positive and negative aspects of one impersonal force.

Herodotus provides us with a valuable piece of religious history concerning the transition from impersonal forces to personal gods with names. He informs us that in very ancient times:

> the Pelasgians offered sacrifices of all kinds, and prayed to the gods, but without any distinction of name or title—for they had not yet heard of any such thing. They called the gods by the Greek word *theoi*—"disposers"—*because they had "disposed" and arranged everything in due order, and assigned each thing to its proper division* [italics added]. Long afterwards the names of the gods were brought into Greece from Egypt, and the Pelasgians learnt them—with the exception of Dionysus, about whom they knew nothing till much later; then, as time went on, they sent to the oracle at Dodona (the most ancient and, at that period, the only oracle in Greece) to ask advice about the propriety of adopting names which had come into the country from abroad. The oracle replied that it would be right to use them. From that time onward, therefore, the Pelasgians used the names of the gods in their sacrifices, and from the Pelasgians the names passed to Greece.
>
> But it was only—if I may so put it—the day before yesterday that the Greeks came to know the origin and form of the various gods, and whether or not all of them had always existed; for Homer and Hesiod are the poets who composed our theogonies and described the gods for us, giving them all their appropriate titles, offices, and powers, and they lived, as I believe, not more than four hundred years ago. The poets who are said to have preceded them were, I think, in point of fact later. (Herodotus II, 50–55)

Here we gain insight into the long process leading from the older, rather indistinct and impersonal forces to the highly differentiated personalities of the Olympian gods. F. M. Cornford has suggested that the proper term for each of the earlier indistinct forces is not *theos*, but *daemon*, since the daemons of which Herodotus speaks had, as yet, no figures or individuality. They were good, local spirits, responsible for the area of earth inhabited by their worshipers. It was the *Moira* of such daemons to fulfil their specific functions as guardians in war and as fertility spirits in times of peace. Greek polytheism remained, in Cornford's words,

> *a system of "departments" (moirai) clearly marked off from one another by boundaries of inviolable taboo, and each the seat of a potency which pervades that department, dispenses its power within it, and resists encroachment from without.*4

As we shall see, Greek polytheism not only laid the foundation for the very beginnings of philosophy, but also provided the religious underpinnings for Plato's own distinctive theories.

Plato's Predecessors

Some two centuries before Plato, philosophy emerged in Ionia, in the commercial, seaport cities of Miletus, Ephesus, Klazomenae, and Samos. All of the Ionian philosophers were interested in the nature of the universe. The first thinkers to address this question were Thales, Anaximander, and Anaximenes—the so-called Milesians—each of whom posited a different basic "substance" underlying all things. Although these pioneers concerned themselves with "nature" (*physis*), they certainly were not physicists in the modern sense. Nor were they "materialists," as they are sometimes called. The Greek word *physis*, as we have seen, implies growth and process; and the separation of nature and mind was totally foreign to them. To all Greeks, including these philosophers, nature was animate. In accordance with their polytheistic beliefs, the entire *physis*—land, sea, mountains, rivers, trees, and bushes—was inhabited by divine beings. For the Ionians, all "matter" was animate, even stones, for they too exhibit force. The terms *hylozoism* and *panpsychism* have been applied to this worldview, since everything in the universe is living and infused with mind. Nature devoid of mind was simply unthinkable. To the question "What is the world made of?" Thales replied that it was made of water. He gave no detailed explanation of the way things are created from water, but there can be little doubt that he shared the worldview in which the moving force was analogous to the human soul. Even Aristotle said that everything is filled with "god" and that the magnet has a soul, since it attracts iron.

From the work of Thales's younger contemporary, Anaximander, one sentence is preserved:

> The beginning of that which is, is the boundless, but whence that which is arises, thither must it return again of necessity; for the things give satisfaction and reparation to one another for their injustice, as is appointed according to the ordering of time.7

What is especially striking about this passage, as Cornford observed, is the *moral* language with which the process of birth and perishing is described. When things break away from the boundless, they must make reparation and pay for the injustice. The words imply that the transformation of the boundless into the manifold world is an injustice, for it takes place through "misappropriation." Equally striking is the fact that the process is described in the language of both morality and necessity. A superior power ordains both what *must* be and what ought to be. The conceptions of *Moira* and Right are united.

Anaximenes differs from Anaximander in that in common with Thales he wants the "primary substance" of the universe to have a definite quality; but he agrees with Anaximander that the substance must be boundless and in perpetual motion. He finds those qualities in "air," the cause of all life and movement: "Just as our souls, which are made of air, hold us together, so does breath and air encompass the world."[6] We see, then, that although there is something of a simple curiosity and a rational approach in these three pioneers, their theories of the nature of the universe remain deeply rooted in Greek religion.

The Pythagoreans were a religious brotherhood whose doctrines were held to be sacred and secret and not to be divulged to the profane. The founder, Pythagoras, was an Eastern Greek by birth who left his native island of Samos early in life and migrated to southern Italy about 530 B.C. where he settled and founded his brotherhood in the town of Croton. Persecuted for political reasons, his followers dispersed, and by the fifth century B.C. had formed communities in various parts of Greece. What distinguishes the Pythagoreans from other pre-Socratic philosophers is their pursuit of mathematical studies and their doctrine of the immortality and transmigration of the soul not only in the bodies of humans but also in the bodies of other creatures. They believed that all life is related, and hence abstained from eating animal flesh. Indeed, the entire universe is a living being. It is *one*—eternal and divine—while humans are *many*— divided and mortal. Not mortal, however, is the human soul, which owes its immortality to the fact that it is a fragment of the divine soul, imprisoned in a mortal body. The aim of human beings, therefore, is to purify themselves from the sensual, to liberate themselves from the prison of the body and to rejoin the universal spirit. In the pursuit of this aim, the soul must undergo a series of transmigrations until, ultimately, it loses itself in reunion with the divine.

These beliefs were shared with other mystical sects, notably those who taught in the name of the mythical Orpheus. But the Pythagoreans differed from all others in advancing the doctrine that the nature of things is *number*. Their founder was a mathematical genius who most probably arrived at this proposition through his studies of music in religious, ceremonial contexts. Pythagoras and his followers recognized that musical pitch depends on the length of the strings or tubes of musical instruments, and that the intervals of a scale can be expressed arithmetically as ratios between the numbers 1, 2, 3, and 4, which added together make 10, the perfect number for the Pythagoreans. Thus a law of quantitative ratio became the key to the infinite variety of quality in sound.

In a fundamental departure from the Ionian view, the Pythagoreans placed the stress on *quantity*. Each thing in the universe was different from another not because of its material elements, which were common to all, but because of the proportions in which the elements were mixed. It was quantity, therefore, that determined the quality or *structure* of being; and since structure, or form, could be expressed numerically, it followed that the nature of things resided in numbers. This general doctrine became the cornerstone of Greek medicine: The key to sound health was the maintenance of the right quantitative relationships between opposite qualities such as hot and cold, wet and dry. It is almost certain that Socrates' conception of the soul was profoundly influenced by Pythagorean doctrine.

Xenophanes, too, translates religious ideas as he ponders the nature of things. His leading theme is the unity of all things in the All-One, a divine or supradivine principle without beginning or end, always the same and unchanging. This principle, sometimes misleadingly referred to as Xenophanes'"One God," was not beyond the world, but organically inseparable from it. His All-One always remains motionless, and though it is immanent in nature, it controls the universe with the power of its "mind" or soul.

Although each of the early Greek thinkers introduces something new in his conception of the Cosmos, he also retains the fundamentals of Greek religion. Heraclitus is no exception. He claimed that he had discovered the hidden law of nature that all things inevitably live by conflict, which is essential to life and therefore good. "War is the father of all"; "Strife is justice." Permanence and stability do not exist; and whatever lives does so by the destruction of something else. Hence there are two basic Heraclitean principles: Everything is born of strife; and everything is in a state of constant flux. And yet, this is not, for Heraclitus, a mindless process, for he does speak of the *Logos* as an intelligent, organizing principle of the whole.

Evidently there was something unnerving for Parmenides—as it was later for Plato—in the Heraclitean doctrine that one can never step into the same river twice, because the second time it is not the same river. If the universe, like a river, is in constant flux, that means that at each razor-edge moment the universe changes. There are no stable "things" in the universe, only transient moments. Thus Parmenides advances a view that largely returns to the divine principle of Xenophanes, characterized by repose and unchangeability. For Parmenides, the whole of reality consisted of a single, motionless, and invariable substance. His polemic is equally directed at those Ionian thinkers who had asserted that the world *was* one thing but *became* many. Against this view Parmenides presents the following formal argument: How can a thing be said to change? To change means to become what something is not; but to say of "what is" that "it is not," is simply untrue. Today this sounds like playing with words, but at the time the argument was taken seriously. Parmenides insisted that change and movement are unreal because that would entail the contradiction of something becoming what it is not; and to say of "what is" that "it is not" is nonsense. Plato, in his dialogue *The Sophist*, attempts to clear up the point that although Parmenides and his opponents used the same word "is," they meant two different things. Plato felt an urgency to mediate between the two positions by acknowledging that change in the world was undeniable, but by maintaining, as well, that there exist unchanging, absolute standards by which the world of change is to be understood and judged.

That the four elements—earth, water, air, and fire—constituted the world was, by the time of these early philosophers, firmly a part of the popular consciousness. Building upon the popular conception, Empedocles proposed that these elements are the real and ultimate constituents of the universe. Unlike the Ionians, however, who posited a self-moving primal substance, Empedocles proposed two separate, motive causes, Love and Strife. This prepared the way for Anaxagoras, the first thinker to have made a clear distinction between matter and mind; and having separated matter from mind, he went on, like Empedocles, to maintain that there must be a moving cause apart from the matter which was moved. For Anaxagoras, whatever was not "matter" must be mind (or "soul"), which rules the world and has brought order out of chaos or confusion. This view, we need to stress again, is entirely within the framework of the polytheistic worldview. No Greek philosopher ever spoke of the creation of the world in the absolute sense, as a god who created something out of nothing, as in the monotheistic view of the Hebrew Bible. For the Greeks, the creation of the world is always the imposition of order on an already existing primal condition. Anaxagoras, then, far from being a "materialist," is unabashedly theistic.

Of all the early Greek thinkers, Democritus comes closest to the standpoint customarily referred to as philosophical materialism. He is the originator of the concept of the "atom," the smallest, indivisible particle. Democritus, unlike Empedocles and Anaxagoras, transferred the principle of motion to the atoms themselves, which, thanks to their different sizes and weights, have been in a ceaseless, eternal state of rotary motion. Through this motion, similar atoms are brought together with atoms of different shapes to form atom-complexes, or worlds. Because the movement of the atoms had no beginning, and both the multiplicity of atoms and the empty space have no limits, there must always have been an infinite number of such worlds in a wide variety of conditions and forms. According to this truly brilliant conjecture by Democritus, the ultimate realities are those tiny, imperceptible, solid bodies (atoms) clashing and recoiling in endless motion in infinite space. And yet, even Democritus was not a thoroughgoing materialist. For although he regarded the soul as something physical—consisting of fine, smooth, and round atoms of "fire"—he nevertheless placed great value on the soul and on mental life. Although the soul-atoms are dispersed after death, the soul is the noblest and most divine part of the human being. Not only that, but also in all other things there is as much reason and soul as there is " Warm." Aristotle informs us that Democritus said that there must be much reason and soul in the air, for otherwise we could not absorb air by breathing. In still other respects, moreover, Democritus is not as remote from Socrates and Plato as is often assumed, since he regarded human thought as superior to sensory experience, and peace of the soul to bodily pleasures.

Finally, it is worth noting that although Democritus could not quite share the popular notion that people had about the gods, he did propose that beings of human form inhabit space, but that they are superior to humans in size and length of life, and partly benevolent and partly malevolent. What the people call gods were, for Democritus, images that these superior beings project, and which appear to human beings either in their waking state or in dreams.[7]

As we reflect on these pre-Socratic thinkers, we see that all of them, without exception, sought to gain insight into the nature of reality by reformulating religious ideas. And as we shall see, this is no less true of Socrates and Plato.

The Sophists

If we look at early Greek philosophy as a whole, from Thales to Democritus, we see that it is preoccupied from beginning to end by the question "What is real?" And while answers to the question always contain a religio-moral component, inquiries were rather sharply focused on the *physis*. With the Sophists, however, we have a marked change of focus as thinkers begin to speculate almost exclusively on ethical, social, and political issues. How would one begin to explain this transformation of philosophical thought? For many centuries Greek society had been governed by ancient customs believed to be divinely inspired. The lives of human beings were guided by a traditional structure of authority (*Diké* or

Right), and the formal enactment of law (*Nomos*) lay in the future. But history, much of it tumultuous, was gradually undermining the stability of the old order. Colonization uprooted people from their traditional homes and ways, placing them in newly formed states where it was plain for anyone to see that the laws were formally enacted by men. Legislators like Solon had also become active in many city-states. The comparatively new phenomenon of formally enacted laws seems to have prompted the question of whether there was any common, moral denominator to the laws, which obviously varied from city to city. The problem of the *physis*, which had occupied the Ionians, had now become for the Sophists the problem of the human social order.

To the process of history that was leading people's minds in this direction, we have to add "anthropology"—that is, the wealth of ethnographic information gathered and recorded by travelers. Herodotus was as much an ethnographer as he was an historian, since his travels led him to observe and record striking differences in customs and conventions. As people became aware of such differences and reflected upon them, we may assume that they were led to question the existence of any universal law. The laws of nature, it seemed obvious, were the same in Greece and Persia: Fire burns everywhere and at all times. But Herodotus and others observed a variety of marriage and burial customs, some people making merry over a funeral and others making lamentation. Nor was there any other social practice that was common and identical everywhere. This could only mean that social institutions were created neither by nature nor by the gods. They were the product of human beings—conventions. Thus, while the study of the *physis* tended toward some common principle underlying all natural phenomena, colonization, together with the growing awareness of the wide diversity in social and political institutions, led to a form of cultural relativism. The great effort of defense against the Persians also contributed significantly to a weakening of the influence of religion on the Greek mind. Apollo was perceived as indifferent, and it was now openly asserted that men, not gods, had saved Greece. A secular outlook was becoming more evident, as in Sophocles, for instance:

> Wonders are many on earth, and the greatest of these is man, who rides the ocean and takes his way through the deeps, through wind-swept valleys of perilous seas that surge and sway. He is master of ageless Earth, to his own will bending the immortal mother of gods by the sweat of his brow, as year succeeds to year, with toil unending of mule and plough. He is lord of all things living; birds of the air, beasts of the field, all creatures of sea and land he taketh, cunning to capture and ensnare with sleight of hand; hunting the savage beast from the upland rocks, taming the mountain monarch in his lair,

teaching the wild horse and the roaming ox his yoke to bear. The use of language, the wind-swift motion of brain he learnt; found out the laws of living together in cities, building him shelter against the rain and wintry weather. There is nothing beyond his power. His subtlety meeteth all chance, all danger conquereth. For every ill he has found its remedy, save only death.[8]

It was in these circumstances that the Sophists appeared as the first professional teachers within Greece. They were neither a movement nor a school, nor did they all share a common set of opinions.[9] As teachers they practiced their craft as individuals, and the main reason why their social role came to be regarded as important was that their teaching was intended to have practical, political significance. They were professional practitioners of *Sophia* (wisdom), and though they were professionals, they were not always paid. Plato and Aristotle, it is true, reproach the Sophists for accepting pay, but the reproach was directed against the later Sophists of the fourth century B.C. from whom they sought to distinguish themselves on the ground that the Sophists taught a narrow technique like rhetoric, while they, Plato and Aristotle, taught people to think clearly. However, we learn from Plato himself that even in the fifth century B.C. the Sophists accepted pay, although they left it to their pupils to fix the amount. Hence, already then there was a prejudice against the name Sophist, which acquired an even more unfavorable connotation in the fourth century B.C.

From the democratic standpoint, the prejudice stemmed from the fact that both the title *Sophistes* and the word *Sophos* implied an attempt to be "too clever." In Plato's dialogue *Apology*, it is precisely the charge of being a *Sophos Aner* (wise man) that Socrates is so eager to deny. But there was more to it than that from a democratic standpoint. The Sophists were for the most part foreigners who resided in Athens as metics, and who had journeyed to Athens because it had become, thanks to the emergence of the Athenian Empire, the intellectual center of Greece. But the pupils they found in Athens were, naturally, those who could afford to pay and thus well off and generally out of sympathy and even hostile to the democratic institutions of Periclean Athens. The Sophists professed to teach the art of public speaking and persuasion, and their rich young pupils were eager to learn eloquence to rebut accusations against them in the popular courts. They wished to learn what the Sophists had to teach them so that they could persuade voters of their view, gain influence over government, and ultimately move the political structure in an oligarchical direction.

However, in the eyes of the common people, the skills taught by the Sophists appeared to be the art of making the worse cause, oligarchy, appear the better. And, indeed, it was out of the ranks of the Sophists' pupils that oligarchical leaders emerged. Thucydides informs us that the person actually behind the oligarchic coup of 411 B.C. was the outstanding orator Antiphon, who

> had a most powerful intellect and was well able to express his thoughts in words; he never came forward to speak in front of the Assembly if he could help it, or competed in any other form of public life, since the people in general mistrusted him because of his reputation for cleverness. (Thucydides VIII, 68)

This does not mean that the Sophists themselves necessarily favored oligarchy. The fact that they were foreigners and "guests" in Athens, and exercised, however inadvertently, an antidemocratic influence in that city, contributed to the odious reputation they earned among the democrats. Some of the Sophists, however, appear to have been beyond reproach in this regard. Protagoras, for example, who was perhaps the greatest of the Sophists, was employed by Pericles to help draft the constitution for the Athenian colony at Thurii in 444 B.C.

Protagoras

Protagoras of Abdera (c. 500–430 B.C.) was a moral and political philosopher and, perhaps, the earliest of the Greek thinkers to profess the dialectical method in discourse. He is known for having criticized the Ionian "physicists," whose attempts to find some underlying unity of the universe Protagoras regarded as futile. The word "empirical" is, perhaps, most apt in describing his approach to knowledge in the human world. It was Protagoras who said, "Man is the measure of all things." What he appears to have meant by this is that it is the common sense of the individual that determines whether or not something exists, as well as its qualities. Things are to each individual what they appear to be. Some commentators have supposed that Protagoras applied this maxim to the moral sphere, which would mean that he advocated an individualist theory of ethics and politics in which each individual is the standard of what is morally right. It is highly unlikely, however, that this was in fact his doctrine. It is true that Protagoras claimed that on every subject it is possible to make two opposite statements (*logoi*), each of which is true for the individual who made it. But he also stressed that one of the two statements would be "stronger," and he believed that it should be made to appear the stronger by means of argument. On the other hand, Protagoras did speak of making the weaker cause the stronger, and there can be little doubt that some of the Sophists did in fact try to impart rhetorical skills that would enable a disputant to win an argument at any cost.

For Protagoras, the stronger statement is "normal" in that it is the assessment of a thing by the average human being. The common sense of an individual is, after all, *common* to other individuals in that particular society. A person's measurement of something or other is not unique, since it is made in accordance with a common standard. It is most likely, therefore, that when Protagoras spoke of making the weaker statement the stronger, he was not advocating the right of every individual to make any view triumph. What he defended, instead, was the right of common sense to justify a belief that was normal because it appealed to normal judgment. His position had definite implications for the right of the common people to participate in politics, although the common people lacked the professional expertise demanded by Socrates. The important difference between the two positions will become clearer when we consider Plato's dialogue, aptly titled *Protagoras*.

Gorgias

From Plato's account one gathers that Gorgias was not so much a teacher of politics, like Protagoras, as a teacher of rhetoric. Relations between the democracy and the privileged classes were becoming more and more strained, and the utility of the art of disputation was, accordingly, increased. Gorgias introduced to Athens methods of persuasion that had been developed during the class conflict in Sicily.[10] In Plato's dialogue *Gorgias*, we find an extreme form of the antithesis of Nature and Law, which Plato ascribes not to Gorgias himself but rather to Callicles, whose views anticipated those of Nietzsche. Callicles rejects all law as a device by which the weak deprive the strong of the just right of their might. Law institutes a "slave morality," which is a false morality, for Nature and Law are antithetical, and Nature is the true ruler of human life. Inequality is the law of Nature and it is only by convention that social equality exists, or that individuals demand an equality of distribution. By nature, humans are unequal, and throughout Nature the strong get more than the weak. When Callicles speaks of strength he means more than physical strength. It is the strength not only of body but also of mind and will (*Gorgias* 491B,D).

Such theories were a reaction against the presumed resentment of everything that rises or strives to rise above the common, which may have been perceived as a characteristic of Athenian democracy. A more extreme position is presented by Plato in the first book of the *Republic*, as having been held by Thrasymachus of Chalcedon, a Sophist of the late fifth century B.C. For Thrasymachus there is no such thing as *natural* right. Right is simply whatever is enforced in the State by the strongest power in its own interest. Unlike Callicles, who defends his theory as a law of Nature, Thrasymachus argues that it does not matter whether the State enforces the right of the strong or the right of the weak, or whether it enforces inequality or equality. Whatever the State enforces is right. If the weak make laws in their interest, those laws are right and just as long as the weak can enforce them; and if they cannot enforce them, the laws cease to be right.

Callicles, as we have seen, attempts to defend his view by citing the example of the animal world. We encounter the same view in Aristophanes' play *The Clouds*, which satirizes the teachings of the extreme Sophists, where a son strikes his father and justifies his action by saying, "Look at the cocks and other animals. They actually fight their fathers. And what difference is there between them and us, except that they don't enact laws?"[11] This general argument drawing upon the example of Nature anticipates the Social Darwinism of the late nineteenth and early twentieth centuries. However, Callicles' conception of Nature was also derived from his observation of the international arena: "...nature itself makes it evident that it is right for the better to have the advantage over the worse, the more able over the less. And both among all animals and entire states and peoples of mankind it is clear that this is the case—that right is recognized to be the sovereignty and advantage of the stronger over the weaker" (*Gorgias* 483D); just as Thomas Hobbes' "state of nature," with its "war of each against all," likewise reflected the fact that States are always in the condition and "posture of gladiators." In these terms the theories of both Callicles and Thrasymachus reflected the prevailing political reality in which Athens, because of its enormously increased power following the Persian-Greek wars, appeared as a tyrant who imposed its will as a matter of right on the other members of the Athenian Empire. The tyrant city, Callicles seems to be arguing, sets an example that the individual is entitled to follow. The speech that Thucydides places in the mouth of an Athenian envoy tends to defend the Empire in terms similar to those of Callicles:

> It has always been a rule that the weak should be subject to the strong; and besides, we consider that we are worthy of our power. Up till the present moment you, too, used to think that we were; but now, after calculating your own interest, you are beginning to talk in terms of right and wrong. Considerations of this kind have never yet turned people aside from the opportunities of aggrandizement offered by superior strength. (Thucydides I, 76)

There are several other such speeches in Thucydides's masterpiece (II, 63; III, 37; V, 89, 105); and although he has not, of course, given us the precise words of the Athenian envoys and politicians, the sentiments and ideas he ascribes to them ring true. For there can be no doubt that the oligarchical clubs and circles in Athens sympathized with the dominated members of the Delian League against the Imperial City, looking upon Athens' democratic government as an opportunistic promotion of the interests of the people by a heavy taxation of the rich. The pro-oligarchy elements regarded the democratic government as opportunistic but not unfair, since they did not necessarily reject the doctrine that "Might is Right." What they resented was not the doctrine but its application, since we know that they took the first opportunity to apply the doctrine themselves, but in the opposite direction.

Later, as we take a closer look at the Sophists and see how Plato dealt with their arguments, we shall find that his general assessment of them was rather unfavorable. Plato is mainly concerned with demonstrating that their arguments from nature are untenable, and that truth and justice are attained by discovering the eternal Standards, Forms, or Ideas, and by constructing our social systems in their light.

Notes

[1]See Werner Jaeger, *The Theology of the Early Greek Philosophers* (Oxford: Clarendon Press, 1947).

[2]F. M. Cornford, *From Religion to Philosophy* (New York: Harper Torchbooks, 1957), p. 13.

[3]See Emile Durkheim, *The Elementary Forms of the Religious Life*, translated by Joseph Ward Swain (London: George Allen & Unwin Ltd., 1915).

[4] Cornford, op. cit., p. 38, italics in original.

[5]Eduard Zeller, *Outlines of the History of Greek Philosophy*, 13th ed., translated by L. R. Palmer (Cleveland and New York: Meridian Books, 1965), p. 43.

[6]Ibid., p. 46. See also W. K. C. Guthrie, *The Greek Philosophers from Thales to Aristotle* (London: Methuen & Company, Ltd., 1962), and Jonathan Barnes, *Early Greek Philosophy* (Harmandsworth, Middlesex: Penguin Books, 1987), a collection of fragmentary texts.

[7]Zeller, op. cit., pp. 85–86.

[8]Sophocles, *Antigone* [356–357] in *The Theban Plays*, translated by E. F. Watling (London: Penguin Classics, 1988), pp. 135–136.

[9]See John Burnet, *Greek Philosophy* (London: Macmillan and Company, Ltd., 1964), p. 85f.

[10]Ibid., p. 96.

[11]Aristophanes, *Lysistrata/The Acharnians, The Clouds*, translated by Alan H. Sommerstein (London: Penguin Classics, 1973 [1410–1457]), p. 170.

3

● ● ● ● ● ● ● ● ● ● ● ● ● ● ●

Socrates

Whereas the Ionians and the Sophists were all foreigners who chose to settle in Athens because it was the intellectual center of Greece, Socrates was a full Athenian citizen. He was born about 470 B.C., and it is certain that he met his death in Athens, on a charge of impiety, in the "year of Laches" (399 B.C.). He was a man of the great age of Pericles, and was over forty when Pericles died. Socrates spent his declining years amid the turbulence of the Peloponnesian War, and as a citizen he carried his share of civic duties. He fought as a hoplite—a heavily armed citizen-soldier—in the Athenian campaigns in Thrace, and again in 424 B.C. at the battle of Delium.

Two things stand out in characterizing Socrates' role as an Athenian citizen. He became a member of the Athenian Council at age sixty-five; and he was also a member, it so happened, of the chief Committee of the Council, which presided in the Athenian Assembly on the day on which ten of Athens' generals were collectively condemned, by a single vote, for their failure to rescue drowning sailors during the naval battle of Arginusae (c.405). Such a collective condemnation was a violation of the Athenian Constitution, and

Socrates, a lone dissenter on the Committee, refused to approve the placing before the Assembly of such an unconstitutional vote (Plato *Apology* 32B). It is possible that he was not only a member of the Committee but also the President for the day of that Committee, and as such the presiding officer of the Assembly on that same day. If that was the case, it was Socrates' personal responsibility to place the vote before the Assembly, and he took it upon himself not to do so. He thus obeyed both his conscience and the democratic Constitution of Athens.

A year later (404), when the Thirty Tyrants were exercising a reign of terror in Athens, Socrates was ordered, together with four other men, to fetch a citizen, Leon of Salamis, from his home for execution; once again he refused to obey an illegal order. The other four men went off to Salamis and arrested Leon, but Socrates returned home. His disobedience was a serious offense; he might even have been put to death for it had the government not fallen soon afterward. Socrates once more obeyed his conscience, but this time under the oligarchical regime (*Apology* 32C–E).

As the son of a sculptor, Socrates learned his father's craft, but he seems to have practiced it briefly or not at all—although it left upon him a lasting impression of what it takes to become a highly skilled and specialized artisan. Socrates devoted his life to the study of philosophy and associated personally with all the thinkers who had made Athens their home in the second half of the fifth century B.C. At first he showed an intense interest in the "physical science" questions of his day; but after about 435 B.C. Socrates turned away from those theories, finding them mechanistic and unconvincing. He now made the transition to philosophy in the broadest sense—an inquiry into all aspects of existence, ranging from the worldly human condition to the nature of the soul, the divine, and the supradivine.

It is not difficult to picture Socrates. He is described as far from handsome, being snub-nosed and having protruding eyes. His gait was peculiar, and the playwright Aristophanes likened it to the strut of some sort of waterfowl. Socrates usually went barefoot and remained within the city of Athens except on military service, and once to attend the Isthmian games. He asserted on one occasion that he was divinely inspired (*Phaedrus* 238C), and it was well known that even as a boy he had a "voice" that he regarded as his divine sign. He believed he was sent to "this city [Athens] as a gift from god" and that he was "subject to a divine or supernatural experience...It began in my early childhood—a sort of voice which comes to me" (*Apology* 31C–D). Socrates then explains, however, that the voice never prompted him to do anything, but rather opposed his doing what he was about to do—namely, enter politics. There can be no doubt that he believed in supernatural beings and supernatural experiences. Subject to ecstatic trances, Socrates would stand motionless for hours buried in thought and quite forgetful of the outer world (*Symposium* 220C–D). He was a firm believer in the immortality of the soul and in the life to come, doctrines not necessarily familiar to the Athenians of his day. He even believed in rebirth and reminiscences from former lives. When asked for his authority for such beliefs, he would refer to Pindar and to priests and priestesses:

> It is said that the human soul is immortal. At a time called death it comes temporarily to an end, at another time it is born again, but it is never finally destroyed. Therefore an individual must live out his life as righteously as possible....
>
> Being immortal, the soul has been born myriad times and has witnessed all things both here and in the other world, and has thus learned everything. So we need not be astonished if the soul can recall the knowledge of virtue or anything else which, as we see, it once possessed. The things of nature are akin, and the soul has learned everything about them, so that when an individual has recalled a single piece of knowledge there is no reason why he should not recover all the rest if he perseveres and does not tire of the search, *for seeking knowledge and learning are, indeed, nothing but recollection.* (*Meno* 81B–D, italics added)

Throughout his life Socrates retained a profound interest in ancient lore and sayings, and he explicitly attributed to the Orphic poets the doctrine according to which

> The soul suffers punishment for its transgressions, and the body is a prison in which the soul is incarcerated, safely confined as the term *soma* indicates, until the penalty is paid. (*Cratylus* 400C)

The soul strives for perfect purity, which it cannot achieve until it is released from the body. It is then and only then that it can dwell with the divine. For Socrates it is this mystical or quasi-mystical conception of the soul that defines the calling of the philosopher. Philosophy is the most sublime of activities, and the person who engages in it will therefore strive for "death" even in one's lifetime by training the soul to concentrate upon itself and thus to attain as much wisdom as possible in this world. Socrates, then, was a religious man—a visionary, an "enthusiast," a mystic.

In the *Phaedo* (96A) we find a sketch of Socrates' intellectual development and an explanation of why he moved away from the physical sciences. Rejecting their "befogging speculations," Socrates turned his back on all such mechanistic accounts and resolved to develop a new method. This must have occurred while he was still quite young, since Plato represents Socrates as discussing his new method with Parmenides and Zeno when they visited Athens shortly after the middle of the fifth century B.C. (*Parmenides* 130A; 135D). Socrates was also quite young when he first came into contact with Protagoras and some of the other Sophists. So we may safely assume that Socrates came to the attention of the most distinguished thinkers of the time and that he had won their respect when he was not much more than twenty-five years of age. Perhaps the one person who influenced Socrates the most was Zeno (*Phaedrus* 261B), the real inventor of the dialectic method—the art of argument by means of questions and answers. Although dialectic is literally the art of conversation, it is conversation guided by rather strict rules. The answerer is required to reply to the questioner as succinctly as possible, to answer the question exactly as it is put, and to refrain from criticizing it or asking other questions in response. Of course, this is a method that can be abused and employed for fallacious ends, but evidently it appealed to Socrates as the best means by which to get closer to the truth and to gain more reliable knowledge.

Socrates so impressed some younger men with his method and intellectual powers that they much admired him and looked to him for guidance. One of these, Chaerephon, was particularly enthusiastic and actually asked the Delphic oracle whether there was anyone wiser than Socrates. The oracle replied that there was no one (*Apology* 21A). Socrates took the oracular response not at face value but with self-deprecating humor, and set out to prove the god wrong. He would seek and find someone wiser than himself and thus refute the oracle. Thus he went to speak to a politician who was indeed wise in his own eyes and in the eyes of other people, but actually quite ignorant in Socrates' judgment. The same experience was repeated with one group of people after another: Poets could give no intelligible account of their own creations; artisans demonstrated that they certainly knew something about their own trades, but on the strength of their knowledge they presumed to know a great many other things of which, again in Socrates' judgment, they were quite ignorant—as, for example, how to govern a society. Socrates' negative assessment of artisans, craftsmen, and other Athenian citizens, together with his other antidemocratic utterances and the nature of the company he kept, will help us to understand the circumstances leading to his prosecution, of which more will be said later.

After such experiences with poets, politicians, and plain people, Socrates came to believe that he understood what the oracle meant— namely, that neither Socrates nor anyone else knew anything, but that Socrates was wiser than others in at least one respect: He knew he was ignorant, while the others failed to recognize their own ignorance. Now he felt he had a mission to his fellow citizens. He was called by the Divine to convince them of their ignorance. Little wonder that in the pursuit of such a mission he engendered considerable hostility and was soon regarded as a "professor of wisdom," which he, however, regarded as a malicious suggestion. This came about as bystanders, witnessing how he disproved the claims to wisdom of others, assumed that he was wise and that he knew everything there was to know about the subject in question (*Apology* 23A). And short of hostility, Socrates appears to have caused perplexity in his interlocutors. It was, they said, as if he had cast a spell upon them so that they soon found themselves helpless to respond effectively. He was likened to a stingray that numbs or paralyzes anything that comes in contact with it (*Meno* 80A).

From Plato we learn that Socrates had embarked on his mission before the beginning of the Peloponnesian War, since he is said to have resumed his mission after his return from Potidaea (*Charmides* 153A). The period when Chaerephon consulted the Delphic oracle, then, would be no later than Socrates' thirty-fifth year, and he seems to have been well known by that time. Plato had not yet been born, so his account of things must have been based on what Socrates eventually told him and, no doubt, on what Plato learned from Chaerephon. With the outbreak of the Peloponnesian War, Socrates was called upon to serve, and he soon distinguished himself as a soldier in the battles of Potidaea (432), Delium (424), and Amphipolis (422). He is described as courageous and as having stood the hardships of the campaigns better than most. Upon his return to Athens he resumed his "numbing" and "stinging" activities and found that many young men from privileged and oligarchically inclined backgrounds were drawn to him, taking great pleasure in hearing the ignorance of others exposed. In Plato's *Apology*, which is Socrates' defense against his accusers, Socrates is represented as insisting that these young men, "whom some people maliciously call my pupils," had attached themselves to him, but that he had never set himself up as anyone's teacher. He then suggests the reason why some people enjoyed spending a great deal of time in his company: They found it amusing to observe him in action, demonstrating that those who thought they were wise were not wise at all (*Apology* 33B–C).

But they appear to have attached themselves to him not merely for the amusement it entailed, but also to gain better preparation for public life. Evidently, some people believed they could learn more from Socrates in that regard than from any professional Sophist. It is certain that Critias associated with Socrates for that reason. To understand how Socrates was very likely perceived as a result of his association with Critias and others like him, we need to pause for a moment to clarify where Critias stood politically.

With the defeat of Athens in the Peloponnesian War the extreme oligarchic party rejoiced in the foreign occupation, seeing it as an opportunity for the subversion of Athenian democracy. Of the exiles, the most prominent and determined was Critias, a member of a distinguished family, a pupil of Gorgias, and a companion of Socrates. Critias had returned from exile bitter and revengeful toward the democracy, and he was the mastermind behind the oligarchic rule of the Thirty Tyrants imposed by Sparta. Originally the purpose of the rule of the Thirty was to frame a new constitution; their powers as a governing body were only to last until they had completed their legislative task. But the majority in the oligarchical party, under Critias' leadership, had no intention of formulating a constitution, which they regarded as a mere pretext for getting into power and retaining it. In opposition to the moderates, Critias unrelentingly resolved to exercise an absolute despotism and to expunge all elements of popular opposition.

First, the Thirty Tyrants put to death men of "bad character," so-called, including some notorious informers; but then they proceeded to execute, with or without trial, not only prominent democrats, but also those of oligarchic sympathies who, although unfriendly to the democracy, were also opposed to injustice and illegality. Soon some men were executed simply because they were rich and their property was confiscated; others fled happy to escape with their lives. Even metics, who had little or nothing to do with politics, were either murdered or expelled. Thus while many Athenians were removed by execution or banishment, others were compelled to assist in the task of arresting fellow citizens so that they might thereby become accomplices in the crimes of the regime. This was the context in which Socrates and four others were commanded with severe threats to arrest an honest citizen, Leon of Salamis. And, as we have seen, Socrates refused without hesitation to do the bidding of the tyrants, while the others were not so courageous. Yet Socrates remained unpunished for his defiance, owing, most probably, to the intervention of Critias, his pupil-companion who could safely indulge his old philosopher-friend since Socrates was neither wealthy nor popular.

There were other well-known and well-to-do figures besides Critias who were devoted to Socrates, notably Alcibiades. During the Peloponnesian War the democratic government of Athens decided that the conquest of Syracuse was necessary as a key to Athens' invincible power in the West. The privileged classes and the pro-oligarchical elements opposed the entire enterprise. They appointed Nicias, a respected general and a decent man, as their spokesman. He sincerely believed that the proposed Syracusan expedition was misguided, foolhardy, and doomed to failure. In an attempt to discourage the enthusiastic supporters of the adventure, Nicias argued that the cost they had estimated was much too low, and that the Athenian Assembly should double its allocation. We learn from

Thucydides (VI, 20–25) that the Assembly, ironically, was so delighted with Nicias's caution that they named him, together with two others, to the staff of generals in charge of the expedition. The other two appointees were Lamachus, a serious and business-like military man, and Alcibiades. Though brilliant, Alcibiades' political career up to this point had been vacillating and unsure. But he had been close to the circle of Pericles, and the Assembly therefore hoped that he would be reliable. When the statue of Hermes—the god of the merchant class and in some ways a sacred symbol of the democratic party—was mutilated, suspicion fell on Alcibiades. The democrats now had second thoughts about going ahead with the Syracuse expedition, since two of the generals, Nicias and Lamachus, seemed to have oligarchic leanings and the third (Alcibiades) was under suspicion. But after deliberation it was decided that the expedition should sail. Lamachus proposed an immediate and direct attack on Syracuse before the Syracusan forces would have a chance to mobilize their defenses. Nicias disagreed, calling instead for a show of force around the coasts of Sicily, where Syracuse was located. Alcibiades wanted a compromise of sorts; but at this point the Assembly voted that he should be arrested and recalled to stand trial on the charge of having participated in the mutilation of the statue of Hermes. He was in fact arrested, but on his return journey Alcibiades succeeded in eluding his captors and, to the astonishment of the democrats, turned up, of all places, in Sparta.

Evidently he managed to ingratiate himself with the Spartan rulers by describing democracy as foolishness and by giving them practical proposals for the conduct of the Spartan campaign, based on his firsthand knowledge of the Athenian forces, their strengths and weaknesses. It was Alcibiades who suggested to the Spartans the fortification of Decalaea on the northern boundary of Attica so as to intercept Athenian trade with the North. That being not enough, he also proposed that a capable Spartan general be dispatched to Syracuse to assist in the organization of that city's defenses against the Athenian invasion. The person chosen, Gylippus, did the job so well that the besieging Athenian fleet was itself bottled up and besieged within the great harbor of Syracuse. With all attempts to break out failing, the Athenian commanders resolved to make a last desperate attempt to escape overland. Owing to the eclipse of the moon, however, and the religious significance this apparently had for Nicias, the departure was postponed until the full moon. An opportunity was lost (Thucydides VII, 50). In a dreadful scene at the Assinarus River, described in vivid detail by Thucydides (VII, 72–87), the beaten and despairing fragment of the once invincible Athenian armada was cut to pieces by the pursuing Syracusan forces. Poor Nicias himself was killed, and thousands of Athenians were taken into captivity and subjected to forced labor in the stone quarries of Syracuse.

Meanwhile, the irrepressible young Alcibiades was building himself a political career in Sparta; but unfortunately for his new ambition, he seduced the wife of King Agis, and therefore had to leave Sparta in something of a hurry. We next hear of him at the court of Persia, giving advice to the Persian king on how best to intervene in Aegean politics in order to advance the interests of the Persian State. Clearly, the political agility of the brilliant but thoroughly unscrupulous Alcibiades must be taken into account as we try, later, to understand the democracy's mistrust of Socrates. For it was widely known that the two men were the most intimate of friends.

The other devoted friend of Socrates was Charmides, Plato's uncle; it is through him that Plato himself came to associate with Socrates. But again we need to stress that, strictly speaking, Socrates had regarded none of these three men—Critias, Alcibiades, and Charmides—as his *disciples*.

The "Spartan" Habits of Socrates' Associates

Socrates often spoke of his relations with these young men in the language of erotic love, although tempered by his usual sly humor. A few examples are in order. In a conversation between Socrates and Critias, the latter states that Charmides "is as fair and good within, as he is without." Socrates replies that he is eager to meet this beautiful young man, so Critias calls Charmides, and everyone present pushes and shoves in an effort to sit next to him. When, finally, Charmides sits down between Critias and Socrates, Plato attributes an extreme awkwardness to Socrates who, when he catches sight of Charmides' inner garment, becomes aroused— overcome by a "wild-beast appetite" (*Charmides* 155C–E). At the end of the dialogue Charmides promises Critias that he will allow himself to be charmed by Socrates and never desert him in things great or small. Socrates asks what the two men are conspiring about, and Charmides replies that they are not conspiring for they have conspired already. Socrates then inquires whether Charmides intends to use force, and when he answers in the affirmative Socrates admits that when Charmides is in a violent and determined mood he is irresistible and will not be resisted (*Charmides* 176C–D).

And in the *Symposium* we hear the intoxicated Alcibiades berating Socrates for having sat next to Agathon, the most handsome man in the room. Socrates then asks Agathon, tongue-in-cheek, to protect him from Alcibiades who, he says, flies into a jealous rage whenever Socrates says a word to some other attractive young man or even merely looks at him. Hearing this, Alcibiades protests that it's the other way around and that it is Socrates who finds it intolerable when he hears Alcibiades say a good word about anyone else. Laughingly, however, Alcibiades then goes on to describe the several elaborate efforts he had made to seduce Socrates, all of which failed (*Symposium* 213C–D, 219B–D). So the personal chastity of Socrates is assumed throughout.

In Sparta and in other Dorian states generally, homosexual attachments were a recognized institution; they originated, presumably, in an era when affective relations among knight, squire, and page were deemed to enhance solidarity and military effectiveness. In Plato's *Laws* (636Bf) the Athenian stranger, who is Plato himself, criticizes the institutions of Sparta and Crete on the very ground that they allowed or even favored the abuse of such relationships. And in the *Symposium* (182B) Plato notes that in Athens and in the Ionian states generally "the very same thing is held to be disgraceful." The Dorian custom had nevertheless made its way into Athens before the time of Solon, although it was condemned both by law and by public opinion (*Phaedrus* 231E). From Plato we learn that it was the fashion in upper-class circles to copy this and other features of Spartan life. And historians inform us that:

> The pursuit of boys was a young man's preoccupation; the older practitioners were liable to be found ridiculous or offensive. The average man settled down easily enough to family life; and no one, familiar with Greek art or poetry, will be disposed to underrate the strength of marital and parental affection that the ordinary Greek felt...
>
> At Athens, it is evident that upper-class boys were subject, as a matter of regular social practice, to something of the strain that is imposed on girls in the more permissive societies of our time. They were free, indeed, from fear of unwanted pregnancy, but surrender was compensated by no physical gratification—at best, by the social gain of having given in to a lover of high standing.[1]

To understand Socrates' attitude in this regard, it has been suggested that we need to appreciate that for him there was no antithesis between "this-worldly" and "other-worldly" love. Socrates, writes John Burnet,

> was a mystic as well as a humourist, and the mystics have always found the language of love more adequate than any other to express their peculiar experience. The love of a fair body is only the earthly type of something far higher. It leads on to the love of a fair soul, to the love of fair studies and fair ways of life, and at last it brings us into the very presence of the "forms" beauty, righteousness, and holiness in that supercelestial region where they have their dwelling place (*Phaedrus* 247C ff.). When thus regarded as the objects of love,

these "forms" are seen to be the realities of which the things in this world are but shadows, and from which they derive such imperfect being as they have.[2]

Socrates in Aristophanes' The Clouds

This comedy by Aristophanes is the only material dealing with Socrates that was composed in Socrates' lifetime. All other materials, including Plato's dialogues and Xenophon's *Memorials*, were written after Socrates' death. *The Clouds* was produced by Aristophanes in c. 423 B.C.; it is a play in which Socrates, then about forty-seven years old, is the central figure. Old Attic comedy dealt throughout with personal burlesque and social satire, and it was essential to the comic-poet's success that the object of his satirical treatment should have achieved some notoriety. The playwright had to count on the audience's recognition of the individual being caricatured. Hence it is a near certainty that Socrates was already a well-known figure when Aristophanes made him the target of his burlesque. In the play Socrates is portrayed as a subversive astronomer who heads up a "school" of followers who concern themselves with the physical sciences and who tend to be irreverent where religion is concerned. In the *Apology*, Plato makes Socrates attribute much of the popular prejudice against him to *The Clouds*. It may, indeed, have had such an influence at the time of his trial when the judges would recall the play and treat it as confirmation of Socrates' alleged atheism. But we gather from Plato that at the time of the play's production it was recognized as the lampoon it was intended to be, and it was taken seriously by no one, and least of all by Socrates himself and his circle. In the *Symposium* Socrates and Aristophanes are portrayed as the best of friends just a few years after the production of *The Clouds*; and everyone takes it in good humor when Alcibiades cites from the play the "waterfowl" gait of Socrates. We may assume, then, that at the time of the play's production no offense was intended by the playwright and no offense was taken by the subject of the play. It was only in the light of the charges later brought against Socrates that the play was resented by Socrates' friends, but even then Plato gave it only little weight in the *Apology*.

Aristophanes did, however, present something of the truth in *The Clouds*. For as we have seen, Socrates, in his youth, was, in fact, chiefly occupied intellectually with the "physical science" movements of his time. In *The Clouds*, Aristophanes is portraying the early Socrates; and what Socrates has to say there, though caricatured, must have had some foundation in fact. We may safely assume that as a student of the *physis* in the spirit of the Ionians, Socrates must have been interested in the things in the heavens and the things beneath the earth. Plato has Socrates declare that these were the main studies of his youth; and Theophrastus, the associate and successor of Aristotle, asserts that Socrates was actually a member of the school of Archelaus, the Athenian who succeeded Anaxagoras when the latter left Athens. So Aristophanes accurately represents Socrates as an adherent of a system recognizable as that of Archelaus and Diogenes of Apollonia—which is why the chorus in the play consists of clouds. Diogenes had revived the view of Anaximenes of Miletus that the world consists of condensed "air," and clouds are one of the first results of the condensation of air. In much the same terms, Plato represents Socrates as saying that he studied whether what people think with is air, and Aristophanes, accordingly, portrays Socrates as swinging in a basket in order to get pure, dry air for his thought.

Aristophanes also knew that Socrates described his philosophical role as that of a "midwife" (*Theaetetus* 149–150), for the playwright includes a jest about the miscarriage of thought. He also ridicules Socrates' followers for going about barefoot and unwashed; and he asserts, finally, that Socrates teaches his pupils to make the weaker argument the stronger, which, as we have seen, is not literally true even of Protagoras. So, if there are no gross distortions of the earlier Socrates, why does Aristophanes caricature him? The most convincing answer is that he did not like the new style of thought and was very suspicious of it. And we may safely assume that the playwright was certainly not alone in holding that view, which, had it been unique, would never have struck a responsive chord in Aristophanes' massive audience. As A.H. Sommerstein remarks in his Introduction to the play,

One of the plays that defeated *The Clouds* in 423—*Connus*, by Ameipsias—also included a portrayal of Socrates which, to say the least, did not contradict that in the *Clouds*; and the same is true of all other references in comedy to Socrates, and indeed to philosophers in general, well into the fourth century. The inference can hardly be resisted that this was also the attitude of the ordinary Athenian to such people. It is understandable. The "enlightenment" of the last third of the fifth century...together with a great deal of truth introduced a great deal of nonsense, and dangerous nonsense at that. The ordinary Athenian saw the nonsense, lumped the truth together with it, and rejected the whole package. The intellectual, like Thucydides, distinguished between the two. Aristophanes did not make the distinction.[3]

The Theory of "Forms" or "Ideas"

A discussion of the Forms should begin here and not in our subsequent analysis of Plato's thought, since there is good reason to believe that it was in fact Socrates' and not Plato's discovery. We take the *Phaedo* at face value, for as A.E. Taylor observed, agreeing with John Burnet, "it is inconceivable that any thinker should...introduce an original discovery of his own to the world by representing it as something which had long been familiar to a number of living contemporaries who were certain to read his work and detect any misrepresentation."[4]

We saw earlier that at least some of the Sophists had regarded law and morality as mere conventions, and that they denied the existence of universally valid standards by which to distinguish between right and wrong, just and unjust. They also preached a doctrine of pure selfishness: "Might is right!" Hence, a skepticism and moral relativism flourished in the latter half of the fifth century B.C., when Socrates was active in Athens. It was in opposition to such doctrines and in recognition of the danger these doctrines posed for society that Socrates (and Plato after him) insisted on the possibility of acquiring valid knowledge and on the existence of absolute standards of right and wrong. With this aim in view, Socrates sought to establish the existence of an objective, universally valid *reality*, which he found in his Forms, or Ideas. Socrates' reasoning went something like this: In order for a definition or concept to be universally valid, it must be a definition of a *constant* reality, independent of any particular or concrete specimens of the thing defined. The best illustration comes from mathematics. In geometry we study lines, triangles, rectangles, and so on. But no line we draw is a perfect one or, indeed, a line at all, since it has two dimensions. No square we draw is a perfect square. What geometry actually studies, however, is the perfect line, square, triangle, and so forth. Therefore, the objects studied in mathematics exist, but not in the physical world and not as the objects of sensory experience. In these terms Socrates has given us the first theory that effectively demonstrates the inadequacy of a strictly empiricist epistemology.

What applies to the objects of mathematics applies equally to virtually all other objects, according to Socrates. When we say "man," "woman," "horse," "chair," or "table," it is not a particular physical object to which we refer, but rather to the universal and perfect form of man, woman, horse, chair, and table. In the *Phaedo*, Socrates illustrates his theory with the example of "equality."

If we look, say, at two sticks and ask whether they are equal, we see that they are not precisely so. But what is it that enabled us to ask that question? We must have had a prior knowledge of what Socrates calls "absolute equality" in order to use it as a standard by which to assess the degree to which the objects of sense "strive" to be like it but fall short and are therefore only imperfect copies. And inasmuch as we have possessed our senses from the moment of birth, we must have had our knowledge of perfect equality before birth. This applies to all absolute standards such as beauty, goodness, holiness, and so forth. All such qualities that we designate as "absolute" were in our mind-soul before birth (*Phaedo* 75A–D). For Socrates, then, whatever else is, say, beautiful "apart from absolute beauty is beautiful because it partakes of that absolute beauty, and for no other reason" (*Phaedo* 100C). The perfect form of "beauty," or any other quality, is not what we call a "universal of discourse" or abstract concept. It is a real, self-subsistent, eternal entity.

And in the *Republic*, arguing in favor of his theory of the Forms, Socrates returns to the example of geometry, the language of which, he says, is preposterous, for one speaks as if one is engaged in actions— squaring, applying, adding, etc.—whereas in actuality the real object of geometric studies is pure knowledge. Indeed, it is knowledge of that which always is, and not of something that at one time comes into being and at another time passes away (*Republic* 527A–B).

In his discussion with Parmenides, Socrates considers the possibility "that each of these Forms is a thought, which cannot properly exist anywhere but in a mind" (*Parmenides* 132B). And although Socrates seems somewhat less than satisfied with his own rejection of that possibility, he rejects it nevertheless:

> Well, my best understanding of the matter is this—that these Forms are, as it were, patterns inherent in the nature of things. But the things other than the Forms are made in their image; they are copies which by partaking of the Forms are simply made in their image. (*Parmenides* 132C–D)

Earlier in the dialogue Parmenides had raised several key questions to which Socrates could reply without doubt; but to other questions Socrates could only reply by frankly acknowledging his puzzlement. Socrates had no doubt that Forms existed for Likeness, Unity, Plurality, Rightness, Beauty, and Goodness. He was puzzled, however, whether Forms existed for Man, Fire, and Water. Parmenides then probes Socrates further, asking him whether there were Forms for hair, mud, or dirt, or other such trivial objects. Socrates responded thus:

> In those cases the things are exactly as we perceive them, for it would surely be too much to suppose that for such things too Forms exist. And yet, I have occasionally wondered whether what is true in one case must not be true in all. But then I draw back from that position

for fear of falling into a bottomless pit of nonsense. At such times I come back to the things we were just now discussing as having Forms and I spend my time reflecting on them. (Parmenides 130B–D)

Inasmuch as Socrates candidly admits his uncertainty over whether his theory of the Forms applies to everything, including hair, mud, dirt, and other trivia, or only to the higher and dignified things, the above-quoted passages are important. In the *Statesman*, the stranger and the young Socrates agree that there are likenesses in nature and society to the *real existents*, that is, the Forms, which the senses can grasp and which are, therefore, relatively easy to understand, (for example, chair, table, and so forth),

> so that when someone asks for an account of these existents one has no trouble at all—one can simply point to the sensible likenesses and get along without any explanation in words. But to the highest and most important class of existents there are no corresponding visible resemblances, no tangible objects which anyone can perceive. In such cases there is nothing visible which can be indicated to satisfy the inquiring mind; the teacher cannot enable the inquirer to perceive something with one or another of his senses and thus give him the real satisfaction that he truly understands the thing in question. We must, therefore, train ourselves to provide and to grasp a *rational* account of every existent thing. For the existents which have no visible manifestation—but which are the most essential and of the greatest value—may only be grasped by means of reason and may be apprehended by no other means. That is the point of our present discussion—to train ourselves to apprehend the supreme class of existents. (*Statesman* 285E–286B)

The theory of the Forms, then, which Socrates and the Pythagoreans are said to hold in common, makes a sharp distinction between the objects of thought and the objects of sense. We know what we mean by "equal," but we have never seen perfectly equal sticks, stones, or anything else for that matter. All the objects of sensory experience that we treat as equal are only roughly so, tending toward the absolute and perfect equal, but actually falling short of it. Socrates' theory of the Forms differs from the Pythagorean doctrine in that he includes moral and aesthetic forms along with the mathematical. Hence, Socrates' Forms or "paradigms" (*paradeigmata*) are the perfect, self-subsistent patterns or standards that the manifold, imperfect things of sense approximate as far as possible, but never attain. For Socrates and Plato there is no way of knowing or judging the phenomena of experience without the Forms or Standards. This implies that standards exist; and once we say that standards exist, we have to say where they exist. One might say that they exist in the minds of human beings, which might be true; but Socrates would insist that the Forms also transcend human minds: They existed before we came along and shall continue to exist long after we are gone. Hence, for Socrates a Form is no mere concept or "universal of discourse". A Form is an *objective reality* to which a concept corresponds, and it exists whether we conceive of it or not.

The Forms as Manifestations of Moira

For Socrates, indeed, the Forms are the ultimate and supreme realities; they are *supradivine,* for they are higher than the gods and remain so eternally. In the dialogue *Euthyphro,* the professional priest by that name suggests a definition of the "right" or the "holy" as that which is dear to the gods, and Socrates responds with this question:

> Do the gods love what is right because it is right or is it right because the gods love it? (*Euthyphro* 10A)

And it is soon established by Socrates that

> it is because it is right that it is loved, and not right because it is loved. (10D)

The gods, far from being omnipotent, are subordinate to the impersonal Forms. Their nature is such that they love the holy because it is holy. Ultimately, the universe is ruled not by divine wills, but by the supradivine, impersonal realities to which they must conform. In monotheism, of course, it is literally unthinkable that anything should be superior to God. As we have seen, however, Greek polytheism took it for granted that the gods were subordinate to *Moira*—the supradivine, impersonal force (or principle) that was at once inexorable and moral. Just as Homer's Zeus must obey Necessity or Fate, Socrates' gods must obey the supradivine, eternal Forms—those self-subsistent realities that serve both gods and humans as absolute standards of knowledge and value. If the Greek gods of the myths reside in their respective domains, heaven being the abode of the most powerful god, the Forms exist in a "place beyond the heavens." For Socrates, that is where true being resides, without color, shape, or tangibility. It is only by means of reason that true being might be apprehended. And it is the apprehension of true being that constitutes the real knowledge nourishing the mind-souls of both gods and humans. While the human soul makes its rounds, it discerns Justice,

Temperance, and Knowledge themselves. That is the knowledge of being that veritably is, not the knowledge that varies with the sensible objects of our world. When the soul has contemplated this super-celestial, supradivine realm, the soul descends again to the heavens and returns home (*Phaedrus* 247B–E).

In the *Timaeus*, a creation myth, it is again emphasized that the phenomenal world cannot exist without the super-celestial realities on which it is utterly dependent. And although the myth speaks of a *demiurge*, or god, he is, again, in no way the maker of the Forms but, on the contrary, dependent on them. To the extent that the phenomenal world is beautiful and its maker good, it must have been fashioned after an eternal, unchangeable Form. In this passage from the *Timaeus*, it appears that Plato recognized the need to include an active principle in the realm of true being; for as G.M.A. Grube has convincingly argued, "by insisting on the necessity of including movement and soul in the 'real,' Plato is opening the gate by which the gods will enter his dialectical discussions and become an integral part of his philosophical system."[5] And yet, even the supreme god of the myth is dependent on the Forms: "Maker or craftsman (*demiourgos*)," Grube continues, "is the name by which the supreme god is referred to throughout. This maker must have an eternal and ever-same pattern before him at the time of creation, and this pattern are [sic] the Forms. So that within the myth itself,...the Ideas [i.e., the Forms] are prior to god and exist before him."[6] In the cosmic scale of existence, the eternal Forms thus constitute the supreme reality, superordinate in all respects to the Maker, to the other gods, to human souls, to human beings, and to other living creatures—in a word, to the entire *physis*. So, we need always to remember that when we read "Maker" or "Creator" in Plato's dialogues, we must not read into the term the Judeo-Christian conception of God. The Socratic-Platonic Forms are the supreme, ultimate, and absolute principles in accordance with which the universe is made and governed. Being supreme and supradivine, they never are, nor can they ever be, subject to any personal will, even the will of a chief god. So although Plato occasionally expresses the divine principle in the singular, this must never obscure the fact that his theory remains throughout rooted in Greek polytheism and characteristic of it. Whether he uses the singular or the plural—*theos* or *theoi*—these words simply denote anything eternal and more than human, and the totality of such things. But they never transcend the status in which they remain subordinate to and dependent on the supradivine, impersonal Forms. In these terms, it may be said that the Socratic-Platonic Forms are manifestations of *Moira*, a translation of a fundamental religious concept into a philosophical one. And as we shall see in our discussion of the *Republic*, even Plato's master-concept of Justice is an application of *Moira* to his ideal State.

The Trial and Execution of Socrates

Socrates was accused of disbelieving in the gods recognized by the Athenian State, of introducing new and different deities, and of corrupting the youth of Athens. There were two components to the accusation, one based on his alleged offenses against the State religion, the other based on alleged offenses against the moral order, but in reality based on political grounds. There can be little doubt that it was the political implications of Socrates' teachings that constituted the real grievance of his accusers. For it was known that he had often criticized the characteristics of Athenian democracy—the use of the lot, the composition of the Assembly, and the ignorance or incompetence of Athenian statesmen. From a reading of Plato's dialogues it seems inescapable that Socrates had taught that statecraft, like any other craft, requires knowledge and training that will produce expertise, which in his eyes neither the statesmen nor the electorate possessed. Indeed, it seems at times that for Socrates the handling of politics required a kind of knowledge that was esoteric and mysterious. Such teachings were bound to offend the collective democratic sentiments, and even more so when it appeared that Socrates' teachings had made influential converts. As we saw earlier, Alcibiades and Critias may not have been Socrates' pupils or disciples, strictly speaking, but they certainly were his associates. Alcibiades was a key figure in the attempt to subvert Athenian democracy in the oligarchical coup of 411 B.C.; and Critias had actually subverted it for a time in the brutal coup of 404 B.C. in which many innocent citizens were executed simply because they were prominent and held moderate political views. Doubtless, these oligarchical revolutions were still fresh in the minds of the Athenians in 399 B.C., the year of Socrates' death.

Moreover, the victorious Spartans were imposing oligarchies wherever they could, and in Athens itself there continued to exist an oligarchical party sympathetic to Sparta. In such an atmosphere of insecurity it is not surprising that Socrates had aroused suspicion; he had preached the need for political knowledge and expertise, which was also the propaganda of the oligarchical circles, and he had had among his intimate associates two men (Alcibiades and Critias) who had achieved notoriety for their hostility to Athenian democracy. Socrates thus fell victim to the fears and weakness of the restored democracy in the aftermath of the Peloponnesian War, and it was political motives that led to his condemnation.

But Socrates' accusers could not come right out and voice their political grievances plainly; for the restored democratic government had granted an amnesty to all the participants in the antidemocratic coup of 404 B.C., under the terms of which no citizen could be prosecuted for offenses committed before that date. The political motive was therefore kept in the background.

For example, Anytus was a decent and honest politician who had been prominent in the restoration of the democracy. As a chief promoter of the amnesty he could hardly allow its conditions to be explicitly contravened, so charges were brought against Socrates on religious grounds. It is true that religion and politics were closely bound up with each other, in that piety for the Greeks consisted in worshipping the deities of the State. This being a civic duty, impiety was the offense of omitting such worship. From this standpoint, the authorities could look upon religious nonconformity as a political offense against the State. But a careful reading of the dialogues reveals that Socrates' religious opinions were certainly not deserving of condemnation. There is no evidence in the texts that he had committed the impiety of refusing formally to "worship the deities which the city worshipped"; and even if he had "introduced other and new divinities," this would have constituted no offense as long as it did not preclude the worship of the civic deities.

Earlier we saw that in his youth Socrates may have been influenced by the Ionian "physicists" who said that water, air, and other forces of nature were gods. In his play *The Clouds*, Aristophanes', evidently referring to this early period, suggests that the young Socrates may have been something of a scientific agnostic. But in his maturity and during the whole of the latter part of his life (from c. 435 to 399) Socrates was so far from being an agnostic that his convictions were rather those of a strongly committed mystic who believed in the Orphic doctrine of the transmigration of souls and their reward and punishment in a future life. The Orphic mysteries were widely diffused in Greece, although perhaps less so in Athens; but there was nothing in them that would necessarily have precluded combining the mysteries with a formal worship of the civic deities. The Pythagoreans had taken over elements of the Orphic teachings; and given Socrates' association with several Pythagorean intellectuals, some Athenians may have looked upon Socrates' religious beliefs as somewhat bizarre. It is almost certain, however, that these religious beliefs had nothing to do with Socrates' condemnation since they were no threat to the stability of the State.

And Socrates' conduct as a citizen, we have seen, was beyond reproach. He had served in the army and in the Athenian Council, and he obeyed his conscience whether the oligarchs or the democrats were in power. And we learn from the dialogue *Crito* that, for Socrates, the laws of Athens were not to be disobeyed except for righteousness' sake. Crito, his old and devoted friend, comes to the prison where Socrates lies doomed; he lays out a plan for Socrates' escape.

It will be easy to bribe the jailers, Crito says, and Crito and his friends are eager to contribute whatever funds are necessary for Socrates to leave Athens and live happily elsewhere. To this Socrates responds by reminding Crito of the principled view he (Socrates) has held for a long time, "that it is never right to do a wrong or return a wrong or defend oneself against injury by retaliation" (*Crito* 49D–E). Although Socrates believes himself to be innocent, he counsels obedience to the State because it is wrong to retaliate and because as a citizen Socrates has, in effect, entered into a contract with the State "to abide by whatever judgments the State has promulgated" (*Crito* 50C). Furthermore, obedience to one's country is an even higher virtue than obedience to one's parents. And if one cannot persuade the State that it is wrong—in the light of universal justice—then one must do whatever it commands and submit to whatever punishment it imposes (*Crito* 51B–C).

The wrong done to him, Socrates argues, was done not by the laws but by men; it would therefore be dishonorable to break his covenant with the State by escaping. It is in this light, too, that we need to understand Socrates' doctrine that politics is an art. For if a citizen is selflessly devoted to the State and its laws, which the citizen will disobey only if they conflict with universal justice, then surely the statesman also owes the State unselfish devotion. Politics as a calling carries with it the moral responsibility to work for the well-being of one's fellow citizens, and not merely for one's own advantage. In these terms the political artisan, like other artisans, seeks the good and the betterment of the subject of one's art.

But Socrates' doctrine of politics as an art, requiring expert knowledge, also lent itself to an authoritarian interpretation, as it did in Plato's hands. What we find Plato advocating—before he somewhat modifies his views in the *Laws*—is a form of enlightened despotism in which the laws become subordinate and even superfluous in the presence of a wise ruler. It is true that this is Plato's view and, perhaps, not that of Socrates; but it does appear to be an inference that Plato drew from his master's teachings. It also needs to be said in this regard that Socrates' doctrine, stressing as it did the need for expert knowledge in politics, had definite antidemocratic implications. And in response to Socrates' doctrine, honest, thoughtful, and committed democrats might have raised the following questions:

Yes, of course, knowledge and wisdom are necessary in political affairs; but is such knowledge the exclusive province of philosophers or intellectuals? And what is the nature of such knowledge? Is its nature such that it can only be learned in the Academy? And isn't it true, Socrates, that in politics, as in all human action, there is necessarily much that is incalculable by means of reason alone? And what about the experience of the people? Doesn't their experience in everyday life, and their reflections upon it, count as a form of wisdom and knowledge? And is it really true, where politics is concerned, that the people's knowledge is necessarily inferior to that of the intellectuals? Is it not possible, on occasion at least, that the judgment of the many will be wiser than that of the few? It appears that you have not given that possibility serious consideration; which may mean that insofar as your Ideal State assigns no political role to the will of the people, your doctrine suffers from a major defect.

These are questions and issues to which we shall return in our detailed analysis of the *Republic* and in Plato's final work, the *Laws*.

Socrates was found guilty of the charges leveled against him, and the penalty proposed was death, although the accusers really had no desire to impose it. It was anticipated that once the charge was lodged in the archon's office, Socrates would leave Athens. He surprised the city, however, by remaining to answer the charge. The trial's proceedings, heard in a court of 501 judges with the king-archon presiding, reached a verdict of guilty by a majority of 60. In accordance with Athenian law, a defendant had the right to propose a lighter punishment than that advocated by the accuser, and the judges were required to select one of the two sentences. Socrates deliberately offered to pay only a small fine (which angered the court), and thus lost an opportunity to save his life. When the court rejected Socrates's proposal he was again condemned to death by an even larger majority. A month later he drank the deadly hemlock while discoursing with his friends till the last hour. In the *Apology* Plato vividly conveys the nature of his master's personality and the general outline of the arguments Socrates made in his own defense. Socrates is represented as having no difficulty in showing that many allegations about him were false; but with the main charge against Socrates of holding and diffusing heterodox views Plato deals briefly and less convincingly.

Soon after Socrates' death, for which his friends never forgave the democracy, his spirit began to exercise an influence, mainly through the work of Plato, his greatest disciple. And as we shall see, Plato turns with admiration not to the free institutions of his own city (Athens) but to the political structure of Sparta. The Lacedaemonian (that is, Spartan) social and political structure, which the Athenians of the Periclean Age had regarded as basically unfree, was selected by Plato as the closest approximation to his ideal society. And this at the very time that victorious Sparta was making itself detested in many cities of Greece for imposing upon them governments very similar to her own, governments in which citizens became subjects absolutely submissive to the power of the State. It is Sparta that becomes the model for Plato's *Republic*, a work that we shall soon examine carefully to see whether it is as much concerned with the liberty of the individual as it is with the authority of the State.

Notes

[1]Antony Andrews, *Greek Society* (Harmandsworth, Middlesex: Penguin Books, 1967), pp. 238–239.

[2]John Burnet, *Greek Philosophy* (London: Macmillan & Co., Ltd., 1964), p. 113.

[3]Aristophanes, *Lysistrata/The Acharnians and The Clouds* (London: Penguin Classics, 1973), p. 16.

[4]A. E. Taylor, *Socrates* (Garden City, New York: Doubleday Anchor Books, 1953), p. 161.

[5]G. M .A. Grube, *Plato's Thought* (Boston: Beacon Press, 1958), p. 161.

[6]Ibid., p. 163.

4

• • • • • • • • • • • • • • • •

Plato

Plato, the most gifted pupil of Socrates, was born in 428 or 427 B.C. to a distinguished Athenian family. On his mother's side he was closely related to Charmides and Critias, who figure prominently in the dialogues and who gave their names to two of them. Plato was brought up in an aristocratic environment, acquiring early a taste for literature and an interest in philosophy. In keeping with Greek customs he was active in gymnastics; and though originally he was named Aristocles after his grandfather, he soon received the nickname "Plato," owing to the broadness of his chest and shoulders. In his youth he had composed lyrical and dramatic poems, and his extraordinary literary skills are evident throughout his writings. He had also studied philosophy with Cratylus the Heraclitean. But the decisive event of his youth was the acquaintance he made at age twenty with Socrates. Earlier we noted that Plato's close relative, Critias, was a prominent leader of the oligarchical clique that ruled Athens in 404 B.C. In due course we shall therefore want to address the question of whether Plato had inherited an antidemocratic prejudice from his family and whether Critias' career tells us anything at all about Plato's political theories.

From Plato's letters we may gather that for a while he had considered pursuing a political career in Athens; with the death of Socrates, however, he changed his plans and turned his attention to the fundamental questions of philosophy. Scholars are largely in agreement that his earliest dialogues are the *Apology*, the *Crito*, the *Gorgias*, the *Protagoras*, and portions of the *Republic*, all of which were composed before his first visit to Sicily in 388 B.C. During the same period, between his thirtieth and fortieth year, Plato is said to have visited Egypt, where he seems to have been impressed with the division of labor among several classes of citizens, and which he strongly advocated in the *Republic*. About 388 B.C. he visited southern Italy and Sicily, the home base of the Pythagoreans. There he was introduced to Dionysius I, the tyrant of Syracuse, whom he had hoped to win over to his political ideas so that he could put them into practice. But those portions of the *Republic* that had condemned tyranny and denounced injustice offended the powerful prince, who turned Plato over to a Spartan ambassador who sold Plato into slavery. He was, however, soon ransomed by a friend who refused to be repaid. Plato then returned to Athens and purchased a grove near the sanctuary of the hero Academus where, in 387 B.C., he founded his famous school, the Academy. Some twenty years later (366) Plato visited Syracuse once again, this time in the hope of winning over to his political ideas the new ruler, Dionysius II, but again to no avail. Plato made still another and final visit to Syracuse (361) to intercede on behalf of his friend, Dion, who had been banished from the court of Dionysius. He failed, however, to bring about Dion's reconciliation with Dionysius, and when Dion was murdered, Plato finally recognized the hopelessness of ever seeing his political philosophy put into practice. He returned to Athens where he continued to teach and write until his death in his eightieth year.

By the time Plato had founded the Academy (c. 387) Athens had already lost her empire; at the same time, however, she had become the commercial and intellectual center of Greece. Plato's school attracted pupils from the country at large, and, doubtless due to Pythagorean influence, seems to have made mathematics the core subject of the curriculum. Although the emphasis on mathematics contrasts with the stress on biological studies of Aristotle and the Peripatetics, Plato's school also gave attention to biology and even to the geological history of Attica.[1] Unfortunately, however, we have no direct evidence of the bulk of Plato's intellectual work in the Academy, to which he devoted the last forty years of his life. All of his lectures are lost to us, which is a serious loss given the fact that the dialogues are no substitute for the systematic exposition of his thought, which must have been communicated over the years in his many lectures.

The dialogues that have been preserved were no doubt composed with an ethical purpose. They aim to impart knowledge that will lead to action and, in particular, to political action, which Plato regarded as the right kind. The earlier aim of Plato's teachings, found in the *Republic*, was to train the philosopher-king whose wisdom and authority would be such as to raise him above the law, or at least above the letter of the law. In his final work, the *Laws*, Plato appears for the most part to have abandoned that aim, proposing, instead, to train the philosopher-legislator who, though he will be guided by the letter of the law, will nonetheless know how to apply it with wisdom and understanding. This is a kind of theoretical "second best" for Plato, which he came to realize was the practical best. The transition to the second phase is found in the *Statesman* (*Politicus*), which may have been written about 360 B.C. There, exemplifying Plato's earlier ideal, the ruler is compared to a ship's captain who

> directs his attention to the real welfare at any given moment of his ship and his crew. He lays down no written ordinances but provides a law in practice through the application of his knowledge of seamanship to the requirements of the voyage. That is the way he preserves the lives of everyone on his ship. Would not a true political structure be just like this and work in the same way if the rulers genuinely grasped what government is, and employed their art as a stronger power for good than any written laws? Rulers with this sound attitude of mind cannot possibly do wrong so long as they adhere firmly to the one great principle, that they must always administer justice impartially to their subjects guided by their own wisdom and the art of government. Then they will preserve the lives of their subjects and change their character for the better, whenever human nature allows for it. (*Statesman* 297A–B)

For Plato, this was, at first, the only true constitution. There being, however, no community in which the citizens can be certain that they have among themselves such an enlightened individual, one must set aside the ideal and choose the "second best," which, under the circumstances, becomes the most just and desirable course. In the words of the dialogue:

> People doubt that any individual will ever be found capable of carrying out such perfect rule. They despair of discovering any one individual willing and able to govern with moral and intellectual insight and to render every person his due with strict impartiality. People are convinced that an individual holding such absolute power will be bound to employ it to the detriment and injury of his personal enemies and to get rid of them. It remains true, however, that if the ideal ruler we have described were ever to appear on earth, he would

be acclaimed, and he would spend his days guiding in strictest justice and perfect happiness the one and only true commonwealth worthy of the name.

We must take things as they are, however, and kings do not arise in cities in the natural way in which the queen bee emerges in a beehive—one individual obviously outstanding in body and mind and capable of taking charge of things at once. That is the reason why human beings come together in order to work out written codes, pursuing with all their might the fading vision of the true constitution. (*Statesman* 301C–E)

That an ideal ruler will be found when needed cannot be guaranteed, so we must have recourse to rules set down in writing. In the Seventh and Eighth *Letters* there is also a new and strong emphasis on the rule of law, and an additional proposal for Guardians of the Law, which is repeated in the *Laws* (753D). In the Seventh *Letter* as in the *Laws* Plato still retains the view that cooperation between a tyrant and a philosopher is necessary. All existing political structures, without exception, are so bad as to be beyond redemption. Plato therefore writes that, as he reflected on these matters, he was forced

to say in praise of the true philosophy that it provides a standpoint from which we can discern in all cases what is just for societies and for individuals, and that accordingly the human species will not see better days until either those who rightly and genuinely follow philosophy gain political authority, or the class that holds political power is led by divine guidance to become real philosophers. (VII *Letter* 326A–B)

This was the conviction Plato held when he reached Italy and Sicily on his first visit. But his failures and disappointments with the Sicilian tyrants led to a basic change in his political theorizing. He now urged, in the light of his Sicilian experience,

Let not Sicily nor any city anywhere be subject to human masters— such is my doctrine—but to laws. Subjection is bad both for masters and for subjects. (VII *Letter* 334C)

And yet, Plato retains the view that law and its philosophical underpinnings are so esoteric a subject that it is only for the select few:

If I thought it possible to deal adequately with the subject in a treatise or a lecture for the general public, what finer contribution would I have made in my lifetime than a work of great benefit to humanity in which the nature of things was brought to light for all to see? I do not, however, regard the attempt to inform humanity of these matters a good thing, for it is only the select few who are capable of discovering these truths for themselves with, perhaps, a bit of guidance. As for the rest, if they were to learn these truths, it would evoke in some an unwarranted and offensive contempt, and in others certain vain and lofty aspirations, as if they had acquired an awesome lore. (VII *Letter* 341C–342A)

The culmination of Plato's thought on this subject is found in the *Laws* where he still upholds the philosopher-king ideal, but concedes that the force of circumstances makes such an ideal impractical. The State of pure justice with its "Perfect Guardians" is therefore abandoned in favor of the law-state with its Guardians of the Law. He continues to believe that the most effective way to create such a law-state is through the cooperation of a tyrant with a philosopher, although once in motion he advocates a fusion of the monarchical and democratic principles.

Apart from the *Letters*, all of Plato's other writings that have come down to us are in the form of a dialogue, which, most probably, was inspired by his master's method of teaching. Socrates, as we have seen, far from having attempted to instill knowledge, claimed that he possessed none. He spoke of himself as a gadfly who sought to sting individuals into the sense of the truth; and he saw himself as a midwife who helped truth to be born. Plato followed in his master's footsteps because he recognized that all groping for truth is, in a large measure, dialogical. What is thinking if not the reflection on experience carried on in the form of an internal dialogue?

A chief feature of the Socratic-Platonic method of argument is the use of analogy. Ostensibly Socrates regularly employed analogies drawn from the arts and crafts, from seamanship and from medicine. Plato, similarly, employs analogy to make a central point. In the *Republic*, for instance, he proposes that women as well as men should be admitted into the class of Guardians. How did he arrive at that proposition? Apparently by reflecting on the fact that the female watchdog is no less capable than the male. And, as we shall see, it was from the selective breeding of animals that he arrived at his peculiar theory of marriage and eugenics. Plato's most prominent analogies, however, are drawn from the arts. Conceiving of politics as the most demanding of the arts, he demands a high order of knowledge and expertise from the statesman, who above all other artists and craftsmen, should know what he is doing, for the consequences of his political decisions ramify far and wide. It was the example of the artist, it seems, that led Plato in the *Republic* to his theory of the desirability of an absolute government. If the artist is most creative when uninhibited by a body of rules, then the Statesman as artist should, ideally, be unencumbered by a body of laws. Pursuing the analogy further, if all artists work not for their own good but for the good of their creations, then the absolute-ruler as artist cannot but work for the common good of all subjects. Later, when we examine this and other analogies as they are employed to establish certain points, we shall see that they are not without their difficulties and even pitfalls. Meanwhile, we may note in passing that although there is considerable truth in the proposition that the artist works best when free of formal rules and constraints, it does not follow that the politician should be allowed to act without the regulation of law—a truth Plato himself almost recognized in his final thoughts on the matter. Before considering in greater detail the path Plato traversed from the *Republic* to the *Laws*, we need to touch upon the earlier dialogues since they address the question of when we may or may not obey the demands of the State.

The Apology *and the* Crito

These early dialogues raise the question of the relation of the individual to the State. In the *Apology*, Socrates is represented as seeking to defend and justify himself at his trial. Suspected of being the leader of an oligarchical coterie, Socrates attempts to refute the charge that he "is guilty of corrupting the minds of the young, and of believing in deities of his own invention instead of the gods recognized by the state" (*Apology* 24B). The central question Socrates confronted at his trial was this: Should he obey the will of the State or his own conscience—that is, his sense of justice with which the will of the State conflicts? We need to remember that Socrates believed that he had been called upon to fulfill a personal mission. These are the words Plato ascribes to Socrates:

> It is literally true even if it sounds rather comical, that a god has specifically appointed me to this city, as if it were a gigantic thoroughbred horse which, because of its enormous size, tends to be lazy, thus requiring the stimulation of a gadfly. It seems to me that a god has assigned me to this city to perform the function of such a fly; that is why I never cease to settle here, there, everywhere, rousing, persuading, reproving every one of you. Another one like me you will not easily find, gentlemen, and if you take my advice you will spare my life. I suspect, however, that you will soon awake from your drowsing and, in your annoyance, you will accept Anytus' advice and finish me off with a single slap, and then go back to sleep till the

end of your days—unless a caring god sends someone to take my place. (*Apology* 30E–31A)

The problem, for Socrates, was whether he should conform by promising to refrain from any further rousing and reproving, or whether he should continue to do what he felt himself called upon to do. His answer was unequivocal:

> Whether you acquit me or not, you know that I am not going to change my conduct, not even if I have to die a hundred deaths. (*Apology* 30B–C)

Socrates thus opposes the law of the State in the name of something higher. But the conditions in which one may justifiably defy the State are further clarified in the *Crito*, where a friend by that name strives to persuade Socrates to escape from the prison in which Socrates awaits execution for the answer he has given to the court. If he follows Crito's advice, Socrates will again offend against the law which has commanded him to remain in prison and to die there as a punishment for his first offense. Shall he defy the law again? His answer is no! What he has once done in response to the demands of his conscience, he will not do in order to save his life. He has engaged in civil disobedience and he is prepared to pay the price for it, which the State, he believes, has a right to exact from him.

In making his case, Socrates first seeks to establish that one must never, in any circumstances, willingly do wrong. To do wrong is in every sense bad and dishonorable for the person who does it. And if, under no circumstances, may one do wrong, then one must not do wrong even when one is wronged. Nor may one do injuries to another, not even in retaliation for an injury done to oneself. Having established this point with Crito, Socrates then goes on to affirm that one must fulfill all of one's agreements, provided that they are right. It follows as a logical consequence, Socrates continues, that if he were to leave the prison without first persuading the State to allow him to go, he would be doing an injury and failing to abide by the terms of a just agreement.

To explain Socrates' position in this regard, Plato places in the mouth of Socrates an argument against Crito's advice, made by the laws and State of Athens. The laws ask him, Is it not true that what you are contemplating will have the effect of undermining the laws and the State as well? Can a society continue to exist if legal judgments have no force and are nullified by private individuals? When you, as a citizen, entered into a contract with us, did you not undertake to abide by whatever judgments the State handed down? And if you now refuse to abide by our judgment, and are thus and to that extent trying to undermine us, what charge do you bring against us to justify your conduct? And now, as the State continues to make its case, we hear a fundamentally sociological argument: Was it not your society that gave you life in the first place? And though you are a deviant individual, is it not true that it is society in the largest sense that has given you your intellectual and other powers? Do you not, therefore, owe society a debt for the goods you have received from it, namely, your cultural and physical education? Because your society wants to put you to death in the belief that it is just to do so, do you expect to retaliate against it and its laws in return? And will you, who presumes himself to be a true devotee of goodness, claim that you have a right to do so? Do you not realize that if you cannot persuade your society otherwise, you must do whatever it orders, and that if you offend against it in any way, you must submit to whatever punishment it imposes? Does not the society even have a right to lead you out to war, where you may be wounded or killed? In war, in the law courts, and everywhere else you must do whatever your country commands if you cannot persuade it, in accordance with universal justice, that what it commands is wrong.

Furthermore, although we have done so much for you and your fellow citizens—the State's argument continues—we have also proclaimed, as a free society, that if any citizen, on attaining manhood, finds himself dissatisfied with our political organization and its laws, he may take his property and leave. Your country has granted you the freedom to emigrate, and yet you have chosen to remain—which we take to mean that you have, in fact, undertaken to accept your society's authority. We therefore maintain that you or anyone else who disobeys us is guilty of offending the very society which has given birth to him, and nurtured and protected him. What is more, such an individual has violated the *social contract* he has made with us, for he disobeys without persuading us, in the light of universal justice, that our decision is wrong. And few people in Athens have entered into such a contract as explicitly as you have, Socrates. That you have been exceptionally attached to your country is clear from the fact that you have never left it, except to fulfill your military obligations. All your actions, and especially your having sired children here, affirm that you have chosen us and that you have undertaken to fulfill all your responsibilities as a citizen.

Moreover, you had the opportunity at your trial to propose the alternative penalty of banishment—that is, you could have done then, with the sanction of the State, what you are now proposing to do without it. But as you rejected the option of banishment, preferring death instead, any attempt to leave the prison now is a gross violation of the contract you have made with us, a contract you have made in deed if not in word. And we must stress again that were you to escape, you would in that case be breaking a covenant with us, which you made under no compulsion or misunderstanding. You have had ample time, seventy years, to leave the country if you have been dissatisfied with us or if you have believed that the contract between us is unfair. It is known, furthermore, that you often held up Sparta and Crete as models of good government, and yet you chose to remain in Athens and to make neither of those countries your home. So, should you decide to heed your friend's advice and avoid the penalty we have designated, you would be committing a breach of faith.

Furthermore, let us suppose that you have indeed escaped to a neighboring State such as Thebes or Megara, both of which are well governed. Is it not likely, once the reasons for your having left Athens became known, that all good patriots would eye you with suspicion as a subverter of law and order? By escaping, are you not, in effect, confirming the opinion of the jurors who tried you, that they gave a correct verdict? For should you show so little disregard for our laws as to avoid the penalty we have imposed, it might well be supposed that you had in fact conveyed corrupting ideas to the young. And how would you reconcile the things you have been saying here in Athens—that goodness and integrity, institutions and laws, are the most precious possessions of humanity—with your conduct? Do you not think, Socrates, that you will appear as a hypocrite? We, your guardians, therefore urge you to listen not to your friends but, once again, to your conscience. Consider what is *right*, and not the preservation of your life. Then you will not only have a cleaner conscience in this world but it will be better for your soul when you reach the next world. As matters now stand,

> you will leave this place, when you do, as the victim of a wrong done not by us, the laws, but by your fellow men. But if you leave in that dishonorable way, returning wrong for wrong and evil for evil, breaking your agreements and covenants with us, and injuring those whom you least ought to injure—yourself, your friends, your country, and us—then we shall be angry with you in your lifetime, and our brothers, the laws, in that place beyond will receive you with hostility, for they will know that you have tried your best to destroy us. Listen, then, to our advice and not to Crito's. (*Crito* 54B–C)

All of this, then, is the argument Plato ascribed to the State, which, in the dialogue, is the reasoning Socrates shares with Crito, who in the end is persuaded and has nothing more to say.

Now, although we have used the terms "contract" and "covenant" in our explication of this text, a qualification is in order. It is true that for Plato the mature individual, as a child of society, owes it a debt for one's education and for all the other good things that he or she has received since one's youth. As one is bound to repay this debt, the person has entered into an implicit covenant to obey the laws. Under the law, a person is free to emigrate if he or she so chooses; but if the individual remains, that person has, in effect, entered into a binding agreement (*synthéke*) to discharge the State's obligations. In these terms a "contract" does exist between the individual and the State.

In Plato, however, there is no idea that the State originated as a contract of *individuals*, and that the claims it makes upon individuals are based on that contract. This mechanistic conception of society, rather characteristic of the Sophists, is vehemently rejected by Plato, who conceives of society as an organic, functionally integrated unity.

Moreover, for Plato, the relation of the State to the individual is not a relation between two parties to a contract, but rather one between father and child; and just as a father has authority over a child, the claims of the State take precedence over those of the citizens. Indeed, for Plato, the dominant claim of the State upon its members is far stronger than is suggested by the father-child analogy, since compared with one's mother and father, one's

> country is something far more valued and sacred and to be held in greater honour among both gods and reasonable individuals. (*Crito* 51A–B)

Other Early Dialogues

The *Republic*, the *Statesman* (*Politicus*), and the *Laws* are the three great dialogues that deal most directly with problems of social theory. The *Republic* belongs to the earlier period of Plato's life and may have been completed by the year 386 B.C. The *Statesman* has been dated about 360 B.C.; and the *Laws*, Plato's final work, was published posthumously in 347 B.C. There are, however, several early dialogues, probably written before the *Republic*, which also concern themselves with matters of social and political theory. Two of these, the *Apology* and the *Crito*, we have just considered, and it remains for us to touch upon the others before we approach the *Republic*.

The central question of the *Charmides* is "What is *sophrosyne*?" This Greek word has conventionally been rendered as "temperance" or "self-control." Scholars acknowledge, however, that these translations do not quite capture the original Greek concept, the spirit of which is expressed in two Delphic sayings: "Know thyself" and "Nothing in excess." *Sophrosyne*, then, is the precise opposite of the characteristics which the Greeks most detested: pride, arrogance, insolent self-assertion, and self-indulgence.

Many definitions of self-control are suggested in the course of the dialogue, but one deserves special notice inasmuch as it anticipates the definition of justice dominating the *Republic*. There "self-control" means, simply, confining oneself to the work of one's own particular capacity and station. This implies that since each individual specializes in only one function, all individuals are interdependent. In the *Charmides*, self-control is defined by someone as attending to one's own business (Charmides 161B). But this definition is neither accepted nor even discussed. Instead of taking it in the sense central to the *Republic*, it is twisted into the opposite sense, that each individual should do everything for himself, make his own clothes and shoes and everything else he needs. In a word, each individual should be economically self-sufficient. To this Plato objects that a State based on such self-sufficient individuals cannot be a well-ordered State. Why not? Judging from the argument Plato later makes in the *Republic*, an aggregate of economically self-sufficient individuals or families is no real State because there exist no organic ties among them. But this point is dropped and given no further attention. If there is any central concern at all in this dialogue, it may, perhaps, be found in one of Socrates' final rejoinders to Critias—that it is not knowledge pure and simple which makes individuals act rightly and which gives them happiness, even if it is knowledge of all the fields of study. There is only one kind of knowledge that will lead to such results, and that is the knowledge which enables a person to distinguish between good and evil (*Charmides* 174B–C). It is disappointing, however, that there is no elaboration of this point, no raising of substantive issues by means of which to clarify what is meant by these abstract terms.

In general, it needs to be said that the application of the Socratic method in this dialogue sheds little or no light. The method at its best is designed to stimulate thinking, which will aid the partners in dialogue to discover and eliminate the defects of their reasoning and thereby gain a more adequate grasp of the matters with which they are concerned. In the *Charmides*, however, the method yields no such grasp. As one commentator has observed: "Socrates shows himself a master of quibbling often enough to keep up a sense of irritation in the reader, and to leave him after pages of hair-splitting definitions with very little idea of what all the talk has been about. He will almost certainly echo Socrates' conclusion, 'I have failed utterly to discover what *Sophrosyne* is.'"[2]

The same method is applied in the *Laches*, but with results that are somewhat more fruitful. The key question is: "What is courage?" Two of the speakers, Laches and Nicias, are distinguished generals who have undoubtedly demonstrated courage in battle as has Socrates himself as a soldier in the field. And yet all three have great difficulty in defining the concept.

Despite the difficulty of definition it gradually becomes clear that courage is something other than blind endurance and fearlessness. It is less than virtuous to face risks in ignorance, without knowing whether the purpose to be served by bravery justifies the risks to be taken. If courage is to be a virtue, it must be based on knowledge. In the words Plato ascribes to Nicias, "courage is the knowledge of that which inspires fear or confidence in war, or in anything" (*Laches* 195A). When Laches suggests that animals are courageous, Nicias disagrees because, he counters, if animals have no fear it is due not to courage but to ignorance of the dangers facing them. They are devoid of understanding in much the same way as are little children who frequently also have no real sense of the hazards they face. Just plain fearlessness, says Nicias, is not to be confused with courage, which presupposes thought and reflection. Courage, then, a virtue possessed by very few, contrasts with the fearlessness-lacking-foresight characteristic of animals, many children, and even many men and women. Such fearlessness is, in effect, rashness and recklessness, not courage. Actions cannot be courageous without also being wise (*Laches* 197A–C). Courage, then, is knowledge of what is and what is not to be feared, in war as in all other occasions. Courage as a virtue, therefore, cannot be attributed to animals, children, or to any human being who has not attained the knowledge that is the necessary condition of courage. Courage requires the ability to distinguish between good and evil; and the brave individual must be able to recognize the evils that are to be feared, and the good that is not to be feared.

In the *Euthydemus*, Socrates is represented as contending with Euthydemus and his brother, who are "fighters with words," and once more we find ourselves in a quest for the meaning of abstract concepts. Knowledge is the central concern, and Plato argues that no knowledge is beneficial unless we know the purpose for which that knowledge should be used. Even if we knew how to turn all the stones into gold, that knowledge would be worthless to us unless we also knew how to use the gold for some worthwhile purpose. Thus

> even if we knew how to make humans immortal, that would bring us no real benefit without the knowledge of how best to use immortality....What is needed, therefore, is a kind of knowledge that combines both how to make something and how to use it. (*Euthydemus* 289A–B)

The upshot, which will be amplified in the *Republic*, is not merely that knowledge is necessary, but that a *master knowledge* is fundamentally necessary to social life. What is that "master knowledge"?

Simply stated, a knowledge of the proper use to which any branch of knowledge should be put. We can see where Plato is heading: What is needed is a higher knowledge, that will determine the ends of all other forms of knowledge and control them. It is primarily the statesman's responsibility to gain the knowledge of the true good which gives the citizens happiness. Plato is thus gradually moving toward a conception of the State perfectly controlled by a perfect knowledge, a knowledge of the final purpose that each and every social activity should serve. This, of course, is an adumbration of the State envisioned by Plato in the *Republic*—a State ruled by philosopher-kings in the light of the Form of the Good. But before we turn to the full-blown account of that vision, we need to see how Plato deals with the doctrines of the Sophists.

The Meno, Protagoras, *and* Gorgias

All three of these dialogues address the actual practice of states and societies; and all three share the aim of exposing defects in their operation and of demonstrating the need for true knowledge as a guide to right action. Plato seeks in these dialogues to vindicate Socrates' teaching by contrasting it with the practice of actual social and political life. Socrates had taught that a supreme form of true knowledge exists, and that it is in the light of such knowledge that humans ought to guide their actions. The justification of Socrates' doctrine required an answer to two questions: (1) How do humans apparently achieve a measure of practical success in life and politics without such knowledge? (2) Can the supreme form of true knowledge be taught and communicated? The *Meno* attempts to provide answers in a discussion of political virtue, or the qualities of a good statesman. Plato acknowledges that good statesmen exist; but he maintains that such statesmen most often fail to transmit their qualities to their sons and successors. Must we not assume that they would transmit those qualities if they could? And if they fail to do so, does that not strongly suggest that Socrates was advocating the impossible? Plato, of course, answers the last question with a resounding no. If good statesmen try, but fail, to impart a knowledge of statesmanship, the reason is not that such knowledge is not transmissible, but rather that the statesmen have no knowledge to impart.

To understand Plato's view in this regard, we have to grasp the Socratic doctrine of the *two knowledges*. In his conversation with Meno, Socrates distinguishes between "true opinion" and "true knowledge." True opinions might be serviceable for all practical purposes. They are

> fine and they accomplish all kinds of worthwhile things so long as they stay in their place. But, alas, they do not remain there long, for

they escape from our minds. They are therefore worth little unless one can tether them by showing that they are anchored in reason. Once they are thus tied down they become knowledge. What distinguishes knowledge from mere opinion is the tether. (*Meno* 97C–98A)

True opinion must be anchored by a reasoning that grounds it in principle. If this can be done, it is no longer mere opinion, and becomes true knowledge. For Plato, what good statesmen possess is not reasoned knowledge, based on principle, but only "true opinion" (*orthé doxa*), and that is why leaders like Themistocles "are unable to make others like themselves." What such leaders possess is well-aimed conjecture, not knowledge. Their so-called knowledge is of the same nature as that of the prophets and tellers of oracles who, under divine inspiration, do in fact utter many truths, but have no real understanding of what they are saying. Such leaders may frequently enjoy considerable success in what they counsel or do, but that is because they are, like prophets, acting under divine influence, inspired and possessed by a deity (*Meno* 99B–D).

(Here we must pause and digress for a moment before presenting the balance of Plato's argument. The passage just cited demonstrates once again that for Socrates and Plato, knowledge divinely inspired is inferior to a higher form of knowledge. Socrates is represented as saying that prophets and tellers of oracles possess only "true opinions," not "true knowledge." Hence, divine inspiration yields a lesser truth than do the Forms. This, as we suggested earlier, is in full accord with the basic tenets of Greek polytheism in which the gods are subordinate to *Moira*. The Socratic-Platonic Forms are, in these terms, manifestations of *Moira*. And this is in sharp contrast to Hebrew monotheism where nothing is higher than God, and where there is no truer knowledge than that which God has conveyed directly to the prophets and they, in turn, to the people.)

To return to Plato's argument, he maintains, in the *Meno*, that "true opinion" cannot be taught, and that since it is untethered by reason to principle, it may fail at a crucial moment to give adequate guidance for proper action. What Plato appears to be calling for is a knowledge superior to that which human beings gain by reflecting on their day-to-day struggles with reality. Plato does not explain, however, why such knowledge, derived from reflecting on the struggles of everyday life, would not meet his requirement of a reasoned knowledge guided by principle. Is it not true that the knowledge of everyday life is, in fact, embodied in principles that can be handed down from one generation to another? The fundamental question that arises here—and to which we shall have to return several times—is whether the so-called true knowledge is of such an esoteric sort that it is only attainable by an intellectual elite, as

Plato believes. This Socratic-Platonic doctrine assumes something which is never demonstrated—namely that intellectuals (philosophers) occupy an epistemologically privileged position vis-à-vis the people. What is foreshadowed here in the *Meno* becomes a full-blown theory in the *Republic*, where Plato gives to the philosopher-kings exclusive access to valid social knowledge.

The Protagoras

The problem of knowledge is further addressed in the *Protagoras*, where Socrates and the great Sophist, who gives this dialogue its name, often show themselves to be largely in agreement; and where, surprisingly, Protagoras is several times represented as having better arguments than Plato's master.

Protagoras opens with the statement that his role as a Sophist is to teach the art of politics (*politiké techné*); and that it is thanks to his instruction that people learn to attend properly to their personal and household affairs "so as to become a real power in the city, both as speaker and man of action" (*Protagoras* 318E). Against this claim Socrates raises the following objection, that whenever the State is faced with the need for a construction project, the Assembly consults architects, and when the matter before it is shipbuilding, it consults naval engineers, because construction and shipbuilding require technical knowledge that can be taught. And if any non-expert in the Assembly tries to give advice on these subjects, that individual is shouted down contemptuously or ejected. But when a political question having to do with the government of the country comes before the Assembly, those who get up to give advice may be carpenters, blacksmiths, shoemakers, merchants, shipowners, rich or poor—and yet no one questions their right to speak on political matters for which they have no expertise. The reason must be, Socrates argues, that people believe that government is a subject that cannot be taught (*Protagoras* 319C–D).

In a long and remarkable speech Protagoras replies rather effectively to Socrates' objection and, indeed, challenges the heart of the Socratic-Platonic doctrine. The speech rests on the assumption held in common by Protagoras, Plato, and Aristotle as well, that the art of politics, the art of acting rightly in the State (society), is the same as acting rightly in general. Protagoras therefore argues that the art of politics, in the broadest sense, is not at all like the specific arts of architecture, shipbuilding, medicine, or what have you; the political art is something that every normal human being has the capacity to learn. He makes this claim by positing an original State of Nature in which human beings, though they possessed religion and language, had no political art and, therefore, no social organization by means of which to protect themselves from the wild beasts who almost destroyed them. For the sake of self-preservation they eventually formed city-states, but

> lacking political skill, they knew not how to keep from injuring one another; so their societies broke up and they continued to be helpless before the beasts. Zeus, observing all this and fearing the total destruction of humanity, sent Hermes to impart to human beings the qualities of mutual respect and a sense of justice, so that they might restore the cities in peace by creating bonds of friendship and cooperation. (*Protagoras* 322B–C)

For Protagoras, then, it is only the few experts who can give wise counsel when it is a question of skill in building or any other craft; but when it is a question involving political wisdom, which must always follow the path of justice and moderation, we listen to every individual's opinion, for we believe that everyone shares in the virtue of respect for others and a sense of justice. Otherwise, society could not exist.

And against Socrates' claim that the political art cannot be taught to everyone, Protagoras submits that "punishment" proves the opposite. We punish a wrongdoer not for what he has done in the past, unless it is "taking blind vengeance like a beast." No, says Protagoras, the whole point of punishment, looked at rationally, is to deter the same individual or, by the spectacle of his punishment, other individuals from doing wrong again. This shows that virtue can in fact be instilled through education. Protagoras reminds Socrates that this is the educational philosophy of his fellow Athenians who impose punishment with the aim of correcting the conduct of wrongdoers—which implies that they too believe that goodness is something that can be taught. It follows that if the qualities of mutual respect, justice, and goodness can be imparted by teaching, the Athenians act reasonably in accepting the advice of smiths and shoemakers on political matters. (*Protagoras* 324B–D)

As he proceeds in his argument, Protagoras further reminds Socrates that every citizen from earliest childhood on is taught the difference between right and wrong, honorable and disgraceful, holy and impious, "do this, don't do that." If the child learns to act properly, well and good. If not, the child is straightened out with threats and penalties. Later, in school, the youngster learns reading, writing, arithmetic, music, gymnastics, and what not. And all along the State compels young people to learn the laws of society and to guide their lives accordingly. The State sets up laws that are the invention of the good lawgivers of ancient times and compels the citizens to rule and be ruled in accordance with them. And whoever deviates from these rules is punished; and notice that the name given to punishment is "correction," implying that a penalty corrects or guides. Seeing, then, that all this care is taken in inculcating social virtue, Protagoras asks why anyone should doubt or be surprised that such virtue is teachable. Indeed, surprising it would be if the socio-moral virtues were not teachable; for if society is to exist at all, no one may be a layperson in knowing the fundamental virtues. "All human beings are teachers of virtue to the best of their ability" (*Protagoras* 327E). All of us, after all, have a mutual interest in the justice and virtue of one another, and "therefore everyone gladly talks about it to everyone else, and instructs him in justice and the law" (*Protagoras* 327B).

But one of Socrates' questions remains unanswered still: If, as Protagoras maintains, social virtue and knowledge are teachable, how come the leading statesmen of Athens, say Pericles, failed to transmit his political ability to his sons? To this question Protagoras responds with the analogy of flute-playing. Even if we were all equally eager and willing to instruct one another, would that be enough, he asks, to ensure that the children of good players would become good players in their turn and superior to the children of poor ones? Certainly not, Protagoras insists, for it is only the children with a natural talent for the flute who would excel while the lesser and untalented would never rise above mediocrity. Is it not therefore obvious that the child of a good performer would frequently turn out to be a poor one, and vice versa? But in any event—and this is a main point in Protagoras' argument—all of these performers would be good enough in comparison with those who had learned nothing at all of flute playing (*Protagoras* 327B–C). So, if Pericles failed to impart his extraordinary political ability to his sons, it was not because he lacked knowledge or because such knowledge is incommunicable. Rather it was because there is such a thing as talent and because extraordinary ability is not, after all, distributed equally to all humans. But even if, perhaps, Pericles' sons inherited less natural talent than their father, they nevertheless received the common endowment of humanity, sufficient talent, that is, to grasp the fundamental socio-moral virtue and to communicate it to their sons and to others.

In effect, then, Protagoras has provided a strong argument in support of a democratic polity; for the underlying assumption of democracy is that every normal adult possesses the ability to learn the socio-moral virtues and to apply them. But Plato was no democrat, and Socrates is represented as rejecting Protagoras' distinction between the art of politics and all other arts, and rejecting, too, his proposition that social knowledge and virtues are naturally inculcated in the day-to-day life of any society. Politics, like other arts in Plato's view, requires special training that will produce real knowledge and expertise that can be passed on to the next generation. Politics and certainly statesmanship, therefore, are something for which only the few have the ability. A good State (society) cannot rest merely on the general knowledge of the citizens; a good society requires rulers trained in accordance with philosophic knowledge that can be systematically transmitted from one generation to the next. This view will bear further critical examination in our analysis of the *Republic*. Before leaving this dialogue, however, we need to look at one more Socratic thesis.

Socrates believed that no person can know what is right and yet do wrong. Protagoras is said to agree with him in this regard. When Socrates says, "If an individual can distinguish good from evil, nothing will compel him to act otherwise than as knowledge dictates, for wisdom is all the motivation he needs," Protagoras replies that this is also his view and that individuals should be ashamed to speak of wisdom and knowledge "as anything but the most powerful elements in human life" (*Protagoras* 352C–D). But then Socrates reminds him that most people reject this view, maintaining, instead, that many individuals recognize the good but are nonetheless unwilling to act upon it. The explanation most frequently given for this state of affairs, says Socrates, is that those who act contrary to what is good do so because they are overwhelmed by pleasure or pain.

For example, an individual may be overwhelmed by the desire for food, drink, or sex, and although the person recognizes that an overindulgence in these things is bad, the person nevertheless partakes of them excessively. Why are they evil in excess? Because in spite of the momentary pleasures they provide, they bring disease and other troubles in the future. They are evil not on account of the pleasures they produce, but on account of their consequences, just as a moderate indulgence in food, drink, or sex may bring with it a momentary feeling of deprivation and pain, but actually be the best choice of action on account of the consequences (*Protagoras* 352C–353E). When, therefore, Socrates says that no one can know what is right and yet do wrong, his real meaning is this: When people make a wrong choice between good and evil, the cause of their mistake is lack of knowledge, or ignorance. Ignorance is defined as holding a false opinion, and being mistaken on matters of great moment. And the matters of greatest moment being political, it is in politics, Socrates wishes to argue, that ignorance is the greatest evil since it leads to the worst consequences.

Did Socrates overlook something in this conception of things? He seems to believe that if an individual is subjected to the two opposing elements of desire and reason, desire would win out only if the individual were ignorant of the unfavorable consequences of satisfying his desire— whether for food, drink, sex, material gain, or political power. Some scholars have suggested by way of criticism of this doctrine that "reason needs as it were an executive arm to enforce its decisions, and this is provided by...will-power, which Socrates so strangely left out of account."[3]

The Gorgias

Gorgias, for whom Plato named this dialogue, was the first teacher of rhetoric in Athens, where oratorical skills were obviously quite useful in gaining political influence or office. Oratory was an integral part of the political life of Athens. In the popular law courts and especially in the popular Assembly an impressive public speaker could carry the day even though his less impressive rival made more sense where the country's interests were concerned. Plato was quite aware of this phenomenon and therefore saw in the rhetorician a serious rival to the true statesman. For Plato, rhetoric is not or should not be a part of politics, for it is the mere semblance of politics. Rhetoric is defined by Gorgias as the power to persuade—by means of words—judges, councilors, a gathering of citizens, and, of course, the multitude. A rhetorician is interested, first and foremost, in persuasion, and that is its sum and substance. Clearly, both Socrates and Plato must take a very unfavorable view of rhetoric thus defined.

There are two forms of persuasion, one producing belief without knowledge, the other producing knowledge. And surely knowledge and belief are not the same. Rhetoric persuades but does not instruct about right and wrong. This much Gorgias grants to Socrates, who then opens the dialogue with a gambit familiar to us from previous dialogues: Whenever the city needs to choose doctors or shipwrights or other professionals, it obviously selects real experts. And when it is a question of constructing fortifications or facilities for harbors and dockyards, master-builders are consulted, not rhetoricians. And, again, when the city needs advice about the choice of generals, or strategic and tactical problems, it will consult military experts, not skilled orators. And since Gorgias sees himself as a rhetorician and trainer of rhetoricians, Socrates feels justified in asking him what someone might gain by associating with him, and on what subjects one would then be able to advise the city—the implication of the question being that the rhetorician has no expertise in anything really worthwhile. But Gorgias counters rather effectively that the walls of Athens and its harbor and dockyard facilities are due to the advice of Themistocles and Pericles, not to that of architects. So it is in fact orators who give momentous advice and carry their motions.

Gorgias then asserts that rhetoric is a master-skill that can control all other faculties. If, for example, a rhetorician and a doctor were to visit any city and contend before the Assembly as to which of the two should be chosen as physician, there can be no doubt that it is the skilled speaker who would be chosen. In fact, Gorgias insists, the same result would occur no matter what kind of craftsman the orator is competing against,

for there is no subject on which a rhetorician would not speak more persuasively than any other craftsman, *before a crowd.* (*Gorgias* 456C, italics added)

And just as other skills such as boxing are abused, by employing them for aggression instead of defense, so can rhetoric be abused. But that does not make the teacher guilty or the skill evil. One should make proper use of rhetoric as of athletic prowess and other gifts.

But what is the proper use of rhetoric? Socrates asks. If verbal victory in and of itself is the aim, rather than carefully investigating the subject in question, is that proper use or abuse? Gorgias has said that where health is concerned a rhetorician will be more persuasive than a doctor "before a crowd," which must mean before the ignorant, for surely a rhetorician will not be more persuasive among the knowledgeable.

"Therefore," Socrates continues, "when the rhetorician is more convincing than the doctor, the ignorant is more convincing among the ignorant than the expert" *Gorgias* (459B). Gorgias grants that this is the conclusion to be drawn in this instance. But Socrates counters that the same conclusion is also to be drawn in other instances: "Is not the position of the rhetorician and of rhetoric the same with respect to other arts as well? The rhetorician cares little or not at all about the truth, for he is primarily interested in persuading the ignorant that he is more knowledgeable than the expert" (*Gorgias* 459C).

For Socrates and Plato, then, rhetoric is a sham art which flatters the senses but has no interest in knowledge or truth. One can dress up an unhealthy body to give the appearance of health instead of engaging in gymnastics to produce real health; one can appear to care for the health of the body by cooking up concoctions and pretending they are medicine. The relation of dressing to gymnastics, and cooking (that is, quackery) to medicine, is the same as that of Sophistic rhetoric to truth, knowledge, and justice. Rhetoric may pretend to seek truth and justice, but actually it has no compunction about making the worse cause appear the better. The rhetorician imparts to politically ambitious pupils technical skills that will enable them to sacrifice truth and justice in the pursuit of power.

In the same dialogue Polus applauds the proposition that success, however attained, is what matters, although he admits that if it is attained at the cost of injustice, that would be discreditable or shameful. Socrates then presses him by asking whether it is more shameful to do or to suffer wrong, and although he gets Polus to admit that to do wrong is more shameful, Polus balks at agreeing that if it is more shameful it is also worse (*Gorgias* 474C–D). His reasoning seems to be that in committing injustice the perpetrator suffers no harm or evil. Plato, of course, vehemently rejects this notion as he will continue to do in the *Republic*.

In both the *Gorgias* and the *Republic* one of the meanings of "injustice" (*adikia*) is "unrighteousness" or, more precisely, *social* unrighteousness—the failure to observe the system of ethics and morals on which the system rests. For Plato—and this is a fundamental point—the interdependence of individuals is such that one can hardly do injustice to another without harming oneself. In the *Gorgias* Plato argues that the perpetrator of injustice is always unhappy. In words Plato ascribes to Socrates,

> the wicked individual, the evil-doer, cannot avoid unhappiness, and he is all the more unhappy if he fails to pay with punishment for his offense. He is, however, less unhappy when he accepts the due penalty from the gods and from his fellow citizens. (*Gorgias* 472E)

The perpetrator of injustice possesses a diseased soul. Wrongdoing itself is evil, but it takes second place to the first and greatest of all evils, which is to do wrong and to escape punishment. Whether it is a tyrant or any other offender against Right, the doer of wrong is more wretched than his victim, and he who escapes punishment is more miserable than he who is punished. Plato believes that punishment heals the soul, the diseased state of which had caused the crime in the first place. His reasoning in this regard will become clearer in our analysis of the *Republic*, but we may briefly state the argument here: When an individual or group offends against society, a wound is inflicted upon both the body politic and the soul of society. If the offense goes unpunished, the society remains wounded and unhappy. It is only by punishing the offender, and thus reaffirming the integrity of its rules of justice, that the society can heal its wound and regain happiness. For Plato, individual citizens are integral parts of the social organism. When, therefore, an individual offends against society, he actually offends against himself and his own soul. If the commission of an injustice disrupts the original harmony of a society's soul and punishment restores it, the same is true of the individual soul.

In the *Gorgias*, therefore, Socrates urges that the wrongdoer ought willingly to ensure that he will be properly punished for his offense, and the sooner the better. In presenting himself before the judge it is as though the wrongdoer is presenting himself to the doctor to prevent the evil poison from becoming ingrained and causing a festering and incurable abscess in his soul (*Gorgias* 480A–B).

So the culmination of the conversation with Polus is a strong condemnation of rhetoric in the pejorative sense. It is a false art which makes the ignorant appear knowledgeable, and, what is all the more reprehensible, makes the better cause appear the worse before a court of law and in political settings. This is the point at which Callicles enters the conversation in earnest and espouses a more radical position than Polus, a position similar to that of Thrasymachus in the *Republic*.

Callicles has just begun his career as a politician who speaks before the Assembly and practices rhetoric (*Gorgias* 500C). He finds Socrates' refutation of Polus' argument unconvincing and, indeed, naive; for if one observes the laws of nature, one can see clearly that social conventions have turned nature upside down. They have inverted nature's ways and created values accordingly:

> In my opinion those who made the laws are the weaker party, the majority. They therefore frame the laws in their own interest and for their own advantage. And they try to prevent the stronger from gaining the advantage over them by teaching that such conduct on the part of the strong is shameful, evil and unjust. In this way the weak and inferior gain satisfaction by striving for equality of status. That is the origin of the convention that it is unjust for the few who are strong to seek advantage over the many who are weak. But in my opinion, Nature herself demonstrates that it is right for the better to have the advantage over the worse, the more capable over the less. We see this to be true among all animals, and among States and peoples as well—that right is simply the ascendancy and dominion of the stronger over the weaker. (*Gorgias* 483B–D)

Originally, humans also followed the laws of nature, so that the "good" referred to the noble, the powerful, and the strong. But now, says Callicles, anticipating Nietzsche almost verbatim,

> We select the best and strongest among ourselves, catching them like young lion cubs, and by spells and incantations we enslave them while inculcating the notion that they must content themselves with equality and that that is just and right. But mind you, should an individual emerge with a sufficiently strong endowment, he will throw off these controls, break loose from these unnatural fetters and trample down our contrived ordinances. He who was once our slave will rise up and reveal himself as our master and thus give expression to true natural justice. And I believe that Pindar agrees with this view for he writes, "Law is the sovereign of all, of mortals and immortals alike," and it is law, says Pindar, that "Carries all, justifying the most violent deed with victorious hand; this I prove by the deeds of Heracles, for without paying the price"—it goes something like that for I do not know the poem by heart. But it states that Heracles drove off the oxen of Geryon, which he had neither received as a gift nor paid for, because it is natural justice that the cattle and all other possessions of the inferior should belong to the superior and stronger. (*Gorgias* 483E–484C)

That is the real truth, reflecting nature's laws, and Socrates would realize it if only he would abandon philosophy and rise to greater things. For it is all right to engage in philosophy in one's youth, but if one persists in it, it will surely blind and ruin any man. What grown men need is not philosophy but rather to learn from the experience of coping with practical affairs and the harsh forces of real life. Callicles thus bases his view partly on nature and partly on international relations—for example, "What justification had Xerxes in invading Greece or his father in invading Scythia?" (*Gorgias* 483D).

In the dialogue, Socrates then asks Callicles whether in his conception of things the more powerful, the stronger, and the better all amount to the same thing; and when Callicles replies in the affirmative, Socrates tries to ensnare him by getting him to agree that the many are more powerful than the one, and, therefore, that the laws of the many are those of the most powerful. And since for Callicles the powerful and the better are the same, the laws of the many are also better and naturally noble. Furthermore, it is the view of the many that justice means equal shares and that it is more shameful to do than to suffer wrong. And since the many are the more powerful and better, it follows that it is not merely by convention but also by nature that it is more shameful to do than to suffer wrong; and it is also true of nature's justice to share equally. So Callicles is mistaken in asserting that convention and nature are opposed (*Gorgias* 488C–489B).

But Callicles, calling Socrates' argument "drivel," responds contemptuously: "Do you think I mean that, if a rabble of slaves and masses who are of no earthly use except for their bodily strength are gathered together and make some pronouncement, this is law?" (*Gorgias* 489C). When Socrates points out that Callicles is forced into that position by his own definition, he shifts ground and assures Socrates that it is not quantity but quality that he is talking about when he says that the stronger are also the better, and that wisdom is such a quality—wisdom in the affairs of state and the best methods of administering it; and not only wisdom but courage and competence to accomplish one's aims without flagging through weakness of the soul. It is the wise and courageous men who should govern states, and this is the meaning of justice, that they should have more than the others, the rulers more than the subjects. Callicles thus insists that the stronger, wiser, and more courageous are better, and therefore also more deserving.

Socrates is willing to agree that the wise, courageous, and competent are better and that they should carry authority; but this must not be understood in the aristocratic sense. For Socrates, "better" must mean morally better, and "wiser" must mean in "true knowledge," not just "true opinion." What is more, Socrates also rejects Callicles' claim that wiser rulers also deserve greater material rewards than do others. The wiser have a right and even a duty to rule, but not the right to profit materially from their rule. This point is illustrated in the following way. If we had to distribute scarce food and water to a number of people, we would want to choose the most capable persons among us to decide how the distribution should be done. There being a doctor in our midst, who knows our physical needs best, we appoint him to distribute the food and water. But it does not follow that because the doctor now has authority over distribution that he also has the right to take more for himself (*Gorgias* 490B–491A).

Callicles, however, rejects these propositions, insisting that for him wisdom means not only a superior intellect but also greater strength of character and will; and insisting, too, that the wiser and stronger should also profit from their rule. No person, he asserts, will take upon himself the burden of the affairs of state unless he can personally gain from it materially. For Callicles it is material things and bodily pleasures that are the most important in life: "Luxury, intemperance and license, when they have sufficient power behind them, are in fact virtue and happiness, and all the rest is bunk, the unnatural catchwords of mankind, mere nonsense and of no account" (*Gorgias* 492C). Whereas Callicles cannot see any intrinsic rewards in an individual's taking upon himself the burden of statesmanship, Socrates sees the inner rewards to the soul as the whole reason for an individual's assumption of political responsibility. For Socrates a sound-minded individual does what is right as a duty to himself, to society, and to the gods, and is, therefore, at peace with himself, and just and pious, all at the same time. And therein lies happiness too. Whereas Callicles believes that hedonism brings happiness, Socrates takes the strong position that if an individual wishes to be happy, he or she must pursue and practice temperance, and flee from indiscipline with all the speed in one's power. Indeed, people should have no need of being disciplined since they discipline themselves. Those who allow their appetites to be undisciplined can never attain satiety, for they are trying to fill a sieve. And there is, of course, an important moral implication of hedonism: An individual who pursues a life of self-gratification is an egotist who is therefore incapable of fellowship and friendship. For Socrates, the entire universe—the heavens and the earth, gods and humans—rests on friendship, temperance, and justice, which is why the sum of all things is called the "ordered universe." Callicles, however, espouses a doctrine according to which the unrelenting pursuit of self-interest is the paramount virtue. He therefore lacks the wisdom to see that the putting into practice of his doctrine would undermine the order of the universe (*Gorgias* 507E–508A).

Although Socrates strives to demonstrate the truth of this proposition, and others by means of rational discourse, we must remember that he is a religious man who believes in the immortality of the soul. As such, he enjoins Callicles to be concerned with how his soul will fare in the next world: "It is not dying but evil-doing that is to be feared; for to arrive in the next world with a soul charged with many evil deeds is the worst of misfortunes" (*Gorgias* 522E). Death, for Socrates, is the separation of the soul and body, each of which in separation retains much the same condition as when the individual was alive. If, in life, a body was large or fat; or scarred from wounds inflicted for wrongdoing; or its limbs were broken or distorted, the same things will be evident in the corpse. And the same applies to the soul. Once it leaves the body, everything in the soul is manifest—all the characteristics that an individual's soul has acquired through experience in life. When, therefore, the souls appear before their judge, the judge will scrutinize them all. And if there are marks and scars due to perjuries, crimes, and other evil deeds, the judge sends them away in ignominy straight to the prison house, where they will suffer punishment—the aim being to improve them and to serve as an example to others who, fearing the same fate, will change their ways in time.

> Those who have been guilty of the most heinous crimes and whose offensive conduct is beyond correction will suffer throughout eternity the most excruciating and terrifying tortures in the prison-house in Hades. As warning-examples, they have been selected from the souls of tyrants, kings and potentates, for it is precisely they who, owing to the license they enjoyed in their lifetime, are guilty of the most outrageous offenses. (*Gorgias* 525C–D)

As Plato sees it, this is no mere "tale" that Socrates relates to Callicles. It is to be taken quite seriously as expressing the deep meaning of Socrates' utterances and actions. That is why Plato represents him as always carefully considering how to live his life, so as to be able to present to his judge, when the time comes, a soul as free from wrongdoing as possible (*Gorgias* 526D–E).

In the *Gorgias*, this is the positive side of the Socratic-Platonic outlook; but there is also a negative-critical side which, through the dialogue with Callicles and Polus, is actually directed against Athenian democracy. Writing after the defeat and decline of Athens, Plato has Socrates prophesy:

> when the crisis of her weakness and disability comes, they will hold their present leaders responsible while singing the praises of Themistocles, Cimon, and Pericles who were the real causes of Athens' misfortunes. (*Gorgias* 519A)

When the Athenians have lost what they once possessed in addition to what they have since acquired, they will blame individuals like Callicles and Alcibiades, forgetting that it was not they who were the original authors of Athens' troubles. The old statesmen may have filled the city with harbors, dockyards, walls, revenues, and similar rubbish, but they were no good in improving the citizens' virtue. For Plato, as we see, the corruption goes back quite far, to Cimon, Themistocles, and Miltiades (*Gorgias* 503B–C; 516D–E). Even Pericles, the greatest figure of Athenian democracy, is not spared:

> Well, you know as well as I that Pericles was highly respected at first and was never convicted of any wrongdoing by the Athenians.... But towards the end of his life, after he had made good citizens of them, he was convicted of theft and narrowly escaped execution. (*Gorgias* 515E–516A)

Plato seems to be referring here to the last two years of Pericles' life, when his policy was for a time rejected, and he was removed from office, prosecuted, and convicted for taking bribes. And though he was briefly returned to office a few months before his death, Pericles had lost his influence and was blamed for all of Athens' misfortunes. But what offended Plato most was Pericles' policy at the height of his influence. By paying the people for serving in public office, Plato alleges, Pericles made the citizenry idle and greedy. Indeed, from Plato's standpoint, *one could not point to a single individual who had ever proved himself to be a good statesman in democratic Athens* (*Gorgias* 516E–517A). In what appears to be an exceedingly pessimistic mood, Plato goes even further and has Socrates say, "...there is never a leader of a city who would unjustly be condemned by the city he leads" (*Gorgias* 519C). The defective nature not only of democratic politics but of politics in general meant, for Plato, that a radically new conception of government and the good society was necessary. That was the aim of the *Republic*, to which we now turn.

Notes

[1]John Burnet, *Greek Philosophy*, (London: Macmillan & Co. Ltd., 1964), p. 223.

[2]Benjamin Jowett, *Charmides*, in *Plato: The Collected Dialogues*, edited by Edith Hamilton and Huntington Cairns, Princeton: Princeton University Press, 1987, p. 99.

[3]W.K.C. Guthrie, *The Greek Philosophers from Thales to Aristotle* (London: Methuen & Co., Ltd., 1962), p. 115.

5

● ● ● ● ● ● ● ● ● ● ● ● ● ●

The Republic

Plato's *Republic* was composed when he was about forty years of age. It is called in Greek *Politeia* ("the State") and bears the additional title *e peri dikaiou* ("Or Concerning Justice"). The Greek was rendered in Latin as *Res Publica*, from which the English title is derived. Actually, however, the *Republic* concerns itself with much more than the title suggests; for it has something interesting to say about all aspects of the human condition. It is a work which offers a philosophy for humanity by addressing one central question: What is a good human being, and how is a good human being made? Given the fundamentally social nature of humanity, Plato understood that a human being could be made good only through membership in a certain type of society. The central question therefore presupposed another: What is a good society, and how is a good society, or State, made? As a follower of Socrates, Plato took it for granted that a good human being must have knowledge; so Plato had to come to grips with a third question—what kind of knowledge must a human being possess in order to be good? The *Republic*, then, is a treatise on the ultimate knowledge to which the good society must lead its citizens if they are to become good and virtuous. In these terms it is a treatise on education, but one that recognizes that a far-reaching reconstruction of economic and social life will be necessary if the educational scheme is to work satisfactorily.

To understand what Plato is affirming, we must know what he is arguing against. For the *Republic* is in many respects a polemic against the younger Sophists of the kind we have already met in the *Gorgias*. It was they, not Socrates, who, in Plato's judgment, were the real corrupters of youth. Their insidious teachings had to be refuted; their influence on the young destroyed. These Sophistic teachers of rhetoric were providing politically ambitious young men with a rationale for the selfish pursuit of power—that those who gain power may employ the State apparatus as a means to their self-aggrandizement. As for "right" or "justice," that is whatever the strongest power in the State enforces, in accordance with its own interests as it sees them. Whatever it enforces is right. Naturally, Plato despised this doctrine and proposed in opposition to it a conception of justice in which politics is a calling. The true statesman enters politics not for his own gain, but to fulfill an essential function for the general benefit. Plato was the first thinker to conceive of society as a living organism in which individuals, through their specialized roles in the division of labor, contribute to the well-being of the whole. The organic analogy implied a close interdependence, such that individuals secure their own ends by securing those of their fellows. In a good society a ruler attains his own full stature by preserving and promoting the commonweal (*Republic* 497A). At the same time Plato had to repudiate the relativism of the Sophists in which laws of justice are mere conventions imposed by the weak upon the strong, contrary to the laws of Nature. For Plato there exist eternal and absolute laws of morality that govern the universe and that may be grasped by the human soul. A good society is no mere aggregation of individuals to be exploited by the strongest. Quite the contrary; it is a community united in the pursuit of moral excellence, and rationally and unselfishly guided toward that goal by those who are truly wise.

In Plato's eyes, contemporary societies, and especially democratic Athens, were altogether the opposite of his ideal. Indeed, the reason why the Sophists were popular is that they simply reflect and repeat the opinions of the multitude, which Plato sees as a "great beast." It is, says Plato, as though these private teachers who work for pay lived with a great strong beast, studying its moods and desires and learning what makes it fierce or gentle and how one may safely approach it; and after acquiring such knowledge they come to believe that this is wisdom which they may then proceed to impart to the young, calling the things that pleased the beast good and the things that vexed it bad (*Republic* 493A–C). Thinking primarily of Athenian democracy, Plato sees two basic defects, the first being that the leaders themselves possess no expert knowledge and, on top of that, cater to the sentiments of the ignorant multitude so that ignorance reigns throughout. The second defect is manifest in the fact that cities are divided against themselves, separated into two hostile camps, as it were, rich and poor, oppressor and oppressed. Eliminating these two defects, then, was Plato's primary theoretical and practical aim. In politics, amateurish incompetence must be replaced by expertise, and civil conflict by social harmony. To Plato, amateurism and ignorance were the chief characteristics and, hence, the basic flaws of the democratic polity of Athens. The fact that any citizen, whatever his ability, might be selected for government office by the chance of the lot, and the fact that any citizen might speak in the Assembly and sway its decisions, meant, in effect, that the mob ruled. The leaders themselves not only failed to possess specialized knowledge but they somehow regarded wisdom as the ability to discern the moods and pleasures of the motley multitude in their Assembly. And the power of the mass public was such that even honest and thoughtful individuals who doubted the popular wisdom were swept along by its torrent (*Republic* 492B–C).

For Plato, everything has its own function, a capacity to accomplish some worthwhile end. The function of any specific tool, for instance, is the work it can perform better than any other tool. One might use an ax to trim vine branches, but neither an ax nor any other implement will do the job as well as a pruning knife fashioned for that purpose (*Republic* 353A–B). By analogy, an individual might be a first-rate craftsman, but does that mean he is fit to govern his fellows? Certainly not, says Plato, for there is a double injustice here: He not only fails to fulfill his own function, but he usurps that of the more capable individual. In Plato's view, therefore, justice means that an individual should do the work in the station of life and occupation for which his capacities make him fit. And although Plato occasionally allows for the possibility that a child of the lower classes might have the capacity to join the ranks of the philosopher-kings, he shows considerable contempt for the system instituted by Pericles in which ordinary citizens were paid their subsistence so that they could participate in government and the administration of justice. Plato's view is antithetical to that of Athenian democracy, which, as it developed, steadily moved away from the concept that public affairs of any kind required a special expertise; the democracy preferred to seek its commonweal in the common sense of the people and the use of the lot.

But if Plato saw flaws in democracy, he was equally critical of oligarchy, characterized, as it was, by the abuse of political office for selfish purposes, by extremes of wealth and poverty, by open hostility between rich and poor. There was even incessant rivalry and dissension within the ranks of the oligarchy itself. The privileged classes' love of wealth infected politics: The rich, seeking to become still richer, seized offices of State for the "spoils" it might bring. As Aristotle noted somewhat later, "nowadays owing to the benefits to be got from public sources men and from holding office, people wish to be in office continuously" (Aristotle *Politics* III.IV.6). In such circumstances, the State, instead of serving its real function as the neutral and impartial arbitrator between classes, became the instrument of the privileged and powerful class. Far from mediating between the classes and moderating the tensions between them, the oligarchical State aggravated those tensions by supporting the rich and powerful against the others. How could there be social harmony in such circumstances? Every city actually consists of two cities at war with one another, "the city of the rich and the city of the poor, and in each of these there are many" (*Republic* 422E–423A).

Plato strives for objectivity as Aristotle later defined the concept:

> it is the special mark of one who studies any subject philosophically, and not solely with regard to its practical aspect, that he does not overlook or omit any point, but brings to light the truth about each. (*Politics* III.V. 4–5)

Accordingly, Plato notes that it is not only oligarchies but also democracies that are subject to selfishness. Like the governing class of an oligarchy, democratic leaders also use politics as a means of economic gain by confiscating, on some pretext, the property of the rich and by imposing upon them heavy "liturgies"—a wide range of public services paid for out of their own pockets. Some of these were periodic and predictable, like paying for the training of choruses for an annual festival, for which a "*Choregus*" (patron) had to be found or the festival could not be held. Other liturgies came irregularly, like the nominal command of a ship in wartime, which meant, in practice, paying the costs of its maintenance and repair. Although the State provided for the hull and rigging and the subsistence of the crew, the wealthy nominal commander was expected to make up for any deficiencies that might occur, lest the State have its property returned damaged or the worse for wear. So in oligarchies and democracies alike there was fertile soil for social tensions (*stasis*) that could explode into large-scale bloody violence.

In the face of this reality Plato set himself the philosophical mission of providing a theoretical ground plan for a different kind of society, one in which the State becomes a truly mediating, moderating, and impartial authority. This was to be a type of State quite antithetical to the prevailing one in which people turn to politics for their own advantage and not for the good of the society as a whole. When this wrong reason for aspiring to political office becomes the general rule, as in fact it has, says Plato, civil and internecine strife destroy both the society and the office-seekers themselves (*Republic* 521A). In such States, Plato observes, leaders are like watchdogs which,

> owing to the lack of discipline or some other evil condition, themselves attack and injure the sheep and behave like wolves instead of dogs. Is it not imperative, then, that we do everything in our power to prevent our political officers from transforming themselves from benign helpers into savage masters? (*Republic* 416A–B)

From Plato's standpoint, the direction of social reconstruction was clear: The political amateurishness of democracy, which its defenders called "many-sidedness," and the political egoism characteristic of both oligarchy and democracy, had to be abolished. But it is primarily in opposition to the democratic shibboleth of "many-sidedness" or versatility that Plato begins to construct his ideal state with the doctrine of *specialization*. He divides his ideal state into three classes, the rulers, the warriors, and the farmers—the first two classes being of "gold" and "silver," respectively, and the third of "iron" and "brass." Each class has its appointed function, and each concerns itself exclusively with the discharge of that function. Government, defense, and the provision of sustenance are thus made into professional occupations and assigned to definite classes. Of these Plato is most concerned with the governing and military classes, which are to receive careful and rigorous training for their duties. As important as training and education are, however, they are not quite enough. A basic change in social structure will be required. Plato therefore proposes a system of communism that will free the minds of the governors and warriors from the distractions of material concerns, thus enabling them to devote themselves entirely to the fulfillment of their respective functions.

Plato reasoned, evidently, that specialization implies the interdependence of functions, and interdependence leads to social unity. Given an objective condition of interdependence in which the classes need one another, and a proper moral education, a united, harmonious community will result. Moreover, if the task of governing is turned over exclusively to one definite class, there will be no room for the old struggles for positions of power. If each class stays within its designated boundaries, concentrating on its own responsibilities, there will be no class conflict. A division of labor of this kind, resting on specialization and interdependence, would bring about a situation in which each class would work at its appointed function in contentment; selfishness would disappear and the new society would be characterized by a unique interclass solidarity. In this scheme we again see how profoundly influenced Plato was by the ancient Greek polytheistic concept of *Moira*, that supradivine force which allotted to each of the gods his or her domain and forbade trespassing. By analogy, if members of society remain in their allotted positions, restricting themselves to the fulfillment of their respective functions, they cannot be selfish; for selfishness (*pleonexia*) consists in trespassing upon another's sphere. Plato recognizes, however, that even a rigorous moral education may not suffice to instill the selfless dedication to their calling that he hopes for in those who govern. Not everyone trained for government is allowed to join the governing class. Only those who have withstood a series of severe trials and temptations, and who have held steadfast in the belief that society's well-being and their own are one, will be admitted to this class, which has *no material privileges*. Plato's communism is thus conceived as an additional structural guarantee of selfless dedication; for the governors, possessing no private property and no family, will have no temptation to selfishness. There will be nothing to which they can refer as *mine* rather than ours:

> Then, may we not assume that lawsuits and mutual allegations will disappear from among the governors because everything except their bodies they will own in common? In such circumstances we can count on their being free of the dissensions that emerge among individuals from the possession of property, children and kin. (*Republic* 464D)

The division of labor among the three classes, with its specialization and interdependence, will, according to Plato's vision, abolish not only class conflict but also individual selfishness, engendering in its place individual contentment. And that is what Plato means by "justice": It is the principle of social life according to which each does his or her part in fulfilling the common goals of society. Justice (*dikaiosyne*), courage, self-control, and wisdom are the four virtues constituting moral goodness (*arete*), which is applied to both the soul of an individual and the spirit of a community. Justice, therefore, is also a constituent element of both individual and social morality. Although justice is, strictly speaking, a part of goodness, it becomes almost synonymous with goodness in the *Republic*. This is the positive conception of justice that Plato here affirms in opposition to Thrasymachus, just as earlier in the *Gorgias* he did so in opposition to Callicles.

The Debate with Thrasymachus

Breaking into a conversation Socrates is having with Cephalus, Thrasymachus asserts that "the just is nothing else than the advantage [or interest] of the stronger" (*Republic* 338C). And explaining himself, he reminds Socrates that in some cities tyranny reigns, in other cities democracy, and in still others, oligarchy. But in each and every one of these cases it is simply the strongest party that has gained mastery and has enacted laws in its own interest, proclaiming at the same time that it is just for their subjects to obey the laws, which are actually to the rulers' advantage. And, of course, the rulers proceed to punish severely all lawbreakers and dissenters. This, Thrasymachus asserts, is the real principle of justice that prevails in all States—it is government in the interest of the strongest party. So if one reasons correctly—that is, realistically—one cannot avoid this conclusion (*Republic* 338D–339A).

In other words, might is right: Individuals *ought* to do everything their powers enable them to do, and they deserve whatever they can get. If one looks at the facts objectively, Thrasymachus is asserting, then it is plain to see that individuals act in their own interest, and that the strongest ones are certain to get what they want. And within states, a government decides its own good and lays down as the law whatever is to its own interest, calling "justice" the rights which it is able to claim by virtue of its superior strength. Thrasymachus thus represents, for Plato, a form of ethical nihilism in which justice and injustice are mere words. For if justice is the advantage of the stronger, and a ruler is stronger than the ruled, their resistance to his power is called by him "unjust." But why should it be just for the ruler to get his own way, and unjust for others to try to do the same? Hence, for Thrasymachus, what is good for one is good for all. Those who are truly wise, therefore, will strive for injustice in the conventional sense: They will be "just" and obey the ruler's selfish commands if they must; but if and when they can, they will be "unjust" and satisfy their own desires. Thus Thrasymachus, like Callicles, espouses a doctrine of extreme individualism that, apparently, was sufficiently influential among the youth to worry Plato. This doctrine had to be counteracted, and the best way to do that was to demonstrate that an individual was no island unto himself, but rather a part of a social organism, fulfilling a vital function within it. Happiness, then, far from being unrestrained self-gratification, was to be found in doing one's duty in the station for which one has the capacity. This, in essence, is Plato's central thesis in the *Republic*.

Plato also attempts a logical refutation of Thrasymachus' doctrine. In opposition to Thrasymachus' claim that a government governs in its own interest and for its own advantage, Plato invokes the Socratic conception of government as an art. All arts, he argues, come into being in order to eliminate defects in the materials with which they deal. The doctor attempts to eliminate the defects of the body, the teacher those of the mind. It is the fundamental aim of every art to bring about the well-being of its material. It follows that if government is an art, and a ruler acts in accordance with the aim of his art, a ruler must be absolutely unselfish. He must selflessly dedicate himself to the promotion of the well-being of the society of which he is a part. That is the way Plato replies to Thrasymachus' first claim. Thrasymachus' second claim—that practicing injustice is wiser than practicing justice—Plato answers with an argument designed to prove that it is the truly just person who is, in reality, wiser and happier.

This person is wiser, first, because, unlike the hedonist, he recognizes the need for limits. He is wiser, too, because he strives for excellence (*arete*) in the fulfillment of his calling. If his relation to others within his own specialization is competitive at all, it is only in the sense that he and they both strive for excellence; and in his relation to individuals in other specializations, there is no need for competition, since the respective functions in the division of labor are complementary, not competitive. The just individual, Plato maintains, is also happier. The argument here rests on the assumption that each "thing" has a specific function, and that the virtue of a thing consists in the superlative discharge of its particular function. Like the eye, the ear, the tool, the horse, or whatever, the soul, too, has its appointed function with its corresponding virtue or excellence. The function of the soul is life (*to zen*), and the excellence for which it strives is the good life (*to eu zen*). Nothing can adequately fulfill its own function if it falls short of its proper virtue: an eye deficient in seeing, an ear in hearing, a knife in sharpness, and so on. Likewise, the soul can only fulfill its function if it possesses the virtue of good living. In other words, it is the function of the soul to promote good living, and to the extent that it does so, it also possesses happiness (*eudaimonia*). This argument rests on the functionalist premise that no individual soul can promote his or her own good living without promoting the good living of others. Good living is therefore synonymous with justice, which brings more happiness than injustice.

Now, although Plato's argument in this regard has substance, it also leaves us somewhat uneasy because of its formal-logical character. What we have here is Plato meeting the Sophists on their own ground and attempting to beat them at their own game of words. For that reason Plato himself is not entirely satisfied with his rebuttal. Thrasymachus has, in effect, alleged that justice in the Socratic sense is not something toward which human beings are naturally inclined. Justice, far from being rooted in human nature, is implanted in individuals by social convention, and kept there by the threat of force. Plato therefore has to supplement his formal argument with an analysis of human nature, which he does in Socrates' debate with Glaucon.

Anticipating modern theorists like Hobbes, Glaucon argues in the spirit of Callicles and Thrasymachus that justice is a mere social convention imposed on individuals contrary to their nature. Justice, according to this view, is the morality of the weaker parties who, seeing that they receive more pain than they can inflict (that is, suffer more injustice than they can impose on others), make a "contract" with one another neither to commit nor suffer injustice. For Glaucon, then, it is out of pragmatic considerations that such a contract is made. Justice is not a real good but a practical compromise between the best course of action, which is to do wrong and get away with it, and the worst course of action, which is to be injured but powerless to do anything about it. "Justice," in these terms, is an expedient that one accepts and approves when one lacks the power to do injustice to others. For if individuals truly possessed the ability to realize their will against the resistance of others, they would be foolish to agree never to wrong anyone (*Republic* 359A–B).

Plato, recognizing that no brief rebuttal is possible, uses the balance of the *Republic* to develop a convincing refutation. He begins with an analogy. Suppose that we had to read small letters from a distance and then discovered that apparently these same letters exist elsewhere, large and easily legible. Clearly, we would prefer to read the larger letters first and then examine the smaller ones to determine whether they are actually the same or different (*Republic* 368D). By analogy, the question of justice exists in the individual and in the entire society, and it might be easier first to apprehend the quality of justice in the larger object. So Plato decides first to look for its quality in States and only afterward to examine it also in the individual (369A).

Plato's Ideal Society

To understand Plato's analogy in this regard we need to bear in mind that for him the individual and society are not separate entities that can be conceived apart from each other. In Plato's holistic view, society creates what we call individuals by implanting in them values and virtues; but Plato also insists that what we call society and social institutions are expressions of the human mind: A society's institutions "spring not from the proverbial oak or rock, but from the character of the citizens who dwell therein" (*Republic* 544D). Justice is no artificial thing imposed on the human mind from without; on the contrary, it is rooted in human nature and in the human soul (*psyche*), which consists of three parts. The first is the irrational element, which craves pleasure and satisfaction and from which spring our erotic impulses, hunger and thirst, and our other appetitive desires. The second part, reason (*logos*), regulates the satisfaction of our impulses and appetites. And the third is *thymos*, the part of the human soul which gives us our sense of honor. Although *thymos* may be the source of ambition and rivalry, it also inspires indignation against injustice, thus becoming an ally of reason. These are the three fundamental elements of the soul that, for Plato, provide indispensable guidelines for the social organization of the ideal society.

Appetite being the first, and most rudimentary element of the soul, it must also be the primary basis of the State or society. In envisioning the ideal society Plato therefore begins with the economic foundation. The first and chief human need is the provision of food; second is shelter; third is clothing and the like. And it is now that we hear Plato, through the words of Socrates, making the case for a specialized division of labor. A farmer, a builder, a weaver, and a cobbler will be indispensable. The question then arises, however: Should the farmer grow enough food to provide for the needs of the others, or should he raise just enough for himself and his family, spending the rest of his time in constructing his own house, weaving his own clothing, and making his own shoes? It is agreed that the former way is easier and, indeed, that our individual natures are not alike but different: One individual is fitted by nature for one task, another individual for another task.

Furthermore, for any task there is a right season or favorable moment that, if one lets it slip by, the work is spoiled. It follows that the tasks of the worker will not wait upon his leisure. The worker's business is a primary affair, a full-time not a part-time job. It is evident that society is able to produce more things of higher quality when each individual performs only one specific task to which he or she is fitted by nature, at the right moment and free from other occupations. More than four citizens are therefore required, since the farmer will not make his own plow, hoe, or other implements, and neither will the builder, weaver, or cobbler make their own tools. So, in addition, the society will require many other types of producers, and even these will not suffice for society's needs without traders specializing in the import-export business. And trade implies a maritime industry and markets where the products of labor will be bought and sold. And let us not forget that unskilled workers strong in body will also be needed. All this and more are needed just for the *necessary* requirements. But if one wishes to go beyond the necessary things, our ideal city will also require, Socrates argues, hunters, artists, musicians, poets, rhapsodists, actors, chorus dancers, contractors, cosmeticians, tutors, nurses wet and dry, barbers, cooks, and what not.

Thus here in the first rudiments of the society—its economic structure—Plato proposes in advance the very doctrine of justice which the *Republic* is supposed to prove, the doctrine that each individual should "do his own" (*to autou prattein*) and fulfill a single, specific function. The ideal society first finds its binding force in human need. The specialized division of labor inevitably implies a reciprocal exchange of goods and services and, hence, interdependence. There is a foreshadowing here of Plato's political-ethical theory, which also rests on specialization. If the cobbler, weaver, and builder produce better and more work by sticking to their specialized tasks and minding their own business, why shouldn't the statesman stick strictly to politics and also produce better results? And if economic interdependence and reciprocity are essential for the satisfaction of human needs and wants, why shouldn't the entire society be organized on the same principle? It should, Plato insists. Reciprocity should replace self-seeking, and the mutually beneficial exchange of services between ruler and ruled should supersede the extreme selfishness of rulers who seek to get everything for themselves. Thus "specialization" is Plato's key sociological principle since, for him, it implies mutuality and, hence, social unity.

We need to ask some critical questions about this Platonic doctrine. There can be no doubt that specialization implies a degree of interdependence. But does it necessarily imply unity? Does complementarity of functions necessarily preclude competition and conflict? Why wouldn't the highly specialized division of labor proposed by Plato lead to a *dispersion* of interests? After all, although the farmer, builder, weaver, cobbler, and other artisans and workers may need one another's services, each of them also has his or her own interests. And if these specialists in Plato's third class of producers have their own occupational interests, what is to keep them from pursuing those interests so unrelentingly that the result is a Hobbesian "war of each against all"? All of the specialized occupations in Plato's scheme are supposed to exchange goods and services. But are all such exchanges necessarily equal or equitable? In the exchange relations between two or more of these occupations, is it not likely that, although the parties are interdependent, their interdependence will be asymmetrical? Will not some need others more than others need them? And on the "principle of least interest," doesn't that mean that those with less interest in an exchange—say wealthy merchants in their relations with poor farmers—would have the power to dominate and exploit the others? Since Plato's communism applies only to the first and second class of rulers, does that not leave open the possibility of inequalities in income and wealth both within and between the crafts of the third class? And if the third class includes, say, well-off farmers and poor farmers, highly skilled craftsmen and unskilled workers, wouldn't that state of affairs lead to dissension and conflict? It is true that Plato represents Socrates as zealously devoted to discovering true or absolute justice and goodness, but does he provide any concrete principles, rules, or laws by which to regulate exchange relations in the third class? And if he fails to provide any such principles or rules, wouldn't the inequalities in the third class, by producing social tension and strife, prevent the very unity that Plato so intensely desires? In a later context we shall be in a better position to determine how well Plato has dealt with these questions. Meanwhile, we may observe that in the *Republic* Plato relies entirely on the wisdom of the philosopher-kings and *not* on rules and laws for the regulation of economic relations within the producer class. In the *Republic* he provides only one general guideline: Philosopher-rulers must, above all, guard against the emergence of extreme wealth and poverty in the ranks of the third class.

To that extent Plato recognizes the material causes of domestic strife and, indeed, of war. He has Socrates demonstrate to Glaucon that the addition of new, specialized occupations will, perforce, necessitate the enlargement of the city. The territory which earlier sufficed to feed the population will become too small. Even the ideal city-state will therefore have to prepare for war, which means that the city must be further enlarged by no small increment, but by an entire army. How so? asks Glaucon. Are the citizens themselves not sufficient for defense and war? Socrates' reply, not surprisingly, is in the negative, since he has insisted all along that it is impossible for one individual to do the work of many arts well. And if the business of fighting is an art and profession, and certainly no less important than the cobbler's art, then a professionally specialized military force of *guardians* will be necessary. The State must have warriors whose business it is to make war, and nothing else but war. And they must be selected for this work by virtue of a special aptitude, namely *spirit*, in the sense in which a brave and dignified creature, whether a horse, a dog, or any other, is high-spirited. It is the presence of spirit that makes a soul invincible in the face of adversity (*Republic* 375A–B).

War is learned behavior. Therefore the art of warfare has to be taught and the appropriate spirit of the warrior instilled. The soldier, as guardian of the State, must have a certain temperament and wisdom. Like a watchdog (*Republic* 376A), the guardian must be gentle to those whom he guards but fierce to every stranger. The watchdog is gentle to all those whom it *knows*; it has the cognitive capacity to distinguish between friend and foe. Similarly, the guardians must have sufficient reasoning ability for that purpose. The guardians' capacity for reasoning is, however, less than perfect; for reason manifests itself most purely not in the guardianship but in the government of the State, in the "Perfect Guardian," or ruler. Plato thus introduces the class corresponding to the element of reason in the soul. This is done by splitting the class of guardians into two: the military guardians, characterized by their high-spiritedness, who are now termed "helpers"; and the *philosophic guardians*, characterized by their extraordinary reasoning ability, who are guardians in the full sense of the word (*Republic* 414B).

The philosophic guardian's reason yields not only knowledge but also love. Reason, for Socrates and Plato, contains both an intellectual element and an element of affection and attraction. The watchdog loves those whom he knows, and loves because he knows. This helps us to understand better Socrates' dictum that no one can know what is right and yet do wrong. Reason is the philosophic element of the soul that understands and is thereby attracted to whatever it understands—truth, beauty, justice, and the interest of the State. The best guardians must be very wise and capable where these virtues are concerned, and, above all, watchful of the interests of the State. Only those individuals who have these qualifications are to be selected (*Republic* 412C–E). The ruler, then, must be wise and *loving*. The individuals who will govern the State best are those who care for it most, and who recognize that its well-being is their well-being, and its misfortune their misfortune. If philosophic wisdom becomes the master of government, government will be unselfish; and in place of the political selfishness extolled by Thrasymachus, government will become an art practiced for the good of its subjects.

Reason is the province of the philosopher (philosopher literally means "lover of wisdom") and the true and best ruler must be a philosopher. But "the love of wisdom is impossible for the multitude" (*Republic* 494A) and is reserved for a few select souls. The chief criterion of the true ruler is intellectual ability and philosophic power. And it is here that the idea of Forms enters the picture, for the philosopher-king must know perfect justice, beauty, and temperance in order to shape the character of the citizens to the likeness of these Forms. Plato admonishes his rulers to take the city and the character of its inhabitants and first wipe it clean as one would a slate—no easy task, he recognizes. This would be a major point of difference between Plato's rulers and ordinary reformers. Then in the course of determining the structure of the State, the rulers would mold a new human character as pleasing and dear to the gods as possible (*Republic* 501A–C). Above all, the rulers must know and understand the Form of the *Good*, "by reference to which justice and all the other virtues become useful and beneficial" (505A). Rulers must therefore be selected only after the most rigorous and demanding intellectual tests have been administered (503E–504A).

The Classes of the Ideal Society

We have seen that Plato has developed his scheme in three successive logical stages: the economic, the military, and the rational-philosophic. The last of these is not merely rational in the formal sense but in the substantive; for the ruler-philosopher must be a metaphysical genius capable of grappling with the problems of existence and offering solutions to its meaning. The three stages correspond to the three parts of the mind—the appetitive, spiritual, and rational. Now as regards the classes in Plato's scheme, the guardians, we will recall, were divided into two classes, to which Plato adds a third, an economic or producing class consisting of individuals who lack the special gifts of the ruler or warrior, but who also restrict themselves to one function, namely providing for the vital needs of the society as a whole. Plato's Ideal State, therefore, is characterized by a division of labor among three specialized classes: (1) the rulers or "Perfect Guardians," (2) the warriors (at first called "guardians" and later "helpers," and (3) the producers and distributors of goods and services, all of whom Plato subsumes under the general category of "farmers." In this way the three parts of the individual mind, transposed to the social sphere, become objectified in three distinct classes. What Plato has thus done, in effect, is to attribute each of the elements of the individual mind (appetite, spirit, and reason) to a respective category of individuals. There is a small class of the select few in which reason is essentially prominent; a second and larger class dominated by spirit; and a third, and by far the largest class, in which appetite rules. This transposition of elements from the individual mind to social groups is problematic; for as Ernest Barker has convincingly observed,

> The State may be and indeed is a product of mind; but it does not follow that the State is or should be divided into classes which correspond to the different elements of mind. In each individual mind all those elements are present; but if in the State each man is limited to an activity which corresponds to one element only, is he not forced to live as a citizen with a single part of his mind? The ruler must live by reason: therefore, Plato argues, he must abandon appetite; and he is accordingly brought under a communistic regime which prevents the play of appetite, and thus involves the paralysis of an integral element in human nature. Again the farmer must live for the satisfaction of appetite; he must be regulated in that life by the external reason of the perfect guardian; and thus he suffers an atrophy of his rational self.[1]

It is Plato's conception of human nature and the human mind that led him to transpose elements from the individual mind to the social sphere and to ascribe each element to a separate class. In Plato's view, the mind is no harmonious unity to begin with, as the elements are in a state of tension and conflict. The appetitive side struggles, as it were, with the rational side, and spirit allies itself with one or the other, depending on the circumstances. How, then, are unity and harmony achieved? Harmony comes about only when reason rules the others and spirit becomes its ally; it is when reason and spirit work together in concert and gain control of the appetitive part, which is so active and insatiable an element of the soul. Reason and spirit must be eternally vigilant lest the desire for bodily pleasures grows so strong as to become the dominant element enslaving all the others (*Republic* 441E–442B). That is the way the conception of the tripartite soul led Plato to the three-class social structure. Reason is embodied in the philosopher-kings whose communism presumably serves to immunize them against material, appetitive, and sensate temptations. Government is strictly in the hands of an intellectual aristocracy, while the military and producing classes remain subordinate, just as appetite and spirit are subordinate to the rational portion of the individual mind. Given the hegemony of reason in the Ideal State, each class will know its duties and *limitations*—each will know that it would be unjust to trespass on the sphere of another class.

There are several features of this social scheme that must strike the thoughtful individual as problematic. The class structure of Plato's Ideal State has a rigidity about it that suggests a system of castes. Worse, it postulates a great gulf between the producing and the ruling classes, and presumptuously denies to the producing classes the capacity to participate rationally in the society's political decision making. And there is the additional presumption that the philosopher-rulers will be content to live under an ascetic communism in which human desires and appetites will be curbed in the extreme, and in which they will own no property. Furthermore, Plato's scheme turns out to be quite remote from that of a republic inasmuch as the majority of the members of his society are *subjects* of a single sovereignty, not citizens constituting a general will. The source of Plato's error in this regard lies in his conception of the mind as consisting of separate elements and in his autocratic conception of reason. If, however, we begin with a unified notion of the human psyche and apply it to the structure of society, we shall arrive at a view of society as an entity pervaded throughout by reason. This would be true because all human beings, not just the chosen few, possess the capacity to reason; and this, in turn, strongly suggests that a polity based on the general will of all of its rational citizens would be more just than a polity based on the autocratic will of the chosen few. In Ernest Barker's words:

> we shall conceive the State as a single personality, and we shall ascribe sovereignty, in the manner of Rousseau, to the general will of the whole personality. In a society based on a conception of this character, there will indeed be classes—but each class will be a factor in determining the common will; there will be unity—but a unity consistent with the full individual existence of each member.[2]

In fairness to Plato we need to remember that he explicitly allows for the possibility that children born in the second and third classes might occasionally have "golden" leadership capabilities and that they should therefore be elevated to the ranks of the guardians; just as golden parents might give birth to offspring with a predominance of brass and iron in their souls who, therefore, should be demoted (*Republic* 415A–C).

But no matter how hard one tries to be fair to Plato, one still comes away with the strong impression that his conception of justice is extremely one-sided. Justice, for Plato, is neither more nor less than *specialization*: the duty to fulfill one's specific function and to refrain from meddling in another's. There is no place in Plato's scheme for real individuals, with full, well-rounded personalities, who strive to fulfill the full range of their creative needs as human beings. Plato's individual, reduced as he is to a mere function-server in the total social system, participates not with his whole personality, but only with one part: the Ruler with his reason, the Soldier with his spirit, the Farmer-Craftsman with his appetite.

What is more, Plato's notion of social justice, which never goes beyond his *idée fixe* of "specialization," fails to speak to the essence of what one generally means by justice. The doctrine of specialization provides no key to the question of how one would deal with conflicting interests and wills, either within or between classes. If, for example, we return for the moment to the third class of citizens, we can see no reason to preclude from it significant inequalities and the attendant social strife. What if there occurred within that class something like the developments described centuries earlier by Hesiod and dealt with somewhat satisfactorily by Solon? Plato's third class of citizens consists, after all, of farmers with both large and small holdings, of rich merchants and small traders, of highly skilled artisans and mere wage earners. How would Plato's conception of justice provide any guidance in dealing with the tensions and conflicts that would inevitably occur? There seems to be no place in Plato's scheme for a conception of justice that speaks to the question of how one should mediate between the rich and the poor, the powerful and the weak. And the same criticism applies to the relationship between the classes. For it is taken for granted throughout that whatever political decision is handed down from up high will be ethically and morally right. In effect, Plato's doctrine of "specialization" solves the problem by definition: The intellectual elite knows what is good and right for the whole society; that is their "function." And with regard to the communism foisted upon the philosophers and guardians, is it plausible that by depriving them of family and property, there will be no room for conflicts of wills, for rivalry and dissension? It is a central feature of the *Republic* that it relies exclusively on the wisdom of the rulers for the formulation of policy for the State. There is no rule of *law* in the *Republic*, only the rule of philosophers who are endowed with that special "golden" ability to know the "good" and the "just." In the *Republic*, therefore, we find no principles with which to regulate and arbitrate the relationships of subjects, either within the classes or between them. An objection might be raised that such criticisms are beside the point because Plato had intended this work not as a study of legal rights and duties, but of social morality. Such an objection, however, seems unconvincing because moral education in and of itself is certainly inadequate for the purpose of regulating exchange and other relationships within and between the classes. And as we shall see, Plato himself recognized this truth in his final thoughts on the subject, in the *Laws*.

In the *Republic*, then, it is moral education, not laws, by which the ideal society will be created. And if, as we earlier suggested, Plato's doctrine of "specialization" was consciously or otherwise derived from the Greek belief in *Moira* (according to which even the gods specialize, knowing their respective functions and duties, and daring not to trespass on another god's domain), then it seems to follow that self-control, duty, and discipline would be the cardinal virtues of the moral education contained in the *Republic*. If justice is the principle of social ethics that unifies a society, and if justice consists in the proper fulfillment of a specific function by every member of the society, then it follows that the society must, for the sake of its own unity, implant in all its members the fundamental principle on which it rests; it must train its members to strive for excellence in the discharge of their functions. Education, in these terms, is a process intended to adjust the individual to society. Individuals in Plato's scheme are therefore more in the nature of objects than subjects, since they are, in essence, occupants of functional positions in the social system. As such, they are duty-bound to adjust to the system, since, with the exception of the ruler-philosophers, Plato assigns to individuals no active and creative role in shaping or modifying the system. It appears, then, that there is a a fundamental contradiction in Plato's general theory. On the one hand he assigns a creative role to reason and the human mind; on the other hand, however, he denies a creative role to the bulk of the populace in his Ideal State.[3]

Sparta or Athens

It seems clear that Plato's distaste for Athenian politics turned him toward Sparta for inspiration. In Athens education was largely the responsibility of the family and of private associations through which the youth acquired the moral and substantive culture intended for a free citizenry. To this Sparta offered a sharp contrast. Sparta was first and foremost a war-state, and as such demanded an unswerving devotion and obedience from its citizens.

Early in Spartan history the leadership had instituted a rigorous system of state training in which the Spartan boy was removed from his family at the age of seven and entrusted for his education to a State official (*paidonomos*). In education as in all other matters the Spartan State was supreme, and the family had no control over the education of its children.[4] Living in barracks under custodians, Spartan youth were trained to endure severe physical hardships and to develop their athletic and military prowess to a high pitch. Spartan education was directly designed to inculcate the "high-spirited" military qualities on which the society depended. It is almost certain that Plato modeled his conception of the military "spirit" required by his soldier-guardians after the Spartan example. In Sparta, women as well as men were subjected to this rigorous physical and mental training, which, again, must have been the source of Plato's inclusion of women among the guardians. The subordination of all institutions to the Spartan State meant that the family and the property system were adjusted to the requirements of military discipline and a steady alertness in preparation for war.

In addition, the military training and discipline were designed to deal not only with external threats to the State's security but also to internal threats. Spartan citizens were actually an aristocracy whose estates were tilled by a subject population; and since the helots and Messenians refused to adapt passively to their subjection, an important function of the Spartan military was to deal with resistance and rebellion. The subjected populations made it possible for Spartan citizens to be free from economic burdens and to devote themselves full-time to the military specialization imposed by the State.

Plato was not the only upper-class Athenian to be impressed by Spartan ways. Indeed, throughout Greece it became fashionable for the well-to-do to send their children to Sparta for training. In Athens itself there was an influential Laconizing party, especially among the upper classes; and a Spartan attitude was cultivated in the relations of older men with young boys. The Spartan system, in throwing men and boys together, encouraged the vice of *paiderastia* (pederasty). We hear echoes of this in Plato's dialogues where Socrates, though he is represented as having remained chaste, is nevertheless portrayed as having powerful erotic impulses toward younger men like Alcibiades and Charmides.

The Spartan educational system had a central aim as a war-state dominating within it a large servile population. Education had a correspondingly narrow scope and curriculum. There can be no doubt that Plato's educational scheme was inspired by the Spartan example: Education and everything else must be controlled by the State so that each citizen can be placed in the functional position for which he or she is best fitted. Does Athens figure at all in Plato's vision? The answer is yes, insofar as Plato is concerned that education lead to the development of the whole individual. In these terms it is true that the wide-ranging Athenian and not the narrow Spartan curriculum was Plato's model for the education of the individual. But it is equally true that this aspect of his educational program pales in significance beside the Spartan aspect, which is salient throughout. In writing primarily for an Athenian audience it is likely that Plato deliberately stressed centralized social control as a critical reaction to what he perceived in the Athenian system as an excessive individualism. It is nevertheless hard to avoid the impression that despite his programmatic aim of developing the whole individual, Plato relegates the vast majority of the members of his society to the status of "helots." For the producer class is confined to its "appetitive" capacities and barred from exercising its reason in the political decision making of the State.

Plato's Theory of the Mind

There is, then, a definitely unresolved tension in Plato's theory of education. On the one hand there is the confinement of the human mind to a specialized function throughout the individual's lifetime, a condition hardly conducive to the development of the entire individual. But on the other hand Plato is a pioneer in setting forth a conception of mind as an active and creative entity—a proto-Kantian conception of mind. Plato's theory of the mind begins with the Socratic assumption that the human soul is immortal, and as such has been born or incarnated many times before and has seen *all* things both here and in the other world. The soul has learned everything there is. Knowledge, therefore, is a form of "remembering" or "reminiscing." As the soul has learned everything, it should not be surprising that we can recall the knowledge of anything at all, including virtue. In the *Meno*, Socrates is represented as proving this proposition by testing it out with a slave boy. Socrates shows the boy a square figure, which he draws in the sand at his feet. He then introduces variations in it, each time asking the boy questions about the size of the figures and eliciting correct answers up to a point. And as he proceeds he urges Meno to watch him (Socrates) carefully to ensure that he is not informing the boy of anything, only "reminding" him. Soon, however, the boy is stumped and cannot answer correctly. At first there was no perplexity and the boy answered correctly and boldly. Now he is perplexed: Not only does he not know the answer but he doesn't even think he knows. For Socrates that means that the youngster is in a better position now in relation to what he does not know. So in perplexing him we have done the boy no harm. On the contrary, says Socrates, we have helped him toward finding out the correct answer. Throwing the boy into perplexity was necessary in order that he should recognize his ignorance and feel the desire to know. As Socrates resumes his questioning he elicits correct answers and Meno witnesses that the boy arrived at this knowledge solely with his own thinking, helped only by probing questions. For Socrates this means that all of the boy's opinions and knowledge were somewhere inside him. Knowledge came not from teaching, but from questioning, which enabled the youngster to recover the knowledge from his own soul-mind (*psyche*). This recovery of knowledge was a process of recollection. Since it was known that the boy had never studied geometry but nevertheless arrived at the right answers, that meant that he had acquired his knowledge not in this life, but during some earlier one (*Meno* 82–86).

In Socrates' view the soul has experienced in a former life—learned in ordinary language—all the things that we say we have learned in this life. Learning is a "remembrance" of the things of that life, which come to mind when it is stirred by the stinging of appropriate questions. The mind, then, is certainly no passive receptacle, no *tabula rasa*; it is an active process, the creative work of the soul.

For Socrates and, presumably, for Plato, the mind, as we have seen, consists of three parts, two of which—the rational and the appetitive—are contradictory, and a third, spirit, which is capable of vacillating between them. Unity is achieved by the mind when reason gains the upper hand and guides action toward the ultimate purpose of life, namely the attainment of the Good. In these terms Plato's conception of mind and knowledge is at one with his general social theory: The mind understands objects insofar as it sees a purpose in them and recognizes their function in a general scheme. To know a thing is to see it as a part of a larger context and to understand its role in that context.

However, there are many contexts that would amount to so many disconnected fragments of knowledge if one could not unite them under some higher general principle—in Plato's terms the Form or Idea of the Good. Knowledge thus becomes a unity representing the unity of the world with its single, sustaining purpose. Plato's theory of knowledge has nothing in common with the modern notion that knowledge consists of useful fictions which enable us to comprehend the world *as if* it were governed by "principles" or "laws." For Plato the world is a unity with a purpose, and the good is the *raison d'etre* of all existence. But the question remains: In his translation of this epistemology into the class structure of the Ideal Society, did Plato preserve the ideal of developing the whole individual and the whole of his or her mind? We shall be in a better position to answer this question when we have further reviewed the educational program of the *Republic*.

Education in The Republic

The first stage in the education of the youth, the stage through which the majority of the class of soldiers (or "helpers") pass, is, of course, military training. Here, as we have seen, the aim is to produce a certain temper of "high-spiritedness" and not merely to teach fighting skills. The second stage, which comes in the maturer years, is only for those who will be able to prove their fitness for membership in the class of "perfect guardians," the philosopher-rulers. The curriculum, accordingly, consists of science and philosophy. Plato's first stage is an adaptation of Athenian elementary-school studies in which he emphasizes gymnastics and music. Gymnastics included dietary and medical studies as well as physical exercise and competitive athletic games. Music, similarly, was broader than the modern sense of the term, including as it did music per se and other media of expression such as the plastic arts and speech.

Gymnastics was more than a training of the body. It was intended to improve the mind and produce a certain strength of character; just as the athletic games had a moral value in enhancing social solidarity. Music, poetry, literature, and art are also to be taught more for their moral value than for their own sake. The Greek poets who were at the forefront of literary education were also the teachers of religion. Hence, moral education being Plato's primary aim, he proposes a re-editing of Homer and the Greek dramatists to expunge from their works representations of the gods that Plato finds offensive and that, he assumes, would undermine reverence for them. Plato's Ideal State thus controls education and, through education, religion and literature as well, because certain forms of poetic expression might have an undesirable moral influence on the young. Plato assumes that the soul-mind (*psyche*) absorbs everything with which it comes in contact. Drama, therefore, is especially threatening to his ideal society. The essence of drama is that it is made up of different characters, some good and some bad. As the youth read and observe dramatic plays, they will identify with this one and that, play one character and then another. Clearly, this is quite antithetical to Plato's fundamental principle, that an individual should "play" the one part to which he or she is called, and that part only. Plato perceives drama to be the literary form of democracy, where each individual plays several parts. Drama, therefore, has no place at all in the Ideal State. The State, in a word, is the critic and censor of all artistic expressions, including even music (*Republic* 401B–402C). Music, especially, because it penetrates the soul, must be carefully supervised. Plato thus opposes all innovations in music that run counter to the long established norms. New songs may be permitted, but not new ways of singing. For it is Plato's view that one can never disturb the established musical modes without undermining the most fundamental political and social institutions (*Republic* 424B–C).

Plato's attitude toward music, literature, and the arts seems to be characterized by a severe asceticism in which art must always serve a higher purpose—moral and even political ones. Against this attitude it might be argued that the artistic impulse, above all, needs free play, and if it is restricted by the State it will lose its appeal to the emotions and even fail in its ethical function of orienting individuals toward the Good. Some scholars, however, have defended Plato, maintaining that for him art was no mere servant of the State. His theory of art, it is argued, is governed by his doctrine of the True and the Good. Art is or should be a representation (*mimesis*) of life, and as such must be faithful to the original. An artistic expression must capture the Good that pervades the world. If, therefore, the poets, for instance, portray the gods and humans in such a manner as to ignore the good in them, they have produced caricatures, not true representations. This defense tries sympathetically to understand Plato's theory as he had intended it to be understood; and to that extent it sheds some positive light on his view of the role of art in society. To the extent, however, that this defense glosses over Plato's subjection of art to the State and his apparent lack of concern for freedom of expression, the defense does not commend itself.

In the light of Plato's very broad conception of education, we can better understand why a system of laws finds no place in his scheme. In modern theories such as those of Hobbes, Locke, and Rousseau, the State is formed in order to institute or improve a system of legal justice. Such a system is indispensable in mediating the claims of individuals and classes. But Plato will not provide for such institutions for the same reason that he will not provide for the institution of medicine. The presence of physicians, surgeons, and drugs is a sign of disease of the body, just as law courts are a sign of disease of the soul. Plato wants nothing to do with all those matters that ordinarily require legal regulation (*Republic* 425C–E). For Plato, right education in the State will make laws superfluous, for the true "lawgiver" is not a legislator but a philosophic educator. Once the proper moral values are instilled in members of the Ideal State, reasonable individuals will find themselves capable of solving all problems. Here as elsewhere, Plato pushes a truth to an extreme, which makes it untrue. As he himself later recognizes, the spiritual basis of laws—moral and ethical principles—can never suffice in and of itself and therefore requires an external expression of that spirit in a code of laws.

Education of the Philosopher-Rulers

To understand Plato's program for the education of the philosopher-rulers, we need to return, briefly, to his theory of the Forms. Plato was under

Pythagorean influence, and it was the Pythagoreans more than any other Greek thinkers who placed the greatest emphasis on mathematical studies as the key for unlocking the secrets of reality. Like them, Plato firmly believed that mathematics was the proper preparation for philosophy, especially for comprehending the Socratic theory of the Forms. Truth, for Plato and his master, Socrates, resides not in sensible particulars—this chair, this table, that book, man, woman, or whatever. These are only images cast by the perfect universals of which they partake, and by their partaking of which, they possess such truth as is in them. Reality, as distinct from that which appears to be, cannot be seen, heard, touched, smelled, or tasted; it has to be grasped by the mind. And mathematics, Plato recognized, is the preeminent discipline that directly concerns itself not at all with concrete particulars. Arithmetical numbers, for instance, are not apprehended by the senses; they are the products of reason. Hence, mathematics is an indispensable branch of study since it compels the soul-mind to employ pure thought in order to attain truth and knowledge. The study of mathematics sharpens the intelligence for other studies as well.

"Natural reckoners," says Socrates, "are by nature quick in all their studies. And the slow, if they are trained and drilled in this, even if no other benefit results, all improve and become quicker than they were" (*Republic* 526B). The real object of mathematical studies is pure knowledge—knowledge, moreover, of that which always exists and not of things that come into being and pass away. Mathematics is knowledge of the eternally existent (*Republic* 527A–B).

On the other hand, of course, mathematics has an obvious practical value, especially in military matters (525B). Precisely because it has this twofold character, capable of satisfying everyday needs as well as preparing the way for philosophy, mathematics must be studied by those who are going to be the rulers of the State (525C). But the real value of mathematics in all its forms is that it facilitates the apprehension of the Form of the Good. Thus Plato adds to the curriculum plane and solid geometry, astronomy, and harmonics. Astronomy, however, must not be merely the observation of the heavenly bodies, nor harmonics an attempt to distinguish musical notes by ear. The goal of these studies must be the solution of general problems. In harmonics, for example, students must rise to the general level and consider "which numbers are inherently harmonious and which not, and the reasons why in each case" (531C).

Such studies, beginning at age twenty, when the youth has completed his earlier studies and his two years of military training, would last until age thirty. Only those who had shown the most promise at the earlier stage would be admitted to the higher stage. The education of the rest would be completed and they would remain in the ranks of the army. The chosen few who will be trained for the function of "Perfect Guardian" (philosopher-ruler) will no longer devote themselves to the pursuit of knowledge in separate subjects, for they will now concern themselves with bringing things together and seeing the relations between them. They will be trained, in a word, to become dialecticians:

> He who can see how things are connected and related [says Socrates] is a dialectician; he who cannot, is not. (*Republic* 537C)

They have been prepared for dialectics by the study of mathematics, the main goal of which is the discovery of the common principles of all the subjects previously studied. Dialectics stands above mathematics. The latter trains students to ascend from objects of sense to objects of thought. Dialectics, however, is the means by which we attain the knowledge of the objects of thought themselves—the absolute or pure Forms and, ultimately, the final object of thought, the Form of the Good. The dialectician is one "who is able to provide an account of the essence of each thing" (534B), and who is able to bring this account together with others to yield a comprehensive view of the nature of things (537C). All this will take trainees to the age of thirty-five, and if they have passed all the tests and trials, they will be admitted to the elite ranks of the philosopher-kings, the Perfect Guardians of the State. From the age of thirty-five to age fifty, they will devote themselves to the service of the State, holding the command posts in both the civilian government and the military. But even at this stage the rulers cannot rest on their laurels since they will continue to be tried and tested. All this applies equally to those women who possess the requisite qualities (540C). When these men and women have reached the age of fifty and have demonstrated their superior statesmanship, they will not rest, but rather

> They will be required to turn their gaze upward in order to behold the Good itself and to use it as a pattern for the right ordering of the State, devoting most of their time to their continuing studies in philosophy but also toiling in the service of the State when their turn comes. And when they have successfully educated a new generation to take their place, they will depart to the Islands of the Blessed where public memorials and sacrifices will be established in their honour, as to the divine and godlike. (*Republic* 540A–C)

Although some readers of the *Republic* have imputed to Plato a certain wavering between the ideal of contemplation and that of action, there can be little doubt that the two ideals were united in this work, though not in Plato's own life. His personal disillusionment with politics, which he conveys in his Seventh *Letter*, does not prevent him from proclaiming that philosophers can only do their greatest work in the service of society. For those who have proved themselves to be the wisest and have scaled the ascent which permitted them to attain the vision of the Good must go down again into the cave and share their wisdom and labors with others.

This brings us to Plato's conception of government in the Ideal State. Plato's rulers, as we see, emerge out of his educational scheme. Government is a creation of the educational system because government must be guided by knowledge; and inasmuch as true knowledge is gained only by rigorously trained lovers of wisdom, government must be guided by philosophers.

> Either philosophers must become kings, or kings must become lovers of wisdom and the other virtues. There must be a fusion of political power and philosophical understanding which will preclude the pursuit of either one apart from the other. Otherwise there will be no end of troubles for States and for the entire human race. (*Republic* 473C–E)

Only thus can an end be made to incompetence and self-seeking among politicians; only thus can States gain wise and unselfish rulers who regard political office not as a perquisite but as a duty to be fulfilled for the common good of all.

Now, because these philosopher-rulers have seen the Truth or the Good—words to which Plato characteristically never gives substantive content—the rulers constitute either a monarchy or an aristocracy (445D), and eventually they are treated as one, "if we assume the identity of the aristocrat and the king" (587D). In any case, whether it is government by one or by several, it is *absolute* in the sense that the governing authority is totally unrestrained by any code of law. Plato thus departs from the traditional Greek conception of the State as an association of equals, in which the first among equals is simply the guardian and instrument of the law, which was the true sovereign. Among the Greeks the departure from this tradition was called tyranny, a form of government in which personal rule abolished the sovereignty of the law. In the *Republic* Plato, in effect, advocates tyranny, the most unpopular form of government in the Greek world. And though he is careful to dissociate his new form of rule from typical tyranny, which he regards as the last and most degraded form of government, he appears to recognize that he is proposing a dangerous doctrine. This seems evident from the fact that, although he provides for no written law, he does introduce certain principles to which the philosopher-ruler must unswervingly adhere.

1. They must guard against either wealth or poverty intruding into the society. The reasons Plato gives for observing this principle are

that the craftsman who grows rich would no longer be willing to give his mind to his craft; and if he grows poor, he will not be able to provide himself with the tools and other requirements of his art. From both causes, poverty and wealth, the products of the arts and the artisans as well deteriorate. Thus Plato's reasons are to ensure the quality of the specializations constituting the division of labor. Nevertheless, although he does not say so explicitly, his first principle, if it were realized, would serve to regulate exchange relations within the producer class so as to forestall extreme social inequalities and the extreme forms of social conflict that would inevitably ensue.

2. Rulers must see to it that the State be neither too large nor too small, but just the right size consistent with unity and self-sufficiency (*Republic* 423C–D).

3. Rulers must maintain the rule of justice (that is, specialization) and ensure that every individual is occupied exclusively with the fulfillment of his or her specific function (423D).

4. Finally, the rulers must guarantee the stability of the entire society by preventing any innovation whatsoever in the system of education, the arts, music, or any other sphere for that matter (424B–C).

Plato's Theory of Communism

It is not by means of education alone that Plato hopes to ensure the dedication of the philosopher-rulers. They are denied both family and private property and are enjoined to form among themselves an ascetic communistic regime. This material and economic provision, far from being the main focus, is an auxiliary to the spiritual changes—the basic changes in human character—which he sought to achieve. Plato was concerned with the question of how to render it unthinkable that the rulers would transform themselves from benign "helpers" of society into savage masters of the State. For Plato, moral education is the chief safeguard against such an eventuality. It is the right education that will "make them gentle to one another and to their charges." But though material conditions are not the main thing, a thoughtful person would affirm that in addition to the right education, the houses and possessions of the rulers "ought to be such as not to interfere with the best performance of their own work as guardians and not to prompt them to wrong the other citizens" (*Republic* 416B–D). The idea of communalism and basic economic equality was not entirely foreign to the Greek world. There is reason to believe that in very ancient times, before the Greeks turned to agriculture, land was held in common by the tribes and clans. Even in historical times, in a rather individualistic city like Athens, the State still exercised some control over private property and retained the institution of public or State-owned property in forests, quarries, and mines. And in Sparta, though the land of a Spartan citizen was tilled by helots, the produce went to supply the common tables at which the citizens had their meals. And even later, in Aristotle's time, there was a mixture of both common and private property. Observing that virtue will result in making "friends' goods common goods," Aristotle goes on to say:

> Such a system exists even now in outline in some states, so it is not deemed impracticable, and especially in the ones that are well-administered, parts of it are realized already and parts might be realized; for individuals while owning their property privately put their own possessions at the service of their friends and make use of the friends' possessions as common property; for instance, in Sparta people use one another's slaves as virtually their own, as well as horses and hounds, and also use the produce in the fields throughout the country if they need provisions on a journey. It is clear therefore that it is better for possessions to be privately owned, but to make them common property in use; and to train the citizens to this is the special task of the legislator. (Aristotle *Politics* II.II.5–6)

So it is again Spartan and other Doric institutions that most probably inspired Plato's adoption of the idea.

In keeping with the central theme of the *Republic*, Plato's advocacy of communal property is directed against a conception according to which the self is an isolated unit which is and should be primarily concerned with its own satisfaction. Plato's aim is to supersede that notion and to put in its place a conception of the individual as part of a system—an individual who derives his or her satisfaction from fulfilling a function in that system. That, as we have seen, is what Plato calls justice—individuals doing their own specialized work and never presuming to trespass on a neighbor's sphere.

It thus followed for Plato that communism is a necessary condition of justice; for if the first two classes, the rulers and the warriors, are to do their work wisely and unselfishly, they must live under a communistic discipline. In the life of the society these two classes represent the soul-elements of Reason and Spirit. In order to fulfill the special responsibilities of these elements, they must forego the element of appetite, which has been relegated to the third class—all the participants in the economy whom Plato lumps together under the heading of "farmers." A life in which the economic motive plays no role is the only proper regime for the ruling classes representing the higher elements of the soul (*Republic* 485D–E). Communism thus enables reason to govern the State untroubled by appetite which, in the absence of communism, would distract reason and make it work for selfish ends. Reason, thus liberated from appetite, motivates the philosopher-ruler to work for the well-being of society as a whole.

There is, however, another important reason for Plato's advocacy of communism for the rulers. The experience of history had demonstrated beyond a shadow of doubt that the concentration of political and economic power in the same hands will surely lead to tyranny. It was time to learn this lesson: Economic power must be separated from political power, or corruption of the social order is inevitable. Whenever the two forms of power are combined in rulers, they

> transform themselves from helpers of their fellow citizens into their enemies and masters; and so in hating and being hated, conspiring and being conspired against, they will spend their days fearing far more their own subjects than the enemies without, thus preparing the way for the destruction of both themselves and the ship of state. (*Republic* 417B)

No communism is advocated for the third class of citizens—the producers. They will retain private property; but even for this class Plato proposes that precautions be taken to prevent extremes of wealth and poverty, since such extremes create social strife that necessarily destabilizes the entire social order. Hence, the philosopher-governors must regulate the economy. This is to be done not by means of legislation but solely by their wisdom. Plato fails to provide any specific suggestions as to how the rulers would accomplish this. For this reason and others, Plato's third class creates difficulties for his entire scheme. In the first place, Plato is so preoccupied with the rulers and guardians that he assigns no special virtues to the producers. The ruler's virtue is wisdom and the soldier's virtue is courage; but the producers, having no special virtue of their own, can only share "justice" with the first two classes—the meaning of justice being, of course, that the producers specialize in their respective arts and achieve competence or expertise in them. The minds of the producers, being dominated by the appetitive element, are restricted to their economic functions and assigned no role whatsoever in the polity of the Ideal State. Little wonder that they have been likened to serfs and helots despite the fact that the land and its products are in their hands. It is noteworthy that despite the precautions proposed in order to prevent extremes of wealth and poverty in the producing class, Plato does not rule out the possibility of rebellion on their part. He represents Socrates as advising that when the rulers choose the site for their encampment, it should be

> a position from which they could best put down rebellion against the laws from within and repel aggression from without. (*Republic* 415E)

The rulers, owning no property—neither land nor houses nor gold nor silver (417A)—live encamped in common barracks. They subsist on "wages" paid in kind by the producer class and consisting of food and other necessities of life that are consumed at common tables. All this again strikes a Spartan note. Plato himself raises the question of whether the philosopher-guardians can be happy under such circumstances. He argues that they can, but what he means is that they achieve happiness only through the happiness of the whole. Plato's aim in proposing the Ideal State was not the happiness of any one class, but the greatest possible happiness of the society as a whole. The philosopher-rulers must therefore be persuaded and constrained to do what will make them the best craftsmen in their own work, even if they must forego those things which most human beings regard as essential for happiness.

For all of his insistence throughout the *Republic* that the just individual is the happier, it needs to be said that Plato never quite proves this central thesis. Or, if the thesis is demonstrated, it is only by defining justice in the individual as a harmonious relation of the parts of the soul, which results in health and, therefore, happiness. But this does not accord with the *social* quality inherent in the term of justice. *Social* justice, for Plato, is synonymous with specialization in a division of labor; but specialization in the three classes compels the members of each class to act with only one part of their souls and to renounce the use of the other parts. Given such renunciation, Plato has hardly demonstrated that justice (specialization) in the city as a whole necessarily means that the just individual (the specialized individual) is the happier.

There are also other problems. As Aristotle observed,

> if the family life and property of the Farmers [that is, the producer class] are to be such as they are in other states, what will be the form of their community? *There will inevitably be two states in one, and these antagonistic to one another.* For Socrates makes one set of individuals guardians, a sort of garrison, and another set farmers and artisans and citizens of other sorts. But quarrels and lawsuits and all the other evils which according to Socrates exist in actual states will all be

found among his citizens too. Yet he says that owing to their education they will not need many regulations such as city and market by-laws and the other regulations of that sort, although he assigns his education only to the Guardians. Again he makes the Farmers the masters of the estates, for which they pay rent; but they are likely to be far more unmanageable and rebellious than the classes of helots, serfs, and slaves in certain states today. (*Politics* II.II., 12–13)

Aristotle has not quite finished with his criticisms. He questions Plato's method of appointing the philosopher-guardians, suggesting that it is unsafe and unlikely to achieve his aim:

For he [Plato] makes the same persons hold office always; but this occasions rebellion even among people of no special distinction, and all the more so among high-spirited and warlike men. (*Politics* II.II.15)

Finally, Aristotle asks, what class will be happy in the Socratic-Platonic Ideal State? Although Plato

deprives the Guardians of happiness, he says it is the duty of the philosopher-guardian to make the whole city happy. But it is not possible for the whole to be happy unless most or all of its parts...possess happiness. For happiness is not a thing of the same sort as being an even number; that may belong to a whole but not to either of its parts, but happiness cannot belong to the whole and not to its parts. (*Politics* II.II.16)

So Plato has left unexplained how one can have a system of communism in one part of society joined in practice with a system of private property in the other part. Plato wants to get rid of the prevalent condition in which the typical State is actually "two states" antagonistic to each other. And yet his Ideal State is surely vulnerable to such a division against itself. If, as Plato believed, gross inequalities in property and income tend to produce dissension and disunity, what is there to prevent such results among members of the third class of citizens? That such inequalities would breed strife and rebellion, as Aristotle observed, there can be no doubt. And if that is the case, another interesting question suggests itself: How would the philosopher-guardians, deprived of property and other economic means of exercising their authority, control both the internal strife and rebellious conduct of the third class? If we assumed that the rulers are a strictly spiritual elite, we would find it impossible to explain how they would control the third class. But we must remember that the rulers, far from being a mere spiritual elite, are also a military elite holding a monopoly over the most efficient instruments of violence and methods of warfare. It is a monopoly because there is no people's militia in Plato's scheme, which means that the third class of citizens has been effectively separated—at least in theory—from control of the means of violence. In that light we can see rather clearly how Plato intends ultimately to control the third class—by force and the threat of force. In this fundamental respect Plato's Ideal State is no different from actual states, not of his time nor of our own.

Communism of Wives

A communism of wives is advocated by Plato for the same reason that he proposes communal property. The rulers must not be distracted from their work by temptations of self-interest. Depriving them of property, Plato recognizes, would not accomplish the desired aim if the institution of the family were left intact. Private property and the family are interdependent institutions. Fathers and mothers, in their anxiety for the future of their children, may be easily tempted to become self-seeking. The prevalent form of the Greek family, with all of the weaknesses of a male-dominated society, was nevertheless too strong and exclusive to fit into Plato's Ideal State. The Greek family implied a private household, secluded women, accumulated property, and, in general, too narrow a focus of life to be compatible with the unity of the ideal society Plato envisioned. He therefore rejects the existing situation in which men drag off to their own houses anything they are able to acquire, and have women and children apart, thus introducing to society private pleasures and pains (*Republic* 464C–D). He wants to abolish the troubles that private property and family life entail, such as the conceit of the rich and the distress of the poor as they struggle to procure the necessities of life for their children and for themselves (465C). This, of course, refers exclusively to the first and second classes of citizens, since the producing class retains home and family, just as it retains private property.

Plato's approach to the problem of the family begins with an argument for the emancipation of women. Employing the analogy of watchdogs again, Plato has Socrates ask Glaucon whether we expect the female to join the male in guarding and hunting and other tasks or whether we expect her to remain indoors, presumably incapacitated by the bearing and breeding of whelps. The answer being obvious, Socrates goes on to establish that it is impossible to employ any creature for the same task as another, if we do not assign it the same nurture and education. Then the question is raised whether female human nature is capable of sharing with the male all tasks or none at all, or some but not others. And it is clear that

Socrates is heading in the direction of insisting that the woman is in fact capable of sharing all tasks with the man. But he anticipates an objection: Has he not argued all along that in the Ideal State each individual ought to attend to one's own business, the one thing for which nature has fitted that person? And is it not obvious that there is by nature a difference between men and women? And does not that imply that they should be discharging different functions and not the same?

Socrates shows that such an objection is based on a misunderstanding of his position. When he spoke of similar and different natures he meant it not in every sense, but only as similarities and difference were pertinent to the social tasks themselves. He meant, for example, that a man and a woman who have a proven capacity for the physician's task have the same nature. By this understanding of "nature," a male physician and a male carpenter have different natures. "Similarly," Socrates continues,

> if it appears that a man and a woman have quite different qualifications for the various arts, they would be assigned to the respective spheres in which they have demonstrated excellence. But if the only difference between them is the fact that the male begets and the female bears, we shall insist that this is an irrelevant difference for our purposes and that the woman ought to be included in the ranks of the guardians and ought to follow the same pursuits as the man. (*Republic* 454D–E)

Just as some men have the requisite qualities for guardianship and others do not, the same is true of women. It follows that the capacities of men and women are, on the average, equal, except for brute strength. With this exception, there is no duty we would demand from the philosopher-guardians which an equally gifted and equally trained woman could not fulfill as well as a man. Plato therefore proposes that such women be selected to mate with their male equals and to serve with them as guardians (456B). To deny an equally gifted woman access to the philosopher-guardian class would be a violation of justice in Plato's sense, for she would then be denied the possibility of fulfilling the proper function for which she is qualified by nature.

Female guardians are to be the common wives of the male guardians, and the children shall also be common, but no parent shall know its offspring and no child its parent. Men and women will have barracks and meals in common, will participate together in physical training and education, and will, by innate necessity, come together in sexual union. It is stressed that the innate necessity is that of erotic love and that promiscuity would not be tolerated. Nevertheless, intercourse must be regulated with the aim of yielding the greatest benefit to the State:

In as many cases as possible the best men must be coupled with the best women for the purpose of procreation, while the worst are coupled with the worst in as few instances as possible. And in order to prevent the conflict and dissension which would otherwise arise from the pursuit of such a policy, the method by which it is implemented must be kept secret from everyone but the rulers. (*Republic* 459D–E)

The sound offspring of the best couples will be taken to the nurses' quarter in a separate area of the city, but the offspring of the worst and any of the others born with defects will be disposed of in secret to ensure that what has been done with them will not become generally known. (*Republic* 460C)

There is, then, a strong eugenic element in Plato's program for the philosopher-guardians. He wants to regulate marriages so as to produce "good stock." He not only advocates the disposal of defective infants but also opposes the prolongation by medical means of the life of the chronically handicapped; and he allows for abortion when pregnancy has resulted from intercourse that has taken place outside the prescribed age limits: for men between the ages of twenty-five and fifty-five, and for women between the ages of twenty and forty. All of this Plato envisions as a means of ensuring the solidarity of the rulers of the State. And it is noteworthy that the principle of Plato's eugenics appears to be that there is no "right to life" in the individual as such; there is only such a right in the individual as a citizen able to serve the State.

Apart from the eugenic element, however, there are other serious problems with Plato's scheme of temporary and State-controlled liaisons. He tampers with certain fundamental human relationships, such as that of husband and wife and mother and child. In Plato's communistic scheme men and women come together for sexual intercourse, and then go their separate ways immediately afterwards. There is no provision in this scheme of things for conjugal affection, friendship, and love between parent and child, which Aristotle regarded as fundamental human needs.

The friendship between husband and wife [wrote Aristotle] appears to be a natural instinct; since man is by nature a pairing creature even more than he is a political creature, inasmuch as the family is an earlier and more fundamental institution than the State, and the procreation of offspring a more general characteristic of the animal creation. So whereas with the other animals the association of the sexes aims only at continuing the species, human beings cohabit not only for the sake of begetting children but also to provide the needs of life; for with the human race division of labor begins at the outset, and man and woman have different functions; thus they supply each other's wants, putting their special capacities into the common stock. Hence the friendship of man and wife seems to be one of utility and pleasure combined. But it may be based on virtue, if the partners be of high moral character; for either sex has its special virtue, and this may be the ground of attraction. Children, too, seem to be a bond of union, and therefore childless marriages are more easily dissolved; for children are a good possessed by both parents in common, and common property holds people together. (Aristotle *Nicomachean Ethics* VIII.XII.7)

Plato, in contrast, abstracts the sexual motive from the total relationship and turns the individual into a mere means to the State's ends. He thus denies to the whole personality the love and friendship and personal parental experience that are so essential to the happiness of a family.

More generally, one can question the underlying assumption of Plato's ascetic communism, namely that material conditions are the cause of political corruption and other evils. Plato subjects his rulers to extreme deprivation in the hope that this will produce a totally new human character. Thus, for all of his emphasis on spirit, Plato tends to belittle spirit. He does not fully trust education to change attitude of mind and character so that the very same material conditions that in others were connected with corruption would have an entirely opposite effect on the philosopher-rulers.

Aristotle, on the other hand, seeing things quite differently, recognizes that although material conditions may often be associated with evil, they are not causes or active forces. He therefore justifies private property, in spite of its temptations, as a basis of personality and as an instrument of action.

Similarly, the family may have limitations, but it is an indispensable nursery in which the child develops his or her sense of self. In abolishing the family, then, Plato effectively destroys the context in which human beings first come to know themselves as distinct individuals, and in which they learn to think, act, and exercise their will.

It is not only the family but also other small groups that Plato abolishes. There is no intermediate association, lower than the State, with which individuals can identify themselves. Plato is zealous in his commitment to the creation of a perfectly integrated organic unity. For him there is no greater evil for a State (society) than its differentiation into a plurality of associations (*Republic* 462A–B). For Plato the best society is that whose State is "most like that of an individual human being" (462C). In the Greece of Plato's time there were, of course, families, clans, phratries, tribes and demes, religious associations, manufacturing and trading groups, and other organizations intermediate between the individual and the State. These are genuine historical institutions that find no place in Plato's scheme, although they do find recognition in the theory of Aristotle who regards households and villages as constituent elements of society and who speaks of tribesmen and demesmen as forming associations which are essential parts of it. Plato so thoroughly identifies the guardian with the State that the result, as Aristotle remarks, is not one which Plato would wish for:

> The unity of the State which Socrates praises most highly, both appears to be and is said by him to be the effect of friendship, just as we know that Aristophanes [in Plato's *Symposium*] in the discourse on love describes how the lovers owing to their extreme affection desire to grow together and both become one instead of being two. In such a union both personalities, or at least one, would be bound to be obliterated.... (*Politics* II.I.16–17)

Social unity, for Plato, often appears to be an end in itself rather than a quality that society must possess in order to attain a worthwhile end. So the personalities of the guardians are severely diminished, if not obliterated, in their fusion with the State; and the individual members of the third class of citizens are also reduced to just one part of their minds and personalities—the appetitive.

The Republic*: Utopia or Program for Actual States?*

In the light of the criticisms which from the time of Aristotle have been made of Plato's Ideal State, it might well be asked whether he had intended this work to influence actual life. There are passages suggesting that although Plato recognized difficulties in implementing his program, he believed it was practicable. Greece of Plato's time was torn by factions that created enmity among the city-states. One major aim of the *Republic*, then, was to teach Greeks how to found cities which would be fundamentally different, cities without internal strife and in which the citizens would be philhellenes, or lovers of Greeks, and who would therefore regard all of Greece as their homeland and revere the holy places common to all Greeks. Such cities would refuse to make war upon one another, and would settle all quarrels amicably, striving for reconciliation. This is Plato's pan-Hellenism, which never became a universal vision. He looks forward to a time when Greeks will be reconciled with Greeks, "while treating barbarians as Greeks now treat Greeks" (*Republic* 470E–471B). Plato acknowledges that the realization of his Ideal State would be difficult, but he maintains that it is not impossible and that the social and political structure he has outlined would yield the *best* society and State known to humanity. In order to realize it, however, the Philosophical Muse would have to gain control of the State—the State would have to be mastered by real philosophers for whom justice is the chief and indispensable concern (*Republic* 499D, 502C, 540 D–E). Yet the difficulties of which Plato speaks are such that the project must begin with a social *tabula rasa*. This would mean that all the inhabitants over the age of ten would be sent out into the country where the guardians will take over the children, remove them from the old customs and habits of their parents, and bring them up in accordance with the guardians' teachings and rules.

There are, however, other passages which occur late in the *Republic*, in the Ninth Book, suggesting that the work was in fact intended as an ideal. In response to Socrates' detailed description of the new society and the role of the wise ruler in it, Glaucon says he understands that the city just described is one whose home is in the ideal, "for I think that it can be found nowhere on earth." And Socrates comments that perhaps it is only an extraterrestrial pattern existing for those who wish to contemplate it and strive to become its citizen. But whether it exists now or ever will is immaterial, since it is only that city's politics which the lover of wisdom will call his own (*Republic* 592B). So the *Republic* is an ideal construction, after all, and it will have accomplished its purpose, in Plato's view, if it exists as an influence on our thoughts and actions.

The *Republic* is an inquiry into the nature of justice, in Plato's peculiar meaning of the term. And once the nature of ideal justice is discovered, the point is not to attain it, which is impossible, but only to approximate it as nearly as possible. "Ideal Justice" is a "Pattern" or "Form" that Plato seeks, asking what would be the character of the perfectly just individual and, conversely, the character of the totally unjust individual.

> These are types or models, as it were, so that whatever is discerned in them as happiness or the opposite would necessarily apply to us as we fashioned our lives after one or the other. *But our aim was not to demonstrate the possibility of the realization of these ideals.* (*Republic* 472C–D, italics added)

Practice must fall short of theory in approximating the ideal; for it is in the nature of things "that action partakes of exact truth less than speech" (473A). Plato's method assumes that principles exist, but that limiting conditions prevent the principles from producing the desired results. A thought-experiment is therefore required in which one thinks away the limiting conditions and replaces them with favorable ones. Plato is right to say that the picture emerging with this method is no daydream. It is an abstraction that can be fruitful even if it cannot be realized, for it helps us to think through the fundamental question of whether certain institutions are necessary, or merely institutions that have been with us for a long time and to which we have grown accustomed. It needs to be said, however, that although there is nothing inherently wrong with employing a method of abstraction—it is something we all do, whether consciously or not— Plato's application of the method went too far inasmuch as it thought away institutions such as the family, private property, and democracy, which are still with us today and which we regard as essential for the good life, for freedom, and for happiness. On the other hand, Plato employed his method to think into being institutions that are neither possible nor desirable.

His communism, as we have seen, is problematic throughout. His Ideal State is a three-class system in which the members of each are permitted to use only one part of their minds. It subjects the first two classes to an unbearably ascetic regime in which they are deprived of family and property, and turned into one large single "family" with wives and children in common—a preposterous construction. And the third class, although it retains family and property, is permitted no rational participation in government. And although Plato urges his rulers to guard against the development of extremes of wealth and poverty in the third class, he fails to explain how they are to guard against it in the absence of laws by which to regulate the economy. One seeks in vain for answers to other important questions as well: What advantage will members of the third class gain by submitting to the rule of the philosopher-guardians? If they will gain no advantage, what will induce them to submit? What will prevent the development in the third class of substantial social inequalities and the corresponding social conflicts? In the absence of laws regulating the economic life of the society, what is there to prevent the "dispersion" of interests—the unrelenting pursuit of self-interest by each of the specialized occupations, resulting in a Hobbesian war? And to repeat several questions raised earlier, if the third class sees no advantage in submitting passively to the rulers, will they not tend to rebel? And how would the rulers deal with rebellion? In the absence of a legal and judicial system, it would seem that force and the threat of force would loom large in Plato's scheme.

Social Systems

In the Eighth and Ninth Books of the *Republic*, Plato seeks to measure actual States by the extent to which they depart from his ideal. As he traces successive stages in the corruption of the ideal, Plato explicitly states that even his Ideal State is subject to change and, indeed, to the laws of dissolution, since everything that has come into being must also pass away (*Republic* 546A). Strictly speaking, however, Plato's conception of growth and change is cyclical and logical rather than historical. Neither he nor Aristotle had a genuinely historical approach to social change. As Plato studies the four successive corruptions of the Ideal State—timocracy, oligarchy, democracy, and tyranny—he follows the same logical procedure in each case, describing the origin and attributes of the corrupt form and then portraying the type of individual character to which it corresponds and from which it emerges. For Plato, it is the character of mind of individuals which forms the nature of States, and not the other way around.

Mind or soul being the criterion, Plato begins with the Ideal State in which the three elements of mind—reason, spirit, and appetite—are brought into a harmonious relationship through the hegemony of reason. Just beneath the Ideal State is one in which reason has lost its dominant position to spirit, which has now gained control. The next three forms of the State—oligarchy, democracy, and tyranny—are all based on the supremacy of appetite and the resulting discord in the elements of the soul.

Plato next proceeds to distinguish types of appetite—the necessary, which is beneficial, and the unnecessary, which is not—linking both to the different types of States. This yields the notion that both oligarchy and democracy rest on appetites conducive to production, although democracy represents, in addition, appetites lacking in thrift. In the Ninth Book of the *Republic* Plato goes on to make the distinction between natural and legitimate appetites and desires, and unnatural and illegitimate ones, anticipating Freud almost verbatim. Some of our desires can be adequately controlled by reason; but there are others which are stronger and more numerous, those that

> manifest themselves while we are asleep when the rational part of the soul slumbers but the beastly and savage part asserts itself, endeavoring to satisfy its own desires. In such cases there is no sense of guilt or shame, for it does not inhibit itself from trying, in our dreams, to lie with a mother or with anyone else—man, god or animal; nor does it shy away from bloodshed and other foul deeds. (*Republic* 571C–D)

We learn the nature of the "beastly and savage part" within us from our dreams, for

> there exists in all of us without exception a fierce and lawless bundle of desires which reveal themselves in our sleep. (572B)

And it is this lawless part of our nature that is embodied in tyranny.

The other factor Plato employs to explain the corruption of States is *excess* and what might be called the principle of "contradiction," anticipating Hegel and Marx:

> Usually, an excess engenders a reaction in the opposite direction; and this is especially true in States and societies. (563E–564A)

When an oligarchy, for instance, concentrates property and other forms of wealth in the hands of the few while the great mass of the populace suffers chronic impoverishment, the poor begin to recognize, affirm, and demand their rights as human beings. Soon a kind of "class consciousness" emerges and with it class warfare and revolution, which is easily touched off by the slightest impulse (*Republic* 556E). Thus oligarchy is transformed into democracy,

> a system in which the poor, gaining the upper hand, execute or expel the oligarchs while granting to the people an equal share in both citizenship and offices, which for the most part are assigned by lot. (*Republic* 557A)

The democratic city is full of liberty and freedom of speech, and individuals have license to do as they choose, to lead their own lives the way they please. Plato likens democracy to a "multicolored garment embroidered with a variety of fibers so that this multifarious society with every type of character would appear to be the best and the most beautiful" (557C). But democracy has a basic defect in that it tramples under foot Plato's ideals and allows individuals from any walk of life to participate in politics and to hold office (558B). Democracy, for Plato, merely appears to be a wonderful form of government and society; but actually it is unjust and anarchic, granting equality to equals and unequals alike, and consisting of a motley aggregate of versatile busybodies who honor politicians simply because they say they love the people (558C). Thus Plato gives us something like an economic interpretation of the structural changes which polities and societies undergo. Changes in the distribution of wealth tend to produce political changes. The State declines into inferior forms once the ideal communism of the Ideal State is disturbed. The timocracy introduces private property as a prerequisite for political office; and the oligarchy makes the accumulation of private property and wealth its sole object, which gives rise to a struggle for the redistribution of wealth, to revolution, and to democracy.

Plato's first and least corrupt form is a timocracy, from the Greek word *timé* meaning honor. In Greece it meant that power was given on the basis of a property qualification. Sparta appears to have been the model for Plato's conception of the timocratic State. It is a mixed structure of good and evil, but its most conspicuous feature is its "high-spiritedness," its contentiousness and covetousness of honor (548C). The timocratic man is harsh to his slaves (helots), gentle with fellow citizens, and submissive to officials. He loves political office and honor, basing his claim to them on his military prowess and exploits in war, and on his excellence in competitive athletics and hunting (549A). The soldier, in a word, has dethroned the philosopher.

In oligarchy—the second logical stage in the decline from the Ideal State—the military elite has been corrupted by the commercial motive. The appetite for wealth, which had already existed in the timocracy, becomes the dominant motive. Property and wealth are the sole qualifications for holding political office, so that the rich hold power and the poor are excluded (550C); and the rich put through laws claiming legitimacy for their power by force of arms and by the threat of force (551B). Such a city is not one but two,

> a city of the rich and a city of the poor, dwelling together, but always conspiring against one another. (*Republic* 551D)

And worst of all, such cities produce impoverished, dependent proletarians, beggars, thieves, purse-snatchers, temple robbers, and other artists in crime (552D).

The third stage of decline is democracy; and here we find that all of the features of democracy which Pericles lauded in his funeral oration (Thucydides II, 34–46), Plato views as evil. Plato and Socrates before him had somehow failed to see that it is precisely a democracy which can best combine individual initiative with a common social purpose; that differentiation and specialization of natural capacity, which Plato himself held to be a necessary condition of justice—nay, justice itself—can be most readily achieved in the State in which there exists the most freedom of opportunity to discover one's capacities and thus one's calling. What democracy meant in ancient Greece and still means today is government by the common mind and will of a free citizenry. For Plato, however, democracy is anarchism pure and simple. Liberty and equality, far from being Goods, Principles, or Self-Evident Truths, were rather the negation of principles, since they ignored the proper hierarchical basis of social order. Worse, democracy is in its very essence the negation of "justice" in Plato's sense, for it rests on the absolute rejection of the principle of specific function, which is shown most clearly in its refusal to choose its leaders from among the philosophers (intellectuals).

In the history of ancient Greece tyranny arose as a reaction to oligarchy, a rigid and oppressive aristocratic regime. The people, weary of poverty and oppression, gave themselves over to a strongman who seized power by force and maintained the allegiance of the people, at least temporarily, by improving their lot at the expense of the wealthy. In Plato's view, in contrast, it is democracy, with its excess of liberty, or more precisely its excessive thirst for liberty, that produces tyranny. Plato arrives at this position by arguing that when the people of a democratic city athirst for liberty get bad leaders who disappoint them, they accuse them of being oligarchs (*Republic* 562D). Plato thus represents Socrates as asserting that tyranny arose not in reaction to oligarchy or out of it, but out of democracy, where there is too much liberty, which is evidenced in the fact that male and female slaves are no less free than their masters. Disdainfully, Plato also mentions in this context the spirit of freedom and equal rights in the relations of men to women and women to men; and though it is almost certain that such a state of affairs never actually existed in Athens, Plato's disdain is strangely at odds with his own call for equality of the sexes in the ranks of the guardians. In a democratic city, Plato sardonically comments, even the dogs, horses, and asses exude the spirit of liberty, jostling anyone who does not readily step aside (*Republic* 563B–C).

In the *Republic* Plato's verdict on democracy is one of condemnation. In its prime it is a government of incompetent politicians who, at the expense of the well-to-do, rule in their own interest and only incidentally in the interest of the multitude. And in its decline, democracy prepares the way for tyranny, the most degraded type of State. In his later dialogues, the *Statesman* and the *Laws*, Plato's evaluation of democracy undergoes a change. In the *Statesman*, as we shall see, he distinguishes between two types of democracy, a law-abiding and a lawless type, and though he considers both types inferior to aristocracy (equivalent to timocracy in the *Republic*), he regards both as superior to oligarchy. In the *Republic*, however, Plato makes no such clear distinction, and he considers democracy inferior to oligarchy.

It is quite likely that Plato's conception of tyranny—the lowest and most degraded form of the State—was derived from his reflections on the history of Syracuse and the regime of Dionysius I. At first the tyrant is like the young lion-cub in Aeschylus' *Agamemnon*, smiling on the people's hand that feeds him for need of its support. When he has entrenched himself in power, he embarks on a policy of war, which makes his leadership necessary and distracts the people's attention from their troubles. Then when his old associates who helped him seize power begin to criticize his rule, the tyrant ruthlessly removes them from his path. This proves inadequate as criticism mounts, so he hires mercenaries to protect him; to maintain his power he not only confiscates the estates of the wealthy but also intensifies his oppression of the people, the very power that begat him

(*Republic* 564–569C). In this ahistorical way Plato tries to blame democracy for the rise of tyranny.

Rebuttal of Thrasymachus' Argument

It is Plato's assumption that the Ideal State is perfectly just and perfectly happy; therefore the citizens of such a State are perfectly just and perfectly happy. In fact, however, it is not easy to accept this assumption, since Plato himself only discusses the happiness of the *full* citizens who are the philosophers and the warriors; and he finds it difficult to prove that even they are as happy as they are just. He tries to prove their perfect happiness by arguing that the root of the matter is the happiness of the State as a whole, and that the rulers and "helpers" must be induced to make their specific contributions to the happiness of the whole (*Republic* 419–21C, 519E–520A). This, however, does not prove the identity of justice and happiness.

In another passage (465–466C), he again implies that happiness for the guardian consists less in his own happiness than in his contribution to the general happiness. But here, too, the guardian's justice does not necessarily bring him happiness. When Plato turns, however, to the opposite end of the scale, to tyranny and "the tyrannical man," his argument seems to be more convincing, based as it is on historical fact. The Greeks knew tyranny as the most hateful of States, and tyrants as the most miserable of men. Why is the tyrant miserable? Because in order to be protected he surrounds himself with base companions who hate him and covet his power. He therefore lives in fear and does not sleep well. The tyrant is the perfectly *unjust* man who, in the end, cuts the ground from under himself by alienating the people with his harsh rule. So, if the tyrant is the most unhappy of men, Plato apparently reasoned, then the perfectly just man at the other end of the scale must be perfectly happy; for he gives his best to the community and, on the principle of reciprocity, gains fellowship and community in return.

The central question of the *Republic* is whether the unjust individual, in the depth of his soul, is less happy than the just individual. The question and the answer are "this-worldly," though not perfectly so in the light of Socrates' belief in the immortality of the soul and some sort of judgment day awaiting it. An explicitly religious underpinning is given to the entire argument in Book Ten of the *Republic* where Socrates is represented as stating the conviction that no matter what personal troubles or suffering might befall the just individual, such misfortunes will finally prove to be good both in life and in death. For surely the gods will never turn their backs on an individual who has sought throughout his life to practice virtue (613A–B). In this respect, Plato, like the writers of ancient Israel, believes ultimately that righteousness must be based on religious faith. And as we shall see in our review of the *Laws*, Plato ends his final work proclaiming the certainty that the divine is just and that the entire universe is a scheme in its hands. Justice, therefore, means the fulfillment of the duty allotted us in the divine scheme. And the way of justice is happiness (*Laws* 903–905D).

Plato's National Ideal

In the course of outlining the structure of the Ideal State in the *Republic*, Plato turns his attention to foreign relations. As we remarked earlier, he calls for a policy of amity and perhaps even alliance among the Greek states in opposition to the "barbarians" (non-Greek peoples). He represents Socrates as decrying the disunity of Greece, the bitter wars of the city-states in which they devastate one another's lands and reduce Greek cities to slavery. Greeks should strive for friendly relations with other Greeks. They should refuse to own Greek slaves and they should urge others to follow the same rule. Thus Plato puts forth the proposition

> that the Hellenic peoples are akin and friendly, but enemies by nature to the barbarians. War is the fit term for this enmity. But when Greeks fight among themselves, they are nevertheless friends by nature. The fit term for this conflict is not war but faction. (*Republic* 470C–D)

Although he speaks of "right" in this connection, there is also an element of expediency in Plato's admonition. If the Greeks change their ways and begin to conduct themselves as he advises, they will be more likely to succeed against the barbarians. Plato's Ideal State, then, is strictly for Greeks, who will be, as previously stated, philhellenes, or lovers of Greeks. The Ideal State is a *national* ideal aiming for a condition in which Greeks may allow for some factionalism, but refuse even to think of factional disputes as a cause for war. They shall strive for reconciliation, resolving all quarrels peacefully. Greeks must strive to realize this pan-Hellenic ideal, "while treating barbarians as Greeks now treat Greeks" (*Republic* 471B). Plato thus makes a fundamental distinction between Greeks and all other peoples, and he draws from that distinction the moral that Greeks must not behave toward one another as they behave toward foreign peoples.

Plato's ideal in international relations is therefore the ideal of pan-

Hellenism. He has no principle of *universal* brotherhood, no universalist vision of the kind Isaiah had enunciated several centuries earlier. Plato never transcends the distinction still prevalent in his day between Greek and barbarian.

Notes

[1] Ernest Barker, *Greek Political Theory* (London: Methuen, 1979; first published in 1918), p. 199.

[2] Ibid., pp. 201–202.

[3] For an illuminating discussion of the ideological considerations that might account for this contradiction, see Joseph M. Bryant, "Enlightenment Psychology and Political Reaction in Plato's Social Philosophy," *History of Political Thought*, Vol. XI, No. 3, Autumn, 1990, pp. 1–19.

[4] See Antony Andrewes, *Greek Society*, (Harmandsworth, Middlesex: Pelican, 1979).

6

•••••••••••••••

The Statesman:
A Transitional Phase
in Plato's Thinking

The *Statesman* is a late dialogue, especially interesting for the light it throws on Plato's thinking in the period between the *Republic* and the *Laws*. As a transitional phase, the *Statesman* shows Plato somewhat less hostile to democracy and more realistic with regard to the need for law. The first two thirds of the dialogue tend to tax the reader's patience with page after page of classification and subclassification in order to reach a definition of what the Statesman is. The last third, however, reviews various forms of government and the role of law within them. The best government is still one guided by the Philosopher-Statesman for whom law is not only superfluous but an encumbrance. In these terms, a belief in *absolutism* is still firmly a part of Plato's thought. The true Statesman belongs to that kingly category of individuals who issue their own commands. He is the superior of the military commander, the magistrate, and all other officials, for it is he who ultimately decides if, when, and how the powers of the others will be exercised. That is because the Statesman's knowledge, like himself, is superior and kingly. The supreme function of the Statesman is to take charge of and sustain the society in question, assuming responsibility for all of its inhabitants and for everything that occurs within its boundaries. Plato compares him to an individual in charge of a whole herd of cows or a stud of horses (*Statesman* 261D).

Plato now introduces a myth in order to suggest how humanity has reached the present condition in which a philosopher-king has become indispensable. The first era was that of Cronus, when the gods ruled the world and the burden of its affairs did not fall upon human shoulders. This was a paradisiac condition in which

> there existed neither a political organization nor a family structure with the taking of wives and the begetting of children. For all human beings arose anew out of the earth and subsisted on the bountiful yield of the trees and bushes which required no cultivation, no human toil. In the evenly-blended and mild climate of this era, these proto-humans needed neither clothing nor shelter, for the luxuriant grass-cover of the earth was their bed and abode. (*Statesman* 271E–272A)

But this springtime on earth came to an end with the onset of the second era, the one in which we now live, when the divine shepherds withdrew from the helm. The earth now ceased to provide sustenance spontaneously and human beings had not yet learned how to gain it for themselves, since in the absence of necessity they had never been compelled to acquire the essential skills. It was in these critical circumstances that the gods graciously provided the indispensable gifts and instruction—fire by Prometheus, the secrets of the arts and crafts by Hephaestus, and the knowledge of seeds and plants by other deities. These gifts made it possible for humans to fend for themselves once the divine guardianship of humanity came to an end (*Statesman* 274C–D).

Plato's point in distinguishing the two eras is to argue that with the loss of the guidance of the divine shepherds, the human flock has been untended and unguided by divine wisdom. We are now dependent upon rulers who are human like ourselves, which makes it all the more imperative that we distinguish between rulers who control their human flocks by means of force and violence, and those who exercise a rule to which submission is voluntary. The myth implies that we now live after the "Fall," and that our institutions must be accommodated to a fallen humanity. This enables Plato to make the transition from his previous advocacy of the ideal communism and the rule of philosopher-kings—now apparently relegated to the era before the Fall—to a new phase of theory in which humanity must accept a *second-best* form of government.

But even this second-best form will require the stewardship of a true statesman who can rightly weave the web of State, bringing together the manifold human and social differences into a firm and enduring union.

Employing his favorite method of analogy but this time of weaving, Plato distinguishes the true weaver (that is, the true Statesman) from pretenders to his name and calling—mere politicians. The latter, not surprisingly, are the Sophists, the chief practitioners of a deceiver's craft who often practice their art with such cunning that many people are taken in and fail to distinguish these impersonators from the true Statesmen. If, however, we wish to see clearly the kind of king we are after, says Plato, it is essential that we expose these imposters and thrust them aside (*Statesman* 291C). Included among the so-called impostors are those who are elected by lot.

Plato then proceeds to examine a variety of political systems. Employing the criterion of number, three different systems suggest themselves according as the one, the few, or the many are in power. Adding three additional criteria—the presence of wealth or poverty, the presence or absence of law, and force or consent as the basis of the system—the first two systems may be subdivided as follows: monarchy yields either tyranny or law-based monarchy, while the rule of the few yields either oligarchy or aristocracy. After making these distinctions, however, Plato dismisses them as not of the essence; for none of those criteria should be regarded as *the* principle by which a good State is distinguished. And no individual should be regarded as the true Statesman just because he satisfies any of those criteria. Statesmanship is knowledge, and not just any knowledge but the ability "to apprehend the highest class of existents," namely, the Forms (*Statesman* 286B). Hence the only true form of government is that in which the ruler possesses such an ability:

> On this principle it is the individuals who possess the art of ruling and those only, whom we must regard as rulers, whatever political form their rule may take. It makes no difference whether they rule over willing or unwilling subjects, whether they rule with or without a code of laws, or whether the rulers are wealthy or poor. For that is the way it is with physicians. We do not assess the medical qualifications of a doctor by the degree of willingness on our part to submit to his knife or cautery or other painful treatments. Doctors are still doctors whether they work according to fixed prescriptions or without them and whether they are rich or poor. So long as they care for our health on the basis of sound knowledge, they may purge and reduce us or they may build us up, but they still remain doctors. The one essential condition is that they act for the good of our bodies to make them better instead of worse, and treat human ailments in all cases as healers acting to preserve life. We must insist that in this disinterested knowledgeable ability we see the distinguishing mark of true authority in medicine—and of true authority everywhere else as well. (*Statesman* 293B–C)

Characteristically, Plato can only tell us about this "highest class of existents" by means of analogy. What we have here, then, is the now familiar proposition that the only true State is that which is based on the knowledge of those supreme existents. No State can be called a true State unless it coheres as a solidary unit through the coordinating power of a statesmanship based on such knowledge, which, as we have come to expect, can be attained only by one individual or at most by a very few, but never by the "multitude."

Plato thus continues to cling so firmly to his philosopher-king that he dismisses law and the consent of the governed as principles of politics and as key elements of the good State. They are not only irrelevant and superfluous, but also indisputably detrimental. It is, again, his analogy with physicians, ship captains, and artists that leads him to that conclusion. The true Statesman concerns himself above all, or perhaps exclusively, with the preservation of the State. If rulers follow the principle of essential justice, then

> the most excellent political structure, indeed the only governing structure worthy of the name, must be one in which the rulers are not persons who make a show of political cleverness but persons who actually possess a true understanding of the art of government. On that sound principle we must not take into consideration whether they rule with or without laws, over willing or unwilling subjects, or whether they themselves are well off or poor. They may purge the city for its better health by putting some of the inhabitants to death and banishing others. They may reduce the citizen body by sending off colonies like bees swarming off from a hive, or they may bring people in from other cities and naturalize them so as to increase the number of citizens. So long as they do their work by following the principles of essential justice and so long as they act to preserve and improve the life of the State, we are obliged to call them true statesmen and say that the State they rule alone enjoys good government and possesses a true constitution. All other State structures are counterfeit, although those based on law do approximate the true form. (*Statesman* 293C–E)

Statesmanship, therefore, is an art or "science" vested in an absolute sovereign. It is the essence of every art that the artist works by himself, unencumbered by rules determining the methods of his work. The artist is free to create the best results with the materials with which he works according to his knowledge; hence the Statesman as artist should be free to do with his subjects as he sees fit. It is thus Plato's analogical method which leads him to the position that the Statesman has no need for either a code of laws or the consent of his subjects. Does a passenger have the right to give prior consent to the ship-pilot in order for him to practice his art? Does a patient have such a right with respect to the physician? Naturally Plato answers these questions with a resounding no. Both the passenger and the patient turn themselves over to the expert without any claim to a voice in the methods he uses to exercise his art. Plato assumes here, as he did earlier in the *Republic*, that every artist aims not for his own benefit, but for the benefit of the object of his art. If the pilot and physician know their business, they will necessarily do their best for their clients, who simply acquiesce.

It follows, for Plato, that the Statesman always knows what is best for his subjects. He may compel them to do things contrary to written laws and ancestral customs as long as he believes that his edicts are more "just, effective and noble." And how should the Statesman regard criticism or censure on the part of his subjects? He should disregard them, for it is no less than preposterous that the subjects who lack political knowledge and expertise should question the Statesman or regard it as an indignity or injustice when he compels them to obey (*Statesman* 296C–D). Plato's ruler always does what is really beneficial for his subjects and he is not only the final but the only arbiter of what is just. He is the captain of the ship-of-state and as such he fixes his attention on nothing but the true welfare of his passengers and crew. He lays down no written enactments nor is he guided by them, since his orders are a law in action, the practical application of his knowledge of statesmanship to the needs of the political voyage. For Plato

> rulers of this kind cannot possibly do wrong so long as they adhere to the one central principle that they must always administer justice impartially, preserve the lives of their subjects, and change their character for the better, insofar as human nature allows for it. (*Statesman* 297A–B)

However, the analogy of the ship's captain does not prove the point Plato is intent upon proving. The captain may be more interested in the good of the shipowners than the welfare of the passengers; nor does the analogy of the physician demonstrate that the patient's role is merely one of acquiescence rather than consent. Patients voluntarily entrust themselves to a doctor's care and may, therefore, accept or reject the doctor's advice or treatment. But Plato simply refuses to consider the ruler's authority as based on the consent of the governed. Although it is relatively clear, moreover, what the physician's expertise consists of, Plato never lets us know precisely and substantively what the Statesman's expert knowledge consists of. Insofar as it consists of something more than coordinating a specialized division of labor, it remains throughout an esoteric and mysterious quality.

In the *Republic* Plato had argued that when education has imparted a living knowledge, law becomes unnecessary, and a code of laws is therefore a sign that the subjects have failed to internalize the necessary knowledge. In the *Statesman* Plato's artist analogy takes him further: Law is evil because it hinders the creative application of the ruler's knowledge. A creative application is essential, Plato argues, in order to deal with the enormous variety of persons, cases, times, and situations that general laws can never take into account or provide for. The ruler's wisdom and creativity are therefore indispensable if the aim is to prescribe with perfect accuracy what is good and right for each and every member of the society at any given moment (*Statesman* 294A–B). From Plato's standpoint, law is an evil not only because it impedes the application of free intelligence by the ruler but also because it lays down general rules that either suit individual cases roughly or not at all. Law, in a word, precludes the very flexibility which true statesmanship requires.

By way of a rejoinder to Plato, one might argue that individuals living in any society must know in advance the rules by which they are to act, and by which they may expect other individuals to act. To this Plato would no doubt respond, "But such rules are best imparted through education and internalized by the individual members of society; and I have given such rules in the *Republic* and in my other writings." One can agree that education is an excellent and even the best way to impart such rules; but the truth is that although there is much talk in Plato's dialogues about the Good, the Just, and other high-altitude abstractions, there are precious few ethical guidelines with respect to human relations. There is, then, a basic question here: Should politics be wholly conceived as an art, as Plato conceives it, or should it be regarded as a matter of accumulated experience, concretized in a body of principles and law by which it is best to guide the Statesman's conduct? It is interesting to note that Plato's thinking at this stage is quite different from that of Aristotle, who rejects the grounds on which someone claims that he alone should govern and that everyone else should be governed by him:

> For surely even against those who claim to be sovereign over the government on account of virtue, and similarly against those who claim on account of wealth, the multitudes might be able to advance a just plea; for it is quite possible that at some time the multitude may be collectively better and richer than the few. (Aristotle *Politics* III.VII.12)

The "multitude" is, after all, the repository of accumulated experience and wisdom. And to the question of whether it is more advantageous to be ruled by the best person or the best laws, Aristotle replies by repudiating absolute monarchy and insisting, as a matter of principle, that government should be guided by law. It is Plato's argument that laws enunciate only general principles but do not provide directions for dealing with diverse and newly emerging circumstances. To compensate for this shortcoming of law, therefore, it is advantageous to be governed by a king, because a single ruler is better able to decide about particular cases. To this Aristotle replies:

> but on the other hand in matters which it is impossible for the law either to decide at all or to decide well, ought the one best man to govern or all the citizens? As it is, the citizens assembled hear lawsuits and deliberate and give judgments, but these judgments are all on particular cases. Now no doubt any one of them individually is inferior compared with the best man, but a state consists of a number of individuals, and just as a banquet to which many contribute dishes is finer than a single plain dinner, for this reason in many cases a crowd judges better than any single person. Also the multitude is more incorruptible—just as the larger stream of water is purer, so the mass of citizens is less corruptible than the few.... But the multitude must consist of the freemen, doing nothing apart from the law except about matters as to which the law must of necessity be deficient. And if this is not indeed easy to ensure in the case of many men, yet if there were a majority of good men and good citizens, would an individual make a more incorruptible ruler or rather those who though the majority in number yet are all good? The majority, is it not obvious? But it will be said that they will split up into factions, whereas with a single ruler this cannot happen. But against this must perhaps be set the fact that they are as virtuous in soul as the single ruler. If then the rule of the majority when these are all good men is to be considered an aristocracy, and that of the one man kingship, aristocracy would be preferable for the states to kingship. (*Politics* III.X. 5–7)

Aristotle's conception of "aristocracy" in this passage is not incompatible with democracy. For there is no reason to suppose that the majority consists of anything but good, honest, and decent individuals; just as there is no reason to assume that the majority of citizens somehow possesses less accumulated experience, wisdom, and knowledge than a single individual, however virtuous and knowledgeable that individual may be.

Plato's Weaver Analogy

In any society one will find a range of temperaments and personalities. In the *Statesman* Plato takes up the question of what that implies for the unity of the State; and in answering that question with his weaver analogy he finds another rationale for absolutism. In the Greek view of the artistic ideal, one strives for the "mean" or, in the language of music, for a "harmony" that blends two opposites. It is the function of every artist to create such a blend or harmony in the things with which one deals. Plato, defining the Statesman as an artist, applies this aesthetic doctrine to statesmanship. Like the weaver who unites in harmony the warp and the woof, the Statesman must unite the different types of human nature.

That human beings react to situations in one way or another according to their dispositions is quite evident. They encourage and engage in some forms of action as compatible with their own character, and they recoil from acts arising from opposite inclinations as being foreign to themselves. Thus individuals enter into conflict with one another over many issues. When such conflict arises over matters of great public importance, it becomes, says Plato, the most malevolent of plagues that can threaten the unity of a community. There are individuals who are known for their moderation and who are always inclined to support "peace and tranquillity." They prefer to keep to themselves and to mind their own business. In all their dealings with their fellow citizens they conduct themselves that way, and even in foreign-policy matters they want to preserve peace at any price with other States. What worried Plato was the indulgence of this passion for peace at the wrong times, as when such individuals were in a position to make or influence policy and not only opposed war themselves, but fostered the same attitude in young people. They thus place themselves at the mercy of an aggressor who swoops down upon them, with the result that in a short time they and their children and the entire society have lost their freedom and are reduced to slavery.

But then there is the opposite type of individual whose bent is toward strong action. It is such individuals who forever drag their cities into war, provoking powerful foes on all sides just because they love the military life excessively. The result is that they either lead their country into destruction or bring it into subjection just as surely as did the peace party. For Plato it was undeniable that where matters of high political importance are concerned, the two types of character are bound to become hostile to one another and so take up opposite party lines. Here, of course, the important point for Plato is not that the two types are a good against an evil, as it were, but rather a good against a good. Essential elements of goodness are at variance with one another, and they set at odds the individuals in whom they predominate (*Statesman* 308B).

No art, Plato's argument continues, deliberately chooses to create any of its products, even the least important of them, out of a combination of good and bad materials. On the contrary, every art strives as far as possible to reject bad materials and to use only what is good and serviceable. The materials may be similar or quite different, but they must be of sound quality so that the art may combine and fashion them into a structure proper to its specific function.

It then follows that, statesmanship being an art, it too would never choose deliberately to fashion the structure of a society out of a mixture of good and bad characters. The art of statesmanship requires real knowledge of the range of character in the society in question. Such knowledge is gained first by putting young children to the test in games. Later the young are placed in the hands of competent educators who would continue the task of character-testing and character-education. And, naturally, all this is done under the constant direction and supervision of the ruler-weaver. For although the artist-weaver turns over to the carder and others the materials he intends to use for the fabric, he supervises the work of others at every stage, retaining direction and oversight himself. He guides each of the auxiliary arts in preparing the strands for his own task of fashioning the web.

That is the way Plato sees the true Statesman dealing with those responsible for educating the young. In all circumstances he retains the power of direction for himself. The only form of education and training he will allow is the one in which the educator produces the type of character fitted for his own supreme function of weaving the web of State. He directs the educator to foster and encourage in the young only such activities as will meet the needs of his regime and no others. And should the character-testing reveal that some pupils simply will not learn the virtues but are rather inclined to godlessness, pride, and injustice, the ruler will deal with them accordingly. He will subject them to the severest public disgrace, and if that fails to change their evil ways, he will banish them or even put them to death. Others who prove incapable of overcoming their ignorance or who possess incorrigibly subservient natures will be made slaves to the rest of the community.

All the rest of the subjects—all those who have submitted to the royal weaving process and demonstrated nobility of character—the Statesman-Ruler will combine expertly into a harmonious unity. Those in whom strength and courage predominate will be the warp, as it were, which the leader will weave together with the gentle and moderate "wooflike" strands of the web. The ruler thus weaves and blends together the two groups of mutually opposed characters so as to serve the fundamental need of social harmony. This will be accomplished by uniting that element in their souls which is akin to the divine, for once that is done, the natural human ties follow more easily. Ultimately, says Plato, human knowledge of what is good, just, and profitable is of a supernatural origin. Thus only the true Statesman, through his divine inspiration, becomes the real lawgiver; only he possesses the kingly art and power of uniting the hearts of his subjects. Under the guidance of the wise king the vigorous and courageous characters will be blended with the gentle and moderate so that they all become willing members of a community based on justice.

If, however, it is through education that the souls of the vigorous and gentle will be harmonized, it is by means of definite institutions that social bonds will be forged. The Statesman will establish intermarriage between the two types so that the children of the mixed marriages will share the qualities of each type. Private marriage arrangements will be prohibited in order to prevent the inbreeding of types; for such inbreeding, after many generations, would perpetuate the prevalent situation in which the two types remain polarized. Thus intermarriage together with a moral education that inculcates common values and standards would be the means of forging social bonds. The "king-weaver" must never permit the gentle characters to be separated from the brave ones. He must therefore weave them into a tight, closely textured fabric by working common convictions into their minds.

Finally, when he has woven the web smooth, so to speak, he must ensure that the various offices of State will, in all cases, be shared between them. Whenever a single magistrate is needed, the king must select an individual with a balance of both characteristics and place him in authority. However, when several magistrates are needed, the Statesman will bring together representatives of each type to share the duties. No society can function well unless both types of character actively participate in public affairs. And, of course, the king-weaver alone must maintain control and supervision over the entire social fabric (Statesman 310A–311E).

Plato's suggestion that offices be filled on the principle of mixture has been interpreted by some scholars as a slight hint and anticipation of the mixed constitution that he explicitly advocates in his final work, the Laws. It is clear, however, that the mixing of types in the Statesman does nothing to reduce the absolutist nature of Plato's king-weaver.

If we compare the Statesman with the Republic, we find in the former no community of wives and no community of property. And although there is a eugenic element in the Statesman's advocacy of intermarriage between the two types, it is different from that found in the Republic. In both dialogues, social classes are based on the natural temperaments and gifts of individuals. But in the Statesman Plato speaks of courage and gentleness instead of spirit and appetite, the element of reason appearing only in the Statesman. As for the classes of the Statesman, they represent character types and not social occupations. "Justice," accordingly, in the sense of fulfilling a specific function, is not the ideal of the *Statesman*. What is emphasized there is a blending of different types in a harmonious unity rather than the specialization of different classes in their particular duties.

In the *Statesman* we find two detailed classification schemes of political structure. The first represents the theory current in Plato's day. Its criterion is number, as we have seen, which yields the three forms of rule—of the one, the few, and the many. With the added criteria of force or consent and the legal or nonlegal nature of government, the first two forms are further subdivided into two types (*Statesman* 291). There are, consequently, in this first scheme five political structures or forms of government: monarchy, tyranny, aristocracy, oligarchy, and democracy. The second scheme is Plato's own (*Statesman* 302C–303A), in which seven forms of government are distinguished. Adding a new form of monarchy—that of the Ideal Statesman who governs by perfect knowledge—Plato thus differentiates three forms of the rule of the *one*: Ideal Monarchy, legal monarchy, and tyranny. Democracy, of which there was only one type in the first scheme, is now subdivided by Plato into the two forms of legal democracy and extreme (arbitrary) democracy. What this seems to imply, then, is that Plato has arrived at a transitional phase in his theoretical reflections on politics, which will lead him to the new position he takes in the *Laws*. In the *Statesman* there are States based on law and there are States based on arbitrary rule. Those based on law are "second-best" in that they come closest to the State founded on the Perfect Knowledge of the true Statesman. Those States which are devoid of law fall doubly short of the Ideal State. This suggests a more realistic conception of politics on Plato's part and a new awareness of the virtue of the "second-best" system. Moreover, Plato's attitude has now changed somewhat toward democracy.

At first in the *Statesman* the doctrine of the "second best" seems not to apply to democracy, which is always "democracy" whether the masses control the wealthy by force or by consent and "whether or not it abides strictly by the laws" (292A). Later in the dialogue, however, Plato makes an argument enabling him to see some good in democracy. The rule of the many, he asserts, is the weakest in all respects. It is incapable of any real good or any serious evil as compared with the rule of the one and the rule of the few. Plato's reason is that sovereignty in a democracy is dispersed in small portions and vested in a large number of rulers. If therefore all three political structures are based on law, democracy is the worst of the three; but if all three are "lawless," democracy is the best. It is best to live in a democracy if and when all governments are unprincipled. But when they are principled and lawful, democracy is least desirable and monarchy, the first of the six types, is by far the best. But even here Plato urges us to remember that the real and true best is not this monarchy but the Ideal, Philosophic-Monarchy of the *Republic*, which, like a god among mortals, stands higher than all other governmental structures (*Statesman* 303A–B). In the *Laws*, however, we shall find Plato advocating a law-based union of monarchy and democracy as the form of government just a notch below the Ideal State itself.

7

• • • • • • • • • • • • • •

The Laws:
Plato's Last Thoughts

The *Laws* represents a new and final stage in Plato's theory of the State and the role of law in government. It was written during the last ten years of his life when he was over seventy years of age, and it was published posthumously soon after his death in 347 B.C. The need for such a work probably became evident to Plato as early as 361 B.C. when he was involved with Dionysius the Younger in Syracuse. Plato had arrived in Syracuse believing in the unfettered rule of a single intelligence specifically trained for the work of political rule. He looked forward to the opportunity of tutoring such an intelligence along the lines propounded in the *Republic*. At Syracuse he would demonstrate the value of philosophy and transform a young tyrant into a philosopher-king. Plato failed in this mission, however, and it was his failure that prompted him to modify the position he had held in the *Republic*.

In order to understand why Plato was forced to rethink his theory of government, we need to say a word about his experience in Syracuse. It was Dion, Plato's friend, who persuaded him to leave Athens and to make the journey in 366 B.C. Plato arrived in Syracuse and began his tutorial duties by introducing Dionysius the Younger to mathematical studies, which he, however, found tedious and irrelevant, desiring a faster road to political wisdom. Moreover, as soon as Plato arrived he found the entire court of Dionysius seething with cabals and malicious reports to the tyrant about Dion. Plato informs us in his *Seventh Letter* that he did his best to intervene in Dion's behalf, but to no avail; and within four months of Plato's arrival Dion was expelled dishonorably by the tyrant Dionysius. All of Dion's friends were in terror lest Dionysius should accuse some of them of complicity in Dion's alleged plot. The tyrant tried to ingratiate himself with Plato but continued to reject his instruction. For some time Plato remained in Syracuse, but seeing no prospect for success, he returned to Athens.

Although relations were strained between the tyrant Dionysius and the philosopher, there was no open breach between them. Dionysius had even promised to send for Plato again and to recall Dion from exile with the aim of setting Syracuse in order with their aid. Plato continued his correspondence with Dionysius, but five years elapsed before the philosopher's next visit to Syracuse. In the intervening years he continued to teach in the Academy and Dion remained in exile. Finally, in 361 B.C., Dionysius sent for Plato, but without recalling Dion, who nevertheless urged Plato to accept the Dionysius' invitation. Plato hesitated because Dionysius was not fulfilling his promise of five years earlier to recall Dion. But when his Pythagorean friend Archytas, who played a major role in the politics of Tarentum, wrote Plato urging him to go, Plato finally consented. Arriving in Syracuse, Plato again tried to persuade Dionysius of the importance of studying philosophy seriously, but he soon realized that Dionysius had no real motivation to subject himself to the hard work that this would entail. Evidently Plato's prodding in that regard was not designed to establish a good relationship with Dionysius, and soon a breach did in fact develop between the two men over Dion. Plato became, in effect, the tyrant's prisoner, and it was only through the intervention of Archytas, the philosopher-ruler of Tarentum, that Plato was released and allowed to return to Athens.

Plato never again returned to Syracuse, but he did continue for the next ten years to take an interest in the political affairs of the city. In 360 B.C., at the Olympic Games in the Peloponnesus, he met Dion who urged Plato to join him and others in an expedition against Dionysius—in revenge, as it were, for Dion's expulsion and exile. Plato refused to take any personal part, pleading that it would not be right to repay in such a manner the hospitality of Dionysius. Dion went ahead with the expedition, joined by some of Plato's friends and Plato's nephew, Speusippus, who later succeeded Plato as the head of the Academy upon Plato's death. The venture proved successful and Dionysius was expelled from Syracuse in

357 B.C. We learn from the Fourth *Letter* (320A), written to Dion after the success of the expedition, that Plato regarded Dion's victory with great satisfaction. With Dion, a friend and disciple of Plato's in control, Syracuse might become the model Philosophic State after all. But dissension arose once again. Plato wrote Dion (*Letter* IV, 320D) saying that all eyes were upon him and urging him to surpass Lycurgus and Cyrus where wise statesmanship is concerned. Having heard that Dion's and, hence, his own cause might be ruined by the rivalry between Dion and other contenders for leadership, Plato entreated Dion to act always "in the role of healer and it will turn out for the best."

Dion, however, failed to heal the rifts and was assassinated in 353 B.C. by Callippus, an Athenian who had once been a member of Plato's Academy. It was at this point that Plato wrote "to the Friends and Companions of Dion," at their request, the Seventh *Letter*, offering advice for the future political conduct of Syracusan affairs. The friends of Dion, he urged, must seek to institute the rule of law by empowering a 50-member commission to draft a legal code. This, Plato added, is not the ideal of the philosopher-king he had hoped to realize in Dion, but it is the best and most realistic option under the circumstances (*Letter* VII, 337B–D). A year or two later, in the same vein, he wrote again to Dion's friends, repeating the same advice and advocating above all the institution of the reign of law (*Letter* VIII, 355B–C) and a "mixed" constitution that might reconcile the different factional interests.

Thus we see the bearing of the Syracusan experience on the gradual transformation of Plato's theory. He began by advocating the supremacy of an enlightened monarch and ended by believing in the rule of law and the mixed constitution—that is, a constitution consisting of monarchical, aristocratic, and democratic elements. It is important to note, however, that Plato never altogether abandoned the ideal of the *Republic*; one hears many echoes of the philosopher-king ideal in the *Laws* (709E–712A). There neither is, nor can be, any better and more rapid way to establish a constitution than by means of a "young, temperate, quick-to-learn, retentive, bold, and high-souled autocrat" (709E–710C). And in another well-known passage (739B–E), Plato returns to the principle of communism by affirming that the first-best society is based on a community in women, in children, and in all possessions whatsoever, so that everything meant by the word "ownership" will be eliminated from social life. Later, he underscores that his ideal scheme, as he styled it, will never be realized as long as there exist personal wives and children, and private houses and property. What Plato therefore abandoned in the *Laws* was not the ideal but the hope of its realization. His aim was to outline the "second-best" governmental structure based on the rule of law; and if that could be secured, he believed, the practicable best will have been achieved (807B).

The reason why we must be willing to settle for "second best," Plato explains, has to do with human nature. Human beings must either provide themselves with a law by which to regulate their lives, or live no better than the wildest of beasts. For there is no individual whose nature is such that he or she will both discern what is good for humans as a community and be willing and able to put the good into practice. It is difficult, in the first place, to recognize that a true political wisdom must be concerned with the community, not with the individual, and that common interests tend to unify a society just as private interests undermine solidarity. It is difficult, in a word, to see that it is to the advantage of both the community and the individual that public well-being be considered before private well-being. But even if someone placed in a position of autocratic sovereignty were to recognize this principle, that person would never prove loyal to it, would not promote the common good as the paramount mission. This is the frailty of human nature, which will always tempt such an individual to self-aggrandizement and to the disregard of what is right and good for society. And it is precisely such egoistic self-seeking that, ultimately, will bring the leader and the society to ruin. If ever, by divine grace, an individual were born with both the capacity to recognize the cardinal principle of justice and the altruistic nature required to implement it, that person would need no laws by which to govern. Law has no right to be sovereign over true knowledge, whose place it is to be ruler of all. But, as things are, given the human material we have to work with, "we have to choose the second best, ordinance and law." (*Laws*, 875)

This, then, is the new theoretical position to which Plato has arrived: A society can be governed by philosophy only *indirectly*, through a general and impersonal code of law. This is the *second-best* form of the State, the constitution of which is a proper combination of the different social elements—monarch and people, rich and poor—which invariably contend for political power in actual States. This type of State, based on law and a mixed constitution, becomes the dominant political idea of Plato's final work. The transformation is a fundamental one, taking him from the Perfect Guardian (*phylanx*) of the *Republic*, unrestrained by law, to the Guardian of the Law (*nomophylanx*), who is the servant and even the "slave" of the law. Thus we see the path of Plato's intellectual development from the *Republic* to the transitional phase of the *Statesman* and ending, finally, with the *Laws*. And there can be little doubt that it was the course of Syracusan political history that profoundly influenced Plato's thinking in this regard. His experience with Dionysius the Younger drove the absolute ideal into the background; and the failure of Dion and Plato's other friends after the fall of Dionysius brought the "second-best" idea into the foreground.

The Central Principle of the Laws

As the Athenian (Plato) remarks in one of his exchanges with Clinias, the objective we are keeping in view in our present investigation into legislation "is the moral worth of a social system" (*Laws* 707D). However, the criterion of "moral worth" as stated in the *Laws* is quite different from that of the *Republic* where, we recall, justice means the *differentiation* of function, a differentiation so rigid that the rulers lose basic social rights while the producers lose all political rights. The guardians are allowed no family or property, but possess a total monopoly of government. The producers, in contrast, live in families and possess property, but have no say of any kind over the government. Alongside justice in the *Republic* is the companion virtue of temperance, or self-control, which means the submission of appetite to the rule of reason. In political terms this translates to mean the willing submission of the producing classes, representing appetite, to the governing class, representing reason. The submission of the appetitive to the rational function was supposed to produce harmony in society just as it does in the soul of an individual. If the *Republic* thus stresses differentiation as the basis of social unity, we get a different emphasis in the *Laws*: The various "functions" (interest groups and classes) must be properly balanced in order to produce a harmonious union of them. In the *Laws* self-control emerges as the cardinal principle and precondition of social harmony. Plato remarks admiringly that the Lacedaemonians (Spartans) assign no special distinction to rich or poor, to the plain citizen or to the prince of the royal house. Such social differences being inescapable, it is imperative that all members of society internalize the virtue of self-control, so as to be ruled by it. It is the duty of a society, if it wishes to ensure its harmony and the felicity of its members, to award honor and dishonor in the right way. "And the right way," says Plato,

> is to award the highest honours to excellence in the fulfillment of the virtues of the soul—temperance being a *sine qua non*—the second-highest honours to excellence of the body, and the lowest level of social honour to the acquisition of material goods and wealth. Should any legislator violate this principle by elevating wealth or demoting the virtues of the soul, his action will constitute an offense against both the deities and statesmanship. (*Laws* 697 B–C)

It is only by inculcating the highest virtue of self-control in all members of society that there can be any hope for social harmony *and* individual freedom. Why? Because an individual is a free agent only when he or she is capable of choosing rationally, under the influence of self-control. For we are never less free than when we lose control of our appetites and fall subject to their rule. It follows that the legislator who designs laws to produce in society the highest degree of self-control will achieve three aims in one: The society will have freedom, amity with itself, and understanding (*Laws* 701D). Plato's point is that self-control is essential in all members of society if the legislator is to have any hope of balancing the interests of the various social groups so as to create harmony among them. A society cannot be at once free, healthy, and at peace with itself if it allows the establishment of overpowerful or unmixed sovereignties (693B). Reflecting on the actual range of social systems that lack the desired balance of social forces, Plato rejects what he regards as evil extremes: the Persian system based on an "excess of servitude and autocracy," which reduces the people to utter subjection; and the Athenian system, which "encourages the multitude toward unbridled liberty" (*Laws* 698A, 699E).

The society consisting of balanced social forces will be different from the one Plato envisioned in the *Republic*. The virtue of self-control postulates no absolute and rigid division of labor. In contrast to the *Republic*, both the rulers and the ruled of the *Laws* have social and political rights. The ruler, no philosopher-king, has family and property; and those ruled have a say and a vote in the election of their rulers. The State as conceived in the *Laws* thus loses the unity which Plato envisioned in the cooperation of different elements, each contributing its special and complementary function to the life of the whole; but it gains, by virtue of self-control, a harmony that springs from the proper and legal regulation of the different elements—a regulation that prevents the different elements from pursuing their respective interests so unrelentingly that their relations degenerate into a Hobbesian "war of each against all." For in the absence of legally constituted authority and the corresponding regulation of the various social groups, the

> spectacle of the Titanic nature of which our old legends speak is re-enacted; human beings return to the old condition of a hell of unending misery. (*Laws* 701C)

War and Peace

In the *Republic*, composed in the era of the Spartan Empire, Plato's communism and his advocacy of the military training of youth by the State was largely inspired by the Spartan system. War, in the *Republic*, is a taken-for-granted, permanent attribute of the human condition. Even children should be conducted to war on horseback to be spectators; and wherever it is safe, they must be brought "to the front to give them a taste of blood as we do with whelps" (*Republic* 587A, 467E). Moreover, in the *Republic* Plato adopts a rather tolerant attitude toward the Spartan system of military training, which segregated young men and herded them together in a camp life that fostered homosexuality.

In the *Laws*, composed in the era of Sparta's decline, the principle that a State must be based on the highest virtue of self-control leads Plato to a different position on war and military life. A State that excessively accentuates the virtue of courage and makes war its chief aim cannot be good. This is a point which the Athenian (Plato), conversing as he is with a Spartan and a Cretan, makes against the military states of Sparta and Crete. The Cretan, explaining the purpose of the system of common meals and physical training, argues that all such arrangements have been made with a military purpose and that it is warfare which the lawgiver kept in mind in all of his ordinances. In fact, the lawgiver regarded the "peace" of which most people speak as no more than a fiction; for in reality the normal attitude of one city to all others is one of undeclared warfare and an unceasing disposition to war. The Cretan legislator has therefore designed all institutions, public and private, with a view to war, and has transmitted his laws for observance in precisely that spirit. That is not all. The unceasing disposition to war, both the Cretan and the Spartan agree, applies not only to the relation of cities but also to villages, households, and even to individuals. "Humanity," says the Cretan,

> is a condition of public war of every man against every man, and private war of each man with himself. (*Laws* 626D)

Furthermore, the Cretan continues, self-mastery is honorable just as defeat by self is discreditable and most ruinous. Does the principle of self-mastery apply to cities, the Athenian asks? Most definitely, the Cretan replies.

> Any city in which the better-off elements are victorious over the masses and the lower classes may properly be said to be master of itself and be rightly congratulated on the victory. (*Laws* 627A)

But, the Athenian objects, is it not true that in such a city there is always the threat of internal warfare between the classes and the political factions? And does it not therefore follow that such a city can never be truly mistress of herself? And is this not the kind of war that every individual would desire never to see in his own city, or if it breaks out, to see it brought to an end at once? It seems inescapable, then—the Athenian continues—that the best legislator is the one who can take in hand a city divided against itself, reconcile its citizens by his ordinances without the loss of a single life, and keep people on permanently amicable terms. And he concludes that the best condition is neither war nor faction—they are things we should pray to be spared from—but peace and amicability. And thus the so-called victory of a city over itself is not so much a good as a necessary evil. For the Cretan's view is tantamount to saying that a diseased body, subjected to and in need of constant treatment, is as good as a healthy one that has never been in need of such treatment. If then we take a parallel approach to the happiness of a city, it is evident that its internal health can never be adequately ensured as long as the legislator's principal concern is the preparation for war. One cannot be a true statesman unless one prepares for war solely as a means to peace (*Laws* 628C–D).

In the *Laws* there is a corresponding change of attitude toward the Spartan and Cretan practices associated with the institutions of physical exercises and common meals in the camp life of the warriors. The Athenian (Plato) charges their two cities with having corrupted sexual relations and reminds his listeners that sexual pleasures have been granted by nature to male and female for the purpose of procreation. Sexual intercourse between male and male or between female and female is an offense against nature and a submission to the lust for pleasure (*Laws* 636B–C; cf. 836). In the matter of sexual relations it is nature that must be the good legislator's guide.

In the *Laws* it is clear that Plato's attitude toward war and certain aspects of military life is more critical than it was in the *Republic*. Expressing, perhaps, a prevalent mood of war-weariness, Plato admonishes the Spartan and Cretan citizens of war-states to recognize that there is neither any real amusement nor solace in war, and that it is only in peace that the truly worthwhile things can be accomplished (*Laws* 803D). But there is no vision of Isaiah here in which war will totally disappear from the human condition. Plato's critique is directed not against war itself, but against offensive warfare and against the war-state—the State that fosters a policy of war and lives by war. He therefore provides adequately for the defense of his State and its central city.

A properly defended city is one that blocks a potential enemy's path by means of ditches, entrenchments, and fortifications of various kinds. Plato's aim is to keep a foe well outside the city's borders, so he opposes the construction of walls. A wall invites the inhabitants of the surrounding countryside to seek shelter within it and to leave the enemy unrepulsed. The crowding, moreover, breeds disease and a certain softness of the soul which tempts the townsmen to neglect the nightly and daily vigilance so necessary for an adequate defense. They imagine, somehow, that their safety lies in locking themselves behind the ramparts (*Laws* 778E–779A). In addition, Plato demands a national service in which all citizens—men, women, and even children—will, in times of peace, train themselves for war. A wise State must be under arms at least one day in each month, hardening the minds and bodies of its trainees with rigorous athletic competitions and the simulation of actual warfare. Finally, in the opening chapter of the last book of the *Laws* Plato lays down stringent rules for military discipline, enacting severe penalties for those found guilty of cowardice on the battlefield, and a crown of wild olives for those who have demonstrated valor.

Property and Wealth

Throughout the *Laws* it is Plato's guiding principle that the good society is based on a blend of different social elements. Marriage must be a union of different character traits and social classes. And, above all, an individual "should seek the liaison that is for the city's good, not merely one which strikes his own fancy" (773A–B). Property must be a combination of private ownership and public control (740A); and the rich must voluntarily

> share their privileges in a generous spirit with the distressed poor by a remission of debts and a redistribution of estates. (*Laws* 736D–E)

Returning to his weaver-metaphor, Plato maintains that the woof and the warp cannot be fashioned from the same kind of threads: A good legislator must reconcile economic interests and blend social differences (*Laws* 734E–735A). The property system and social structure of the *Laws* therefore marks a definite departure from the communistic ideal of the *Republic*. In the *Laws* Plato distinguishes three types of sociopolitical structure. The best is still the ideal of the *Republic* in which private property is altogether banished from the life of the ruling classes and which is reflected in the old Greek saying that "friends' property is indeed common property." The second-best is the one being constructed in the *Laws*: The "State we have set about to build, if only it could be brought into being, would be in its way the nearest to immortal perfection" (739E). Though it falls short of the best, still, if we can secure the second-best conditions, "we shall indeed succeed well enough" (807B–C). In this second-best State land and houses will be allotted as private property; there will be no common ownership or tilling of the soil, for that would be beyond the ability of individuals educated under the prevailing system (740A). And yet, although each citizen is to receive his own personal plot in the original distribution, and although he receives it as private property, it is considered, in a sense, the common property of the entire society. For Plato the right of property must be recognized as a social right to be used for the benefit of society. Private property is no absolute right entitling individuals to do with it as they please. And there is an echo of the *Republic* here inasmuch as the produce of the land must support a system of common dining halls so that consumption will be public and common.

The ideal population of Plato's second-best State is, curiously, 5,040 citizens who will receive in the original distribution 5,040 lots of equal size. The population must remain stationary to ensure always that there will be one lot for each citizen. If a citizen has no child to whom to bequeath the lot, he must adopt as his heir another citizen's son. Should there be a tendency to exceed the prescribed population size, births must be controlled or a colony founded. And should the opposite tendency become evident, rewards must be given to the married, and penalties imposed on the celibate. The equality of lots, which Plato is eager to preserve, is combined in his scheme with inequality of personal possessions. It would have been most desirable that all settlers in his sub-ideal colony should have entered with equal means of every kind. But this being impossible (744B), Plato allows every citizen to acquire personal possessions up to the value of four times the value of his lot (744E). The scale of wealth will therefore range from one lot with the minimum of personal belongings to one lot plus four times its value. The result is a system of four classes determined by property qualifications on which Plato eventually bases the franchise and the exercise of citizenship. Although there are classes in this scheme, Plato believes that it will prevent the twin evils of opulence and penury, which inevitably breed faction and conflict, the most fatal of disorders. So intent is Plato on forestalling the extremes of wealth and poverty that he requires the registration of all personal property; and should an individual happen somehow to acquire more wealth than allowed, "he must consign the surplus to the State and the religious institutions if he wishes to retain his good name and avoid legal proceedings against him" (*Laws* 745A).

In one important respect Plato retains the principle enunciated in his earlier works, that politics is a specialized vocation in its own right and therefore the responsibility of a citizen. It followed that no citizen is to practice a craft inasmuch as citizenship itself is a craft and a calling requiring careful study. It makes full demands on an individual's time and attention if he wishes to contribute effectively to the preservation of social order, a matter that should never take second place to anything else (846D). Having thus defined citizenship itself as a calling and having prohibited to citizens the practice of an additional craft, Plato goes on to prohibit any resident alien from being, say, a smith and a carpenter at the same time. In keeping with the central principle of the *Republic*, Plato insists that each artisan must have only a single craft, and must earn his living by that trade and no other (847A). Plato also leaves little room for what he regards as an ignoble method of money-making such as buying and selling. No citizen may possess gold or silver; and though a currency will exist for the purpose of exchange and the payment of wages to slaves or alien settlers, it will be an internal currency only, of value at home but worthless abroad

(742A). In this way, by excluding the citizen from crafts and commerce, and by forbidding the possession of precious metals and the taking of interest, Plato hopes to keep the citizenry free from the temptation of making the accumulation of wealth its life's aim. Given these proscriptions, the citizen will be free to pursue the excellence of body and mind, to which extreme wealth is the worst enemy. "To be at once very rich and good is impossible," says Plato. "The immensely rich are not good individuals...and if they are not good, neither are they happy" (*Laws* 742E–743C). And in social relations riches breed dissension, which undermines the solidarity of a community.

Anticipating the Physiocrats, Plato demands that his sub-ideal society base itself exclusively on agriculture, and even agriculture is to be pursued no further than the needs of body and mind require. In such a society, based on a "natural economy," the work of the legislator will be less than half of what it is elsewhere; for he will legislate only for farmers and shepherds and bee-keepers and be free from the need of dealing with shipping, commerce, trade, loans, interest, and a thousand other such matters (842C). The citizens too, in Plato's sub-ideal State, are as fortunate as the legislators. Indeed, they are a privileged class since every citizen has his lot tilled by serfs who, as tenants, pay a part of the produce as rent.

The serfs of Plato's imaginary colony in the *Laws* are like the helots of Sparta and not, strictly speaking, the personal chattels of the citizens. There are neither industrial slaves nor public slaves in the service of the colony, as there were in Athens. In his discussion of the "slaves" who till the land of the citizens, Plato reflects on the repeated risings of the servile population of Messenia under Spartan domination. To prevent such evils and to maximize the probability that the slaves will submit to their condition quietly, Plato proposes that in order to preclude unity among them they should be neither of one stock nor of one dialect; and that they should be treated properly and with consideration, not only for their own sake but still more for the sake of the masters. Proper treatment means that one should abjure the use of violence against a servant, and refuse to wrong a servant just as one would an equal. Plato then introduces a general ethical principle that has much in common with the teachings of the Hebrew prophets of social justice: It is the dealings with those whom one can easily wrong, writes Plato,

> which reveal an individual's genuine and unaffected respect for right and abhorrence of wrong. The individual, therefore, whose character and conduct are unsoiled with meanness and evil in his relations with slaves is, beyond all others, sowing the seed for a harvest of goodness; and the same may be truthfully said about a master, autocrat or wielder of power of any kind *in his relations with a weaker party*. (*Laws* 777D–E, italics added)

At the same time it is proper that masters should punish slaves when they deserve it, and not spoil them by such mere admonition as one would use toward free individuals. Neither should one become too familiar with servants of either sex (*Laws* 778A).

If one takes the necessity of slavery for granted, as did the ancient Greeks, then Plato's rules for the treatment of slaves are compassionate and sensible. But Plato never transcends the common Greek view of slavery. He links the slave with the child where the role of punishment in education is concerned, implying that the minds of both are similar in their incomplete development (937A). And in his criminal code Plato exhibits a certain inconsistency in his provisions for the punishment of slaves and citizens who have committed criminal offenses. Sometimes he stipulates harsher punishment for the slave: If a citizen takes another's grapes, figs, or other plants without the owner's consent, he shall be fined; if a slave does the same, "he shall receive a lash for every grape of each cluster taken, or every fig taken from the tree" (*Laws* 845A; cf. 872B). But in other instances Plato provides for less harsh punishment: If a slave or alien is caught committing a sacrilegious act, he shall be branded on hands and forehead, scourged and cast out naked beyond the borders. If, however, a citizen is taken in sacrilege, his sentence shall be death (*Laws* 845E; cf. 941D–E). But whether punishments are more or less harsh, it is Plato's assumption throughout that the slave is a different and lower form of human being. This assumption is especially evident in the laws provided for homicide (865–874), of which the following passage is representative:

> The man who slays a slave in the heat of passion shall, if the slave is his own, ritually cleanse himself, and if another man's, pay the owner twice what he has lost....If a slave slays his owner in passion, the kinsmen of the deceased shall deal with the slayer as they please and be clean of guilt, but in no case shall they spare his life. If a free man is killed in passion by a slave not his own, he shall be delivered by his owner to the kinsmen of the deceased, who shall be obliged to put the slayer to death, in a manner of their own choosing. (*Laws* 868A–C)

Plato's construction of his "second-best" State is, as he himself admits more than once, wholly imaginary. As such it is more in the nature of an unrealizable dream than a theoretical plan for a realizable state. For it is most improbable that human beings would tolerate permanently fixed limits on the amount of their property and the size of their families. It is equally unlikely that they would consent to being deprived of gold and silver or having their lots divided into town and country halves (*Laws* 745E–746A). Plato acknowledges the weight of such objections but nevertheless defends his method by arguing that a theoretical plan must first be presented as a perfectly consistent whole. Then if one finds it impossible to put some point of the perfect plan into practice, he can at least strive to approximate what ought to be done and what is most akin in character to the perfect model (746C). So even Plato's "second best" is an ideal that he had no more hope of realizing than his highest ideal in the *Republic*.

Most of Plato's concessions to reality are made in his sketch of the economic life of his sub-ideal society. Although industry and commerce are prohibited to citizens, those indispensable functions are fulfilled by turning them over to the resident aliens. What we find, then, in the *Laws* is a three-class system: (1) the citizens who devote themselves exclusively to the art of politics and the pursuit of excellence in body and mind; (2) the slave or serf who tills the land of the citizen; and (3) the resident alien who attends to commerce and industry. This three-class system is, of course, different from that of the *Republic*, but a central principle of the earlier work still animates the later one, namely that each individual should discharge a single, specific function. It is this principle which accounts for the rule that the citizen shall practice no art or craft other than citizenship; and it is the same principle which accounts for the rule that no alien shall practice more than a single art. So notwithstanding his objections to the commercial state, Plato makes room for foreign commerce and for free trade by assigning them to aliens (*Laws* 847B–C). In these terms, the State as outlined in the *Laws* is no closed society, since it allows the free entry of aliens: "Any foreigner who wishes may become a resident in the country...but he must have a craft" (850A–B).

Finally, we should note that in the State everyone must work and there shall be no begging. The true object of pity, Plato observes, is the virtuous individual who is the victim of misfortunes. The State will therefore do its utmost to assist such individuals. If, however, individuals should attempt to make their living through begging, they will be expelled from the city in accordance with the State's statutes (*Laws* 936B–C).

Marriage and the Family

On the position of women and the institution of marriage, the *Laws* has much in common with the *Republic*. It is the right and duty of women, Plato insists, to take their place alongside men in the general life of the State. In the *Laws* as in the *Republic* women are entitled to the same education as men and are free to follow the same pursuits. On the other hand, the community of wives and children of the *Republic* is left behind, although women are still drawn into public life through the system of common meals, and marriage continues to be controlled by the State in the public interest. Plato accepted the authenticity of the stories told about the societies around the Black Sea in which women, as a matter of course, learned horsemanship and skills with bows and other weapons. It is pure folly, he argues, and an egregious oversight on the part of legislators that they have failed to institute a similar practice in Greek societies, thereby losing the services of half their members (*Laws* 805A–B).

In contrast to the Sarmatian women of the Black Sea, Plato reminds his listeners, the Thracian women are little more than slaves, tilling the fields, caring for the flocks and herds, and performing menial tasks. Athenian women are confined to the home and the superintendence of the spinning and wool work. Spartan women, it is true, take their share of physical training and music in girlhood, but when they have grown up, though they have no wool work to occupy them, they are expected to devote themselves to childbearing, but take no share in the business of war. What a waste of human resources! A good legislator, therefore, must not confine himself to ordinances for the male sex, leaving the other sex to her traditional pursuits and thereby creating a society with a mere half of its potential (*Laws* 805C).

In the State contained in the *Laws* women must receive the same training as men, in a single system of universal, compulsory education. All females are to be trained in gymnastics, girls and young women sharing in the contests and sports of boys and young men. Adult women prior to marriage must participate in the athletic competitions of adult men; women must be trained for actual combat and, when necessary, fight like men (*Laws* 833–834). This is intended as a wise practical policy, for it would be very sad indeed, Plato remarks, if in the presence of a foreign invader the women could not contribute militarily to the city's defense and to the repulsion of the menace (814A–B). On the other hand, Plato, in the *Laws*, fails to assign to women any political role such as voting in the Assembly or holding office. He has dropped the proposal for Women Guardians of the *Republic*.

Marriage in the *Laws* is entirely controlled by the State. Plato provides for special sports and dancing occasions during which young men and women will have the opportunity of seeing and being seen in undress. And before marriage the background and medical history of the contracting partners should be known to ensure that they are a suitable match for the common procreation of children (*Laws* 771E–772D). Once married, it is the duty of the husband and wife to breed children for the service of the State.

Concerned as he is with keeping the population of the State stable, but more concerned with a falling than a rising birthrate, Plato proposes that if a man has passed the age of thirty-five unwed, he should be heavily fined each year of his continuing bachelorhood, and awarded no part whatsoever in the public honors (721D). There is not only a political but a religio-moral reason for this ordinance. Humankind naturally partakes of immortality through procreation, from which it follows that piety strictly forbids a man to deny himself the benefits and blessings of his own act (721C–D). Men have the duty to remain sound in body and sober in mind throughout their lives; for a man who drinks to excess is an awkward and bungling sower of seed who commonly begets pitiful creatures with bodies as twisted as their souls. In general but especially when he is procreating, a man should not only shun hard drinking but any action at all which might jeopardize his health or that of his offspring (775C–E). The virtues of chastity, loyalty, and heterosexuality are underscored at length: Sexual intercourse must be restricted to its natural and procreative function, and the law should be strictly enforced against adultery, against sexual intercourse with concubines, and against unnatural sexual relations between males (841D). As for the young married couple, they should embark on a life of their own. Plato advocates that the young pair should leave their respective parents' abodes and form new households (776A–B). If, however, a husband and wife should become utterly estranged by their unhappy marriage, Plato allows divorce if the guardians of the law and the women in charge of wedlock fail to bring about a reconciliation (*Laws* 929E–930A).

Government in the Laws

The central principle of Plato's final work is the sovereignty of the law: Governments must accommodate themselves to law, and not law to governments. In the *Laws* we find two distinct methods by which a constitution might be established for Plato's new and imaginary colony. The first method proposes the collaboration of a wise legislator with a young autocrat or tyrant of retentive memory, who is quick to learn, temperamentally bold and high-spirited, and possessed of the virtue of self-control (temperance) (*Laws* 709E). Plato assures his listeners that "there neither is, nor can be, any better or more rapid way to the establishment of the constitution" (710B). What prompts this view, evidently, is that prescribing laws is not as difficult as impressing them upon the people and ensuring that the laws be obeyed. Plato's solution is the "young tyrant" who will set an example which, by virtue of his strong personality, the people will be ready to follow. But also, of course, by virtue of his ability to realize his will through the use of actual force if necessary. This is the old ideal of the *Republic*, but with significant modifications. Instead of philosopher-kings who rule permanently, there is a single philosopher (legislator) collaborating with a tyrant who rules temporarily during the birth of the colony. But even as Plato advances this proposal, he reminds

Clinias that it is only a second-best condition, since the best is that in which supreme power is vested in *one* individual who combines in himself the virtues of wisdom and temperance (712A). It is strange that Plato, after the experience with Dionysius, and at a time when he was in touch with Dion and his friends who had overthrown and expelled the tyrant, could still think of tyranny in favorable terms. Plato simply cannot abandon the thesis of the *Republic*. More than once in the *Laws* he speaks of a legislator who is also himself a tyrant, as more powerful and, therefore, more desirable than one who is not (735D).

There is, however, another, quite different method of establishing a constitution which Plato presents at the beginning of Book VI of the *Laws*, where a tyrant figures not at all and where it is the founders of the colony themselves who cooperate with the legislator in the organization of the State. In these passages Plato is concerned with the question of how to fill the various political offices, in circumstances in which the colonists have but recently come together and are unfamiliar with one another (*Laws* 751). The founders, therefore, who are a select minority of the colonists, will choose from among themselves the majority of the guardians of the law who will serve for twenty years. They must also co-opt 100 of the newly arrived colonists, selecting the most mature and able men, and another 100 from their own ranks. The latter will carry the main responsibility in the new State for the selection of magistrates who will undergo proper training before assuming their duties. When this temporary business has been completed, the founders will have done their work "and the new State should be left to carry on by itself and to prosper by its own efforts" (754D).

The following details are important, as we shall see, for they bring to light Plato's bias. Once the colony is settled and has entered its routine, the electoral authority joins the Assembly, which elects the Council and the various magistrates. The Assembly consists of the entire body of 5,040 citizens who are arranged in four classes according to the amount of property they possess. *Attendance at the Assembly's meetings is mandatory for the two highest property classes and optional for the third and fourth classes* (764A). Only those citizens, however, in any class may attend who bear arms in the cavalry or infantry and have gone through military service (753B). The Assembly's major functions are the election of the guardians of the law, military officers, and some local officials. There are 37 guardians of the law who are to be elected in a three-stage ballot: Some 300 candidates are to be eliminated in the first vote and 200 eliminated in the second. Thirty-seven are then selected in the third vote from the 100 candidates who remain (753). The class system comes more directly into play in the election of the Council, which is to consist of 360 members, elected annually, 90 of which are to come from each class. Candidates for the

Council are chosen by public vote but are selected differently from the various classes. The candidates of the first and second classes are to be selected by the citizens of every class, but voting is compulsory for the upper two classes and optional for the lower two. The candidates of the third class are to be selected by the citizens of the first three classes— *citizens of the fourth class being free to vote or abstain. In the selection of the candidates of the fourth class, the citizens of the first two classes must vote or pay a fine; but members of the last two classes may either vote or abstain.* Thus 100 candidates are chosen from each class, from which 90 are finally selected by lot. And that is the way the 360-member Council is elected.

Now this complex system was carefully thought out by Plato to combine universal suffrage with class-based suffrage, or what the Greeks regarded as the democratic method of the lot with the aristocratic method. "Conducted in this way," Plato believed,

> the election will strike a mean between monarchy and democracy, as a good political system always should. (*Laws* 756E)

The monarchical or aristocratic principle is represented by the superior power which the wealthier classes exercise in the selection of candidates; the democratic principle is represented by the stipulation that all citizens *may* participate and that the democratic method of the lot will be used in the final stage of the process.

Plato defends this complex system as an embodiment of the true and best equality. He argues that in assigning more to the greater and less to the lesser, rewards are adapted to the real virtues and abilities of both. The proposed system, he asserts, assigns honors and privileges proportionately, awarding to those of greater worth a larger share and to those of lesser worth a share commensurate with their goodness (757B–C).

There is, however, a real contradiction between Plato's conception of "true equality," as it is here formulated, and his proposals for the election of the Council. For his method of electing the Council is based not on virtue or ability but on wealth and poverty (*Laws* 744B–C). To be sure, it is hardly possible to measure ability exactly, and the question of what one *deserves* is extraordinarily difficult. Indeed, it has been rightly remarked that even if the question were easy, a world in which what one deserved was always precisely measured and rewarded would be a worse world than the one in which we now live. Nevertheless, it seems indisputable that Plato's proposals for the structure of government violate his own chief principle that government must be in the hands of the expert and wise. For in measuring individuals for office by wealth, he employs a criterion which is no index to their ability, virtue, or wisdom.

It is not difficult to see that the governmental scheme of the *Laws* was inspired by the work of Plato's predecessors, the great Athenian lawgivers of the past. The popular Assembly of the *Laws* is modelled after the Athenian Assembly of Solon's time, similarly divided into four classes and possessing similar powers. Plato's Council, however, is modelled after the one instituted in Athens by Cleisthenes, though there is a significant difference. Whereas Cleisthenes' Council was elected according to tribes, the Platonic Council is elected on the basis of four classes. But if there is a definite Athenian influence on the State described in the *Laws*, it is a Spartan influence that we see in its social system. The method of education and training, the common tables, and the status of women are all adaptations of Spartan institutions. Both the society and the State of the *Laws* are combinations of Athenian constitutional forms and freedom with such features of the Spartan structure that made for its comparative stability. In essence, Plato has thus attempted to combine oligarchy with democracy, the two antithetical systems in the Greece of his time. This is evident in the *dramatis personae* of the *Laws*, the Athenian stranger who plays the leading role, and the Spartan Megillus who has much in common with the Cretan Clinias, given the great similarity in the institutions of Sparta and Crete.

What we have, then, in the *Laws* is a governmental structure consisting of a popular Assembly, an elected Council, and an executive body of guardians of the law. There are, in addition, military officials, courts of justice, and local officials. The Assembly is based on a system of classes, and a distinction is made between the classes that *must* and the classes that *may* attend Assembly meetings. Every citizen is a member, however, and every citizen may vote in all of the Assembly's meetings. The Council, the presiding body in the State, is elected by a method that combines the criterion of wealth with universal suffrage. As for the guardians of the law, Plato seems to allow that they be freely elected by and from the entire citizenry. The military officials are recruited partly by popular election and partly by appointment; and the courts of law contain an element of specialized knowledge in the selection of the judges, but there is also an element of popular election. Finally, local officials are elected by all citizens, though not indeed *from* all. Plato's main aim in this complex scheme is to combine knowledge with liberty. But the basic problem with this scheme, as we have seen, is that Plato assigns the function of knowledge or wisdom to the two upper classes, who are higher only in the sense that they possess a greater amount of property and wealth than do the others.

We cannot, therefore, gloss over the fact that there is a large element of oligarchy in Plato's scheme. In theory he wants the rule of wisdom and knowledge, but in practice he identifies wisdom with wealth, thus turning the rule of intelligence into the rule of wealth, which he himself considers the essence of oligarchy. At best the State described in the *Laws* is a mixture of oligarchy and democracy, the members of the first and second classes being "the Few" and those of the third and fourth being "the Many." Moreover, as Aristotle observed, the artifices of legislation proposed by Plato are definitely oligarchical in nature: The rich are compelled to attend the Assembly, the poor are free to absent themselves; local offices such as inspectors of various kinds are open to the upper classes but not to the lower classes; the method of electing the Council favors the wealthy. Assessing fines on the rich and letting the poor go unpunished for failure to attend the Assembly or to fulfill other civic duties is—Aristotle informs us—a well-known oligarchical device designed to make a mere show of the people's participation in government, but its real aim is to concentrate power in the hands of the few. Legislators make a great mistake, says Aristotle,

> in giving too large a share [of power] to the well-to-do but also in cheating the people; for false benefits inevitably result ultimately in true evil, as the encroachments of the rich ruin the constitution more than those of the people. (*Politics* IV.X.5)

Plato's State is not only biased in favor of oligarchy, it is biased against democracy. Plato contends that just as a ship at sea requires a perpetual watch set night and day, so does a ship-of-state imperilled as it is by interstate conflicts and internal conspiracies of every kind. There must therefore be an unbroken succession of magistrates and other officials. "*No large body of individuals,*" Plato maintains, "*will ever be able to fulfill these tasks with dispatch*" (*Laws* 758A–B, italics added). The italicized passage above is true from a technical standpoint. Even Rousseau recognized that popular sovereignty cannot mean that the people are able to govern themselves without delegating authority. But for Plato this is more than a technical point. Whether it is a matter of art, music, or politics, it is only the "best men" who are capable of true judgment. The true judge must not allow himself to be influenced by the gallery nor intimidated by the clamor of the multitude. Nothing must compel him to hand down a verdict that belies his own convictions. It is his duty to teach the multitude and not to learn from them (*Laws* 659A–B).

Moreover, if the guardian of the law fails to persuade, then he must compel the poets and musicians to compose as they ought—that is, as the guardian sees fit (*Laws* 659E–660A). The pretense of knowledge on the part of the multitude has spread from music and has become a general conceit of universal knowledge. Plato contemptuously describes the situation in which the once-silent audiences now presume to know what is good and bad in art. The sovereignty of the best, he says, has now yielded to the sovereignty of the audience. This is bad enough; but what is worse in Plato's eyes is that this presumption has spread from the arts to politics, and to the society as a whole where the common people show no regard for the judgments of their betters, a consequence of the reckless and prevalent excess of liberty (*Laws* 701A–B).

For Plato, the part of the individual soul that feels pleasure and pain is like the citizenry of the State. Just as it is folly in individuals, therefore, when their desires fail to obey reason and knowledge, it is folly in a State when the people fail to obey their rulers and the laws. In Plato's view, there can be no doubt as to who should rule whom: Parents should rule children; the well-born should rule the worse-born; the elder should rule the younger; masters should rule slaves; the stronger should rule the weaker—which is "nature's own rule," says Plato, despite his earlier objections in the *Gorgias* and the *Republic* to the arguments from nature presented by Callicles and Thrasymachus; and the wise should rule the ignorant (*Laws* 689A–690C).

One can, of course, acknowledge that in art, music, or literature, for example, good taste requires education and experience leading to knowledge; and that in politics, similarly, a good and decent society requires knowledge on the part of its governors. But the fundamental problem with Plato's view is his low regard for the people, so low, in fact, that he categorically denies them the capacity to acquire the knowledge necessary for an intelligent participation in politics. If he concedes to the people the right to elect officials, therefore, it is primarily for the purpose of avoiding popular discontent and its consequences. In that light it is fair to say that what Plato proposes in the *Laws* is not a truly mixed constitution if one means by that term a constitution in which each social element has the power to check and balance the other. What we have instead is a scheme in which the popular elements are mainly passive combined with an active, governing upper class. Plato is thus unable or unwilling to see what Aristotle later observed, that the multitude often possesses a faculty for collective judgment superior to that of the few (*Politics* III.VII.12). People are capable of recognizing the relative capacities of political candidates and of understanding political issues. They should therefore be able to choose their leaders freely and call them freely to account.

The State Apparatus in the Laws

Supervision figures prominently in the State that Plato describes in the *Laws*. Property and marriage are subjected to rigid control by the State; and in one passage Plato advocates what appears to be a system of mutual espionage:

He who does no wrong is to be honoured; but he who will not tolerate another's wrong to the State deserves to be rewarded with twofold honour. The first is worth the value of the good actions of one individual; but the second, who reveals the wrongdoing of others to the authorities, is worth the value of the good actions of many. But he who goes even further and assists the authorities in their work of repression is the perfect citizen who should be awarded the palm of virtue. (*Laws* 730D–E)

And, as we shall see, the poet, dramatist, and musician are also brought under the State's control. Indeed, there is so much regulation of all aspects of life that it has some of the characteristics of a modern police state. When we arrive at the Twelfth and final book of the *Laws*, therefore, we find, as Aristotle correctly observed, that although Plato wished to make the social and political structure of the *Laws* more suitable for adoption by actual States, he "brings it round by degrees back to the other form, that of the *Republic*" (*Politics* II.II.2). In Book Twelve of the *Laws* the philosopher-kings of the *Republic* reappear, but in a different guise, that of a nocturnal council of philosopher-astronomers who guide the State because they have grasped the mysteries of the heavens.

The first new body of officials to be introduced in Book Twelve of the *Laws* is the censors, or auditors, who are charged with the responsibility of examining the magistrates in the conduct of their office. Apparently, such a board of examiners was an institution common to both oligarchical and democratic states. For Plato the aim of the new body was to catch crooked officers and to put them straight. It was therefore necessary to find men of superior merit to set over the magistrates (945C). Plato provides that every year all citizens shall nominate any other citizen over the age of fifty whom they consider best in character and conduct. From those nominees who have received the most votes in this first balloting, half of their number is to be chosen by a second balloting, and from this half three are to be elected by a final vote, who are to hold the office of censor till the age of seventy-five. In this way the college of censors, or auditors, annually receiving an increment of three new members, will constitute a body of the best citizens who will supervise the entire administration of the State. This college has the power to impose death sentences for extreme offenses, though a convicted magistrate has the right of appeal before a court of select judges (*Laws* 946D–E). The members of the superior body are to be accorded honors commensurate with their authority; and Plato gives detailed instructions as to how a censor-auditor shall be honored, including the pomp of the funeral ceremony when a censor-auditor dies (947).

This college of auditors, however, does not occupy the summit of the

Platonic State. Above them, in accordance with Plato's fundamental principle, is a nocturnal council, so called because it meets between dawn and sunrise, consisting of men who surpass all others in knowledge and philosophic insight. No precise description of the Council's composition is given; but judging from the two passages in which it is mentioned (*Laws* 951D–E, 961A–B), we may surmise that it comprises (1) the ten senior acting guardians of the law; (2) all the auditors up to the number of forty; (3) the acting minister of education together with two or three of his predecessors; and (4) a certain number of citizens who have served as "observers" of foreign states and who have proved themselves worthy of membership. And as each of the older members has a younger associate between the ages of thirty to forty years, this yields a total of more than 100 members.

Actually, this nocturnal council was mentioned incidentally in Book Ten of the *Laws*, where it is stated that its place of meeting is near the house of correction, a prison for offenders against religion (908A). It is in that general context that Plato discusses good and evil, defending the view that gods do exist and attacking atheism. His discourse proceeds along the following lines: There are many good things in the world, but also many contraries to the good, the latter being even more numerous. Hence the need for a constant watchfulness and undying struggle against evil, in which the gods and spirits are our allies. Salvation lies in righteousness, temperance, and wisdom, and these have their home in the living might of the gods, though a faint trace of these virtues may be seen as dwelling within ourselves. If by his own volition an individual has drunk deep of the virtues, his soul in the afterlife will be transported to a special place of utter holiness; but if in his lifetime he has acted with grave wickedness, his soul will fall into the depths, into the so-called underworld, the region known by the name of Hades. And yet, there are those who teach that the gods, if they exist at all, are as indulgent of the wrongdoer as they are of the righteous, if the wrongdoer's booty is shared with them. Plato compares this conception of things to one in which the wolf offers to share his spoils with the sheep dog if the latter will allow the ravaging of the flock. That is the degree of venality, he remarks, which some have attributed to the gods (*Laws* 906D). Of all the forms of ungodliness, the defender of such a creed is the very worst and may be most righteously condemned. Plato then presents three propositions, the validity of which he claims to have demonstrated: that gods exist; that they are mindful of humans; and that they can never be seduced from the right path.

Plato acknowledges, however, that the main source of his zeal for these propositions is his apprehension that if the skeptics, materialists, and atheists "get the better of the argument, evil individuals may fancy themselves free to act as they will" (907C). It is Plato's fear of nihilism, of a moral vacuum, that prompts him to propose inquisitorial means of discovering words and deeds of impiety. He provides for a law stipulating that if any individual should commit impiety in his utterances or acts, witnesses shall defend the law by reporting him to the authorities. The offenders would then be prosecuted before the magistrate appointed to deal with crimes of this nature. And if any official should fail to take action on the information received, he himself would be liable to prosecution for impiety at the initiative of anyone aware of the dereliction of duty. In the case of conviction, the court would impose a penalty for each impious act, but imprisonment would in all cases be a part of the penalty (*Laws* 907E–908C). It is noteworthy, however, that notwithstanding his belief that religion and morality form an inseparable whole, Plato acknowledges that a complete unbeliever in the existence of the gods may nevertheless be a righteous individual who abhors wrongful acts in all forms (908B–C).

For Plato, the nocturnal council, with its wise and experienced officials, its young associates, and its well-travelled observers, is the brain and directing mind of the entire State. As such it will hold conferences on the subject of the laws, accepting relevant suggestions from the codes of foreign states and clarifying such points of law as might be unduly ambiguous. And returning to his favorite analogies contained in the *Republic*, Plato reminds his listeners of the fundamental need in all matters for specialization and expertise: If we expect a physician to know a great deal about bodily health, and a commander equally much about military strategy and tactics, why should statecraft be different from all other crafts? If an individual lacks the specialized knowledge of statesmanship, does he have any right to the title of Statesman? (*Laws* 962A–B) The true magistrate, guardian, or statesman must, above all, be capable of recognizing the Form of Goodness permeating and unifying all other virtues. To gain such a capability, the individuals who are to become the true guardians of the law will require a certain kind of education. Concerned as Plato is with combatting nihilism, he regards the subject of divinity as preeminent. It is of supreme importance to ascertain the existence of gods and the powers with which they are invested. Mere conformity with the religious traditions might be tolerated among the masses; but no individual would be granted access to the body of guardians who has not learned every available argument for the existence of gods. Only those who have seriously and conscientiously studied the subject of divinity would be admitted to the ranks of that august body (*Laws* 966C–D).

For Plato, there are two grounds for belief in divinity, the first being the Socratic doctrine of the soul, "more ancient and divine than anything that draws eternal being from a motion that once had a beginning" (966E). The second ground is the orderliness of the universe. Here, in order to establish his own view, Plato needs to combat a theory of his time, which might be called "scientific materialism." In a reference to the pre-Socratic "physicists" and, most probably, also to Democritus, Plato recalls that it was once commonly held that those who busy themselves with the study of the planets and other heavenly bodies are turned into atheists by their astronomy and its related disciplines, because the celestial phenomena appear to be governed by laws of objective necessity and not by the purpose of a conscious and beneficent being. But in his own time, Plato happily reminds his listeners, the situation has been completely reversed. Now the view prevails that, were the heavenly bodies without souls and intelligence, they could hardly behave as precisely as they do. And even in the days of the early "physicists" there were thinkers perceptive enough to recognize that the heavenly bodies owe their order to the control of mind, and that they are not merely an aggregation of soulless stones travelling through space (*Laws* 966E–967D). There are, then, two religio-philosophical articles of faith underlying and animating Plato's conception of the individual and his or her place in the universe: (1) the immortality of the soul and its sovereignty over the body; and (2) the presence of a Mind governing the entire universe (*Laws* 967D–E). The true guardians must never for a moment forget these fundamentals as they study the sciences and music, and apply their knowledge to the guidance of legal and moral conduct.

At the end of the *Laws*, however, we find ourselves back to the position of the *Republic*. For we learn at the very end that the most important statute of all has to be added, a statute that is, in fact, the presupposed foundation of all the other ordinances discussed so far in Plato's final work. The foundation stone on which the entire structure rests is the

> nocturnal council of magistrate-guardians, duly educated with the precepts we have described, as the State's custodian and preserver. (*Laws* 968A–B)

Plato's vision will have reached its fulfillment, he avers, when these scrupulously selected and educated individuals will have seated themselves in the State's central fortress as the perfect guardians (969B–C).

The Return to the Republic

The *Laws* thus ends by returning to the doctrines of the *Republic* couched in a new astronomic form. For all of his efforts at designing a sub-ideal State based on the rule of law, Plato returns, in Book Twelve, to the rule of philosopher-kings. The nocturnal council is none other than the Perfect Guardians of the *Republic*, imposed, as it were, on the legal and political machinery outlined in the earlier books of the *Laws* but poorly integrated with it. And if we treat the *Epinomis*, or "Appendix to the Laws," as Plato's own work—which it surely is in spirit—we can see clearly that it is Plato of the *Republic* who is speaking. In this Appendix he returns once again to the proposition that it is only the select few who possess godlike and sober souls and who are naturally inclined toward virtue. It is only these few who have mastered what Plato calls his "science" and which he claims to have adequately explained. These are the individuals who are to occupy the command posts of the State while all others are to follow (Plato *Epinomis* 992C–E).

Plato thus ends his final work with no real belief in the workability of the "second-best" State based on a mixed constitution. Instead, the final proposals of the *Laws* and still more of the *Epinomis* bear the marks of a theocracy—a State guided by a supreme religious assembly acting in the light of divine truth gained from the study of an "astronomy" that is more in the nature of a theology. In the earlier books of the *Laws*, as we have seen, Plato assigned to the people a political role, however passive and shadowy it might have been; but the general change of tone in Book Twelve leads one to wonder whether even that role has been dropped from the theory altogether.

We must end on this critical note and say a few more words about Plato's attitude toward democracy. Plato believed, as we have seen throughout, that there is such a thing as "wisdom" and that government should be placed in the hands of the wise. "Justice" meant that a small group of philosophers should rule in the light of a supradivine, unchanging knowledge, while the vast majority of the populace in the producer class attends to its specialized function in the division of labor, and to that function exclusively. Plato doubted and mistrusted the ordinary individual's ability to participate in politics, and he detested the "versatile busybodies" of Athenian democracy.

Pericles, in contrast, and most defenders of democracy since his time, have argued that finding a collection of "wise" individuals and leaving the government to them would be undesirable even if it were possible, for there is no reason to believe that the One or the Few are always wiser than the Many. That is the ultimate reason for democracy.

References

ARISTOTLE, *The Athenian Constitution*. Translated by P.J. Rhodes. Harmondsworth, Middlesex: Penguin Classics, 1984.

ARISTOTLE, *Nicomachean Ethics*. Translated by H. Rackham. Loeb Classical Library, Cambridge, Mass.: Harvard University Press, 1982.

ARISTOTLE, *Physics* in *The Basic Works of Aristotle*. Edited by Richard McKeon. New York: Random House, 1941.

ARISTOTLE, *Politics*. Translated by H. Rackman. Loeb Classical Library, Cambridge, Mass.: Harvard University Press, 1977.

HERODOTUS, *The Histories*. Translated by Aubrey de Sélincourt. Harmondsworth, Middlesex: Penguin Classics, 1972.

HESIOD, *Theogony* and *Works and Days*. Translated by Dorothea Wender. London: Penguin Classics, 1987.

HOMER, *Iliad*. Translated by Richmond Lattimore. Chicago and London: University of Chicago Press, 1951.

HOMER, *Odyssey*. Translated by Richmond Lattimore. New York: Harper Torchbooks, 1967.

PLATO, *Platonis Opera*. [The Greek Texts of Plato's Dialogues and Letters]. Edited by John Burnet. Five Volumes. Oxford: Oxford University Press. First published 1900. Eighteenth impression 1987.

References are made to the following: *Apology, Cratylus, Charmides, Crito, Epinomis, Euthydemus, Euthyphro, Gorgias, Laches, Laws, Letters, Meno, Parmenides, Phaedo, Phaedrus, Protagoras, Republic, Statesman, Symposium,* and *Theaetetus*.

THUCYDIDES, *History of the Peloponnesian War*. Translated by Rex Warner. London: Penguin Classics, 1988.

Acknowledgments

Selections from the following appear throughout the text:

Aristophanes, *Lysistrata and Other Plays*. From the Introduction by Alan H. Sommerstein. Harmondsworth, Middlesex, England: Penguin Classics, 1973. Copyright © 1973 by Alan H. Sommerstein. Reproduced by permission of Penguin Books Ltd.

Aristotle, *The Athenian Constitution*. Translated by P. J. Rhodes. Harmondsworth, Middlesex, England: Penguin Classics, 1984. Copyright © 1984 by P. J. Rhodes. Reproduced by permission of Penguin Books Ltd.

Aristotle, *Nichomachean Ethics, Volume XIX*. Translated by H. Rackham. Loeb Classical Library, Cambridge, Mass.: Harvard University Press, 1926. Reprinted by permission of Harvard University Press and The Loeb Classical Library.

Aristotle, *Politics, Volume XXI*. Translated by H. Rackham. Loeb Classical Library, Cambridge, Mass.: Harvard University Press, 1932. Reprinted by permission of Harvard University Press and The Loeb Classical Library.

Herodotus, *The Histories*. Translated by Aubrey de Selincourt, revised by A. R. Burns. Harmondsworth, Middlesex, England: Penguin Classics, 1972. Copyright © 1954 by the Estate of Aubrey de Selincourt. Copyright © 1972 by A. R. Burns. Reproduced by permission of Penguin Books Ltd.

Index

A

Abortion, 123
Absolutism, 135
Academus, 66
Academy, 66, 148
Aeschylus, 27, 131
Agamemnon (Aeschylus), 131
Agathon, 50
Agis, King, 50
Agriculture, 6, 8-9, 10, 157
Alcibiades, 48, 49, 50-51, 59, 108
Alcmaeonidae, 14
Ameipsias, 53
Amphipolis, battle of, 47
Analogy, 69-70
Anaxagoras, 34, 53
Anaximander, 26, 27, 31-32
Anaximenes, 26, 31, 32, 53
Antheagoras, 11
Antiphon, 38
Anytus, 60, 70
Apollo, 36
Apology (Plato), 37, 44, 46, 47, 52, 70-71
Appetite, 128
Archelaus, 53
Archytas, 148
Areopagus, 13, 17
Arginusae, battle of, 43
Aristocracy, 3, 137, 141
Aristophanes, 2
    The Clouds, 40, 52-53, 60
Aristotle, 3, 10
    The Athenian Constitution, 13, 15
    concept of aristocracy, 140-41
    criticism of Plato's ideal state, 119-20
    justification of private property, 117, 124, 125
    Physics, 27
    Politics, 4, 7, 14, 94, 120, 125, 141, 165, 166
Army, Athenian, 16
Artisans, 3, 4, 19-20, 156
Assembly:
    Athenian, 43, 44, 48-49, 79, 93, 164
    in *Laws*, 164, 165
Astronomy, 113
Atheism, 168-69

Athena, 27
Athenian Constitution, The (Aristotle), 13, 15
Athenian democracy:
    Assembly, 43-44, 48-49, 79, 93, 164
    Council, 43
    under Cleisthenes, 15-16
    Delian League and, 22
    education and, 109, 111
    empire and, 21-23
    oligarchical coups and, 59
    peace with Sparta, 22-23
    Peloponnesian War and, 1-2, 10, 22, 23-24, 48-49
    under Pericles, 17-19, 23, 38, 90, 93
    Persian-Greek wars and, 10-12, 16-17
    Plato's criticism of, 89-90, 92-93, 131, 171
    under Pisistratus, 14-15
    restoration of, 59-60
    slavery in, 12, 19-20
    Socrates' criticism of, 59-62
    under Solon, 13-14
Attica, 13, 20, 23

B

Barker, Ernest, 104, 105
Boule (council), 16, 17
Burnet, John, 51, 54

C

Callicles, 39, 40, 86-88, 89
Censors, 167
Chaerephon, 46, 47
Chaos, 26-27
Charmides, 50, 65, 108
Charmides (Plato), 47, 50, 74-75
Civil disobedience, 71-72
Classes:
    Greek system, 2-3, 12, 14-15, 22
    in *Laws*, 159, 163-164
    in *Republic*, 95-96, 101, 103-7, 127
Cleisthenes, 15-16, 17
Clinias, 151, 162
Clouds, The (Aristophanes), 40, 52-53, 60
Communism, in *Republic*, 106, 127, 149, 196

family and, 121-125
   property and, 116-121
Connus (Ameipsias), 53
Constitution:
   establishment of, 161, 162
   mixed, 149
Corinth, 8
Cornford, F. M., 27-28, 29, 30-31, 32
Courage, 75-76, 96
Cratylus the Heraclitean, 65
Creation, 34, 58
Critias, 47-48, 59, 65-66
Crito, 60-61
Crito (Plato), 61, 66, 71-74
Croesus of Lydia, 16
Cronus, 136
Currency, 156-57
Cypselus, 8, 9
Cyrus, King of Persia, 16

D

Darius I, King of Persia, 16, 17
Death, 89
Decimal system, 16
Delian League, 22, 40
Delium, battle of, 43, 47
Deme-name, 16
Democracy, 81, 128 (*see also* Athenian democracy)
   bias against, 165
   birth of, 6, 9
   decline of states and, 129, 130, 131
   legal/extreme, 145
Democritus, 34-35, 170
Demosthenes, 11
Dialectics, 46, 114
Diogenes, 53
Dion, 66, 147-148, 149, 162
Dionysius I, 66, 131
Dionysius II, 66, 147, 148-49
Division of labor, 96, 100-101, 104
Drama, 111
Durkheim, Emile, 29

E

Education:
   Athenian model, 109, 111
   character, 143
   moral, 96, 107, 111, 116
   of philosopher-king, 82, 112-16
   Plato's theory of, 109-12
   Sophist, 37-38
   Spartan model, 107-9
   of women, 160
Elements, four, 34
Empedocles, 34
Ephialtes, 17
Erinyes, 28
Erythrae, 9
Ethnographic information, 36
Euripedes, 23, 27
Euthydemus (Plato), 76-77
Euthyphro (Plato), 57

F

Family:
   in *Laws*, 159-61
   in *Republic*, 121-125, 127
Fate (*Moira*), 27-29, 30-31, 57, 58, 78, 96, 107
Foreign relations, in *Republic*, 133
Forms, Socrates theory of, 54-58, 112-13

G

Glaucon, 98-99, 121, 126
God(s):
   Greek, 26, 27-31, 57-58, 78, 106
   Hebrew, 29
Good living, 98
Gorgias, 39-41
Gorgias (Plato), 39, 83-90
Government (*see also* Athenian democracy;
   Democracy; Oligarchy; Tyranny)
   in *Laws*, 161-66
   in *Republic*, 115-16
   in *Statesman*, 145-46
Grube, G. M. A., 58
Guardians, military, 102-3
Gylippus, 49
Gymnastics, 111

H

Happiness, 97, 98, 119
Haraclitus, 33
Harmony, 104-5
Hebrew God, 29
Hedonism, 88
Hephaestus, 136
Hera, 28
Hermes, 49
Herodotus, 1, 2, 8, 9, 10, 30
   as ethnographer, 36
Hesiod, 2
   Theogony, 26-27, 28-29
   Works and Days, 4-6
Hippocrates, 11
Hobbes, Thomas, 40
Homer, 2, 111
   gods of, 27, 28
Homosexuality, 50-52, 108, 154
Human nature, 104, 150

I

Iliad (Homer), 28
Inbreeding, 144
Individualism, 97
Injustice, 84-85, 98
Intermarriage, 144
Ionian Revolt, 17
Irrigation, 10
Isagoras, 15

J

Justice:
   in *Laws*, 151
   in *Republic*, 96-99, 100, 106, 126, 151

K

Knowledge:
    master, 76-77
    opinion and, 77-78
    true, 78-79

L

Labor, division of, 96, 100-101, 104
Laborers, 3, 9
Laches (Plato), 75-76
Laconia, 12
Land, 4, 8-9, 12, 14, 116-17
Laurium, silver mines at, 19, 20
Laws:
    creative applications of, 140-41
    enforcement of, 39-40
    of nature, 86-87
    Nomos, 29, 30
    obedience to, 71-74, 80-81
    sovereignty of, 161
    state based on, 150
    statesman and, 139
Laws (Plato), 61, 62, 67, 68, 74, 147-71
    central principle of, 151-52
    government in, 161-66
    property/wealth in, 155-59
    state apparatus in, 166, 170
    warfare in, 152-55
Legislators, 6-7
Leon of Salamis, 44, 48
Letter (Plato), 68-69, 114, 148, 149
Lysander, 23

M

Magistrates, 5, 6
Manufacturing, 13
Marriage, 123, 144, 155, 160-61
Mathematics, 113, 114
Medicine, 33
Mendaeans, 11
Meno (Plato), 47, 77-79, 109-10
Messenia, 12
Milesians, 31
Military training, 108, 113
Mind, Plato's theory of, 109-10
Moira (destiny/fate), 27-29, 30-31, 57, 58, 78, 96, 107
Monarchy, 2, 7, 12, 137, 145
Moral education, 96, 107, 111, 116
Moral worth, 151
Music, 111-12

N

Nature, 40, 79-80, 86-87
Navy, Athenian, 20, 22, 23, 49
Naxos, 22
Nicias, 48, 49, 75, 76
Nobility, 2-3, 4, 6, 12, 13
Nocturnal council, 168, 169

O

Oedipus Rex (Sophocles), 27

Oligarchy, 128, 137, 164, 165
    corruption of states and, 129, 130
    defined, 3-4, 11
    Plato's criticism of, 93-94
    Sophists and, 37-38
    of Sparta, 12, 22, 23-24, 59
    of Thirty Tyrants, 44, 48
    tyranny as weapon against, 9
Oratory, 83
Oriental despotism, 10
Orthagoridae, 9
Ortyges, 9

P

Pan-Hellenism, 133
Parmenides, 33-34, 46, 55-56
Parthenon, 23
Patroclus, 27
Pausanias, 17, 21
Peace of Nicias, 23
Peasants, 4-6, 8-9, 12, 13
Pelasgians, 30
Peloponnesian League, 12, 16
Peloponnesian War, 1-2, 10, 22, 23-24, 47, 48-49
Periander, 8, 9
Periclean system, 18, 93
Pericles, 17-19, 23, 38, 90
Persia:
    Greek wars, 10-12, 16-17, 21
    Ionian Revolt against, 17
Phaedo (Plato), 45, 54, 55
Phaedrus (Plato), 51, 58
Philaedae, 14
Philosopher-astronomer, 167
Philosopher-king, 67-69, 102, 103, 105-6, 136, 171
    education of, 112-16
Philosopher-legislator, 67
Physics (Aristotle), 27
Pisistratus, 9, 14-15
Plataea, battle of, 17, 21
Plato, 3, 12, 25 (*see also Laws* [Plato]; *Republic* [Plato])
    Academy of, 66, 148
    analogies of, 69-70
    Apology, 37, 44, 46, 47, 52, 70-71
    Charmides, 47, 50, 74-75
    Crito, 61, 66, 71-74
    Euthydemus, 76-77
    Euthyphro, 57
    family background of, 65
    Gorgias, 39, 83-90
    Laches, 75-76
    Letter, 68-69, 114, 148, 149
    Meno, 47, 77-79, 109-10
    and Periclean system, 18
    Phaedo, 45, 54, 55
    Phaedrus, 51, 58
    philosopher-king ideal of, 67-69, 103, 105-6
    Protagoras, 79-82
    Sparta as model for, 62-63, 107-9
    Statesman, 56, 67-68, 74, 135-46

The Sophist, 34
Symposium, 50, 51, 52
    in Syracuse, 147-49
    theory of mind, 109-10
Politics (Aristotle), 4, 7, 14, 94, 120,
141, 165, 166
Polus, 84
Polydamidas, 11
Polytheism, 25-31, 57-58, 78, 106
Poseidon, 28
Potidaea, battle of, 47
Profane, 29-30
Prometheus, 27, 136
Property:
    in *Laws*, 155-56
    in *Republic*, 116-21
Propylaea, 23
Protagoras, 23, 38-39, 46, 53, 79, 80, 81
Protagoras (Plato), 79-82
Public works, 9
Punishment, 80-81, 85
Pythagoras, 32
Pythagoreans, 32, 56, 66, 113

R

Religion:
    combatting nihilism, 168-69
    grounds for belief in, 169-70
    nonconformity, 60
    before Plato, 31-35
    polytheism, 25-31, 57-58, 78, 106
    righteousness and, 132-33
    Sophists, 37-38
    theocracy, 171
Republic (Plato), 39, 55, 58, 62-63, 66, 69,
70, 91-133
    central question of, 91-92
    communal family in, 121-25, 127
    communal property in, 116-21
    criticism of Athenian democracy, 92-93
    criticism of oligarchy, 93-94
    economic structure of ideal state, 99-103
    education in, 107-16
    foreign relations in, 133
    happiness of citizens in, 132-33
    justice, doctrine of, 96-99, 100, 106,
    126
    as polemic against Sophists, 92
    realization of, 125-126
    rulers of ideal state, 102-3, 112-16
    social structure of ideal state, 94-95,
    103-7, 127
    Spartan model and, 107-8
    stages in decline from, 127-31
    as utopia, 126-27
    warfare in, 102
Rhetoric, 83-84, 85

S

Sacred, 29-30
Salamis, battle of, 17, 20
Sarpedon, 27
Scientific materialism, 170
Self-control, 74-75, 96, 151-52

Selfishness, 96
Sexual intercourse, 123-24, 154, 161
Ship's captain analogy, 67, 139
Sicyon, 9
Silver mines, 19, 20
Slavery, 12, 19-20, 66, 157, 158
Social harmony, 93, 151
Socrates, 25
    in Aristophanes' comedy, 52-53, 60
    associates of, 47, 48, 50
    as Athenian citizen, 43-44, 60-61
    dialectic method of, 45-46
    homosexual attachments of, 50-52, 108
    mission of, 46-47, 70-71
    in Peloponnesian War, 47
    physical appearance of, 44
    in Plato's dialogues, 77-78, 79-82, 83,
    84, 85, 87-89, 96, 97, 100, 109-
    110, 121, 132, 133
    religious opinions of, 60
    supernatural beliefs of, 44-45
    theory of forms, 54-58, 113
    theory of mind, 110
    trial and execution of, 60-62, 71, 72-73
Solon, 6, 7, 8-9, 36
    reforms of, 13-14
Sommerstein, A.H., 53
Sophist, The, (Plato), 34
Sophists, 23, 37-38, 54, 92, 98
Sophocles, 23
    Oedipus Rex, 27
    secular outlook of, 36-37
Soul, 98, 105, 110
Sparta:
    education system of, 107-9
    military system of, 152-55
    oligarchy of, 12, 22, 23-24, 59
    peace with Athens, 22-23
    in Peloponnesian League, 12, 16
    in Peloponnesian War, 1-2, 10, 22, 23-24,
    48-49
    and Persian war, 17, 21
Specialization, 100-101, 106, 119
Speusippus, 148
States:
    art of politics, 79-80, 81
    corruption of, 127-131
    ideal. (*see Republic*)
    obedience to laws of, 71-74, 80-81
    second-best form of, 150, 158, 170-71
    true, 138
Statesman:
    ideal, 67-69
    ship's captain analogy, 67, 139
    transmitting knowledge of, 77-79, 81
    true, 92, 137
    weaver analogy, 142-46
Statesman (Plato), 56, 67-68, 74, 135-46
Suffrage, 164
Sumptuary laws, 13
Symposium (Plato), 45, 50, 51, 52

T

Taylor, A.E., 54
Thales, 26, 31

Themistocles, 17, 20
Theocracy, 171
Theogony Hesiod, 26-27, 28-29
Theophrastus, 53
Thirty Tyrants, 44, 48
Thrasybulus, 8
Thrasymachus, 39-40, 96-99
Thucydides, 1, 7, 10, 11, 18, 19, 21, 22,
23, 24, 38, 40, 49
Timocracy, 129-30
Trade, 3, 15, 100
Tyranny:
  history of, 6-9
  in *Laws*, 161-62
  in *Republic*, 115, 128, 130-31, 132
  in *Statesman*, 137, 145

W

Warfare:
  in *Laws*, 152-55
  in *Republic*, 102

Weaver analogy, 142-46
Wisdom, 96
Women:
  in *Laws*, 159-60
  in *Republic*, 121-23
Works and Days (Hesiod), 4-6

X

Xanthippus, 17
Xenophanes, 33, 34
Xenophon, 2, 52
Xerxes I, King of Persia, 17

Z

Zeno, 46
Zeus, 27, 28, 29